# Navigating from the White Anthropocene to the Black Chthulucene

# Navigating from the White Anthropocene to the Black Chthulucene

William Brown

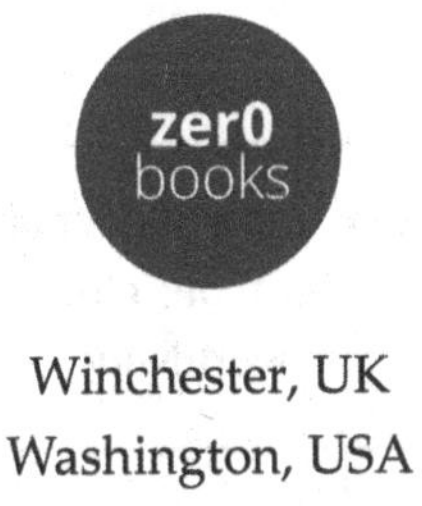

Winchester, UK
Washington, USA

JOHN HUNT PUBLISHING

First published by Zero Books, 2023
Zero Books is an imprint of John Hunt Publishing Ltd., No. 3 East St., Alresford,
Hampshire SO24 9EE, UK
office@jhpbooks.com
www.johnhuntpublishing.com
www.zero-books.net

For distributor details and how to order please visit the 'Ordering' section on our website.

Text copyright: William Brown 2022

ISBN: 978 1 78279 517 9
978 1 78279 518 6 (ebook)
Library of Congress Control Number: 2022936654



Design: Matthew Greenfield

We operate a distinctive and ethical publishing philosophy in
all areas of our business, from our global network of authors to
production and worldwide distribution.

# Contents


Acknowledgements     xi

Chapter 1 Buster Keaton marooned     1
Chapter 2 Killing an octopus     7
Chapter 3 Cthulhu rises in the 1920s     12
Chapter 4 *Habeas viscus*     20
Chapter 5 The ocean as ossuary     28
Chapter 6 Plasticity     33
Chapter 7 Black blood, white Cthulhu     38
Chapter 8 Unity is (a) submarine     44
Chapter 9 Black + Red = Maroon     52
Chapter 10 White face, Black hole     62
Chapter 11 Queer trans*port through the wormhole     70
Chapter 12 The Black Irish?     84
Chapter 13 White Deleuze     90
Chapter 14 White Bergson     108
Chapter 15 The Keaton economy     117
Chapter 16 The Black Outside     126
Chapter 17 White Anthropocene, Black Chthulucene     132
Chapter 18 Submerged Sycorax     140
Chapter 19 The Keaton legacy     151
Chapter 20 Apostasy or apocalypse     166

Endnotes     170
References     205

For Radian and Mila,
and also to DHF

# Also by the Author

*Moving People, Moving Images: Cinema and Trafficking in the New Europe* (with Dina Iordanova and Leshu Torchin)
ISBN: 978-1906678036

*Deleuze and Film* (editor, with David Martin-Jones)
ISBN: 978-0748641208

*Supercinema: Film-Philosophy for the Digital Age*
ISBN: 978-1782389019

*Non-Cinema: Global Digital Filmmaking and the Multitude*
ISBN: 978-1501361654

*The Squid Cinema from Hell:* Kinoteuthis Infernalis *and the Emergence of Chthulumedia* (with David H. Fleming)
ISBN: 978-1474463737

# Acknowledgements

I would like to express deep gratitude to David H. Fleming (my erstwhile partner in Chthulucrime), James Harvey, Matthew Holtmeier and Jamie Ann Rogers for givingly agreeing to read parts or the whole of this manuscript, and whose feedback has surely enriched the work. I was honoured to have been invited by Victor Fan and Ivan Girina to discuss a draft of this book as part of their Media Philosophy reading group, and was fortunate enough to receive further excellent feedback both from them and from Laurence Kent, Thomas Lamarre and Deborah Levitt, who also generously participated. I presented a segment of this work at SCMS 2021 on a panel with Luca Barattoni and Kelli Fuery, who, along with other attendees, including Robert Burgoyne and Chelsea Wessels, offered ideas and encouragement. I furthermore discussed a section of this work during a job interview at the University of British Columbia, gaining some useful feedback from Stephen Heatley, Ernest Mathijs, Shannon Walsh and others (positive vibes from Olivia Michiko Gagnon). Kara Keeling generously offered to read the book close to its completion, for which I am hugely grateful. I would like to thank Charlotte Anne Edwards, Frank Smecker, Andrew James Wells, Christopher Derick Varn, Dominic C. James and John Romans, who were points of contact during the publishing process with Zer0 Books. Thanks also to David Martin-Jones for ongoing academic support and ideas, as well as to Oliver Campbell for his friendship. Finally, I would like to thank Mila Zuo, my companion and my better, for abiding and helping with the inspiration, development and execution of this book, as well as to Radian Winter Zuo Brown, who with her mother brings constant joy to my life.

# Chapter 1

# Buster Keaton marooned

At the beginning of the final third of *The Navigator* (Donald Crisp and Buster Keaton, USA, 1924), Rollo Treadway (Keaton) dons a deep-sea diving suit in order to head underwater to free the titular ship from having run aground on a shoal off the coast of a small Pacific island. As he sets up a men-at-work sign in order to demarcate his submarine workspace, a lobster begins to claw at Rollo's heals. Rollo picks up the lobster and uses one of its pincers to cut a wire. Instants later, a swordfish prods Rollo in the buttocks, prompting him to wrestle with it, before then using this first swordfish as (of course!) a sword in order to fight with a second swordfish that has duly arrived to pester him. Defeated, the second swordfish swims vertically away from Rollo, at which point the film cuts to the surface, where we see dark-skinned native islanders abducting Betsy O'Brien (Kathryn McGuire) from the *Navigator*, and taking her ashore.

During Betsy's abduction, Rollo's air supply is cut off as the oxygen pipes fall limp from the pump that channels air to him. Indeed, when the film cuts back to beneath the *Navigator* we see Rollo inspecting the now-loose pipes and struggling to breathe, before he starts to walk to shore. It is at this point that the hero encounters an octopus. We first see the creature in a separate shot, clearly filmed against a glass pane, since the octopus crawls along its surface, suckers in full visibility. Then we see Rollo, airpipes adrift in the water, heading towards a rock, out from the base of which we see protruding an octopus leg. The leg grabs Rollo and pulls him toward the far side of the rock, squirting a jet of ink into his face for good measure. The ink continues to emerge from the rock, behind which Rollo and the octopus have now both disappeared. We briefly see the top of

Rollo's helmet sticking out above the rock, before a new shot shows him emerging from behind the rock with a knife in his hand. The ink was clearly accompanied latterly by the blood of the octopus, which Rollo has killed with his blade.

Rollo then emerges on to the shoreline of the island, with his strange appearance in the deep sea diving suit initially scaring away the islanders, which allows Rollo to rescue Betsy. Buoyed by air in his diving suit, she then uses him as a raft to swim back to the *Navigator*, but now pursued by the islanders, who have realised that Rollo is just a human. Once aboard the *Navigator*, Rollo hangs upside down from one of the ship's ladders/stairways in order to empty his diving suit of water and to liberate himself from it – a moment to which we shall return – before then staving off the islanders through various ploys, including at one point the firing of a mini-cannon into the chest and face of a native, who falls into the ocean, presumably to his death. The ship overrun by indigenes, Rollo and Betsy flee to one of the canoes that the natives have used to approach the ship, only for said canoe to sink. On the point of drowning, however, Rollo and Betsy are saved by a submarine – and their union is allowed to proceed with nary a hitch (except for Rollo knocking into the sub's steering shaft, which causes it to do a 360° loop). The end.

I start with an extensive description of the final 20 minutes of Keaton's film because there is much that it (along with aspects of the rest of the film) contains for us to pick apart as we evaluate the whiteness of the Anthropocene, and as we use Keaton's esteemed masterpiece, which he reckoned to be his best work (see Meade 1997: 151), in order to navigate from the White Anthropocene to the Black, or perhaps better the Maroon, Chthulucene. Indeed, while the shoal in Keaton's film presents to Rollo an obstacle that he more or less overcomes, in that the *Navigator* runs aground there, an event that in turn leads to his confrontation with the black(ened) natives, I hope in this text to draw extensively upon that sequence from the film in order to make of it an unsettling 'shoal' in the sense described by Tiffany Lethabo King. That is, as King explains, '[a]s a geological and oceanic formation, shoals force one to pause before proceeding' (King 2019: 2). But more than this, to encounter specifically a black shoal, as Rollo/Keaton does following the arrival of the black(ened) natives, involves

> a moment of friction and the production of a new topography... The shoal, like Black thought, is a place where momentum and velocity as normal vectors are impeded. It is the place where an adjustment needs to be made. As an in-between, ecotonal, unexpected, and shifting space, the shoal requires new footing, different chords of embodied rhythms, and new conceptual tools to navigate its terrain. **(King 2019: 4)**

And so, if in *The Navigator* the shoal provides, as we shall see, an opportunity for Rollo/Keaton to prove himself and to win the girl (that is, it allows Keaton to fall back into, perhaps even to justify, the old conceptual tools of antiblackness, anti-Indigeneity and heteronormative patriarchal masculinity), in this book I aim nonetheless, against the tide of Keaton's film, to engage with and to expand upon precisely such a set of new conceptual tools. In this way, the shoal that is this book, if not exactly the shoal in Keaton's film, 'functions as a spatial allegory for the moving and shifting space of the human. Rather than a place of safety, the shoreline is an unstable ecozone and nervous landscape where boundaries between the human and Black and Indigenous bodies continually shift' (King 2019: 78). And through this allegory, we shall navigate, as per our title, from the White Anthropocene to the Black Chthulucene in order to unsettle the interlinked processes of racialisation and colonisation alike. In its coalition of Blackness and Indigeneity (or what, after Glen Sean Coulthard, Frank B. Wilderson III and others, we might call Redness; see Wilderson 2010; Coulthard 2014), this (Auto)Chthulucene might be more clearly coloured maroon, in that black + red = maroon, a term that also connotes, of course, the antihegemonic practice of *marronage*, as we shall discuss in due course.

In this way, *Navigating from the White Anthropocene to the Black Chthulucene* hopes to be what Caribbean poet and historian Edward Kamau Brathwaite would term a *tidalectic* work (see Brathwaite 1999: 44), displacing old concepts from the dry and increasingly barren land of possessive white thought, and replacing them with new thoughts that arise, resurge, emerge and renew by being not solely aquatic as opposed to terrestrial, but aquatic *and* terrestrial, or what Elizabeth DeLoughrey, both alone and in collaboration with Tatiana Flores, calls 'terraquous' (DeLoughrey 2019: 29; DeLoughrey and Flores 2020: 141), as well as perhaps being extraterrestrial. Put differently, *Navigating from the White Anthropocene to the Black Chthulucene* draws heavily on the tools provided by critical race theory, black studies, queer theory, trans* theory and indigenous theory in order to rewrite our understanding of a canonical, white Western cinematic text, namely Keaton's *Navigator*. In the process, we hopefully will create waves that will crash into and erode the whiteness of so much cinema, as well as the studies thereof, and which will surge forward in offering a decolonised and decolonising approach not just to this film, but to film and media more generally.

With regard to the book's title, the meaning of the Anthropocene should to numerous readers by now be clear, in that it demarcates an epoch in which 'Homo sapiens have cast the planet out of the temperate norms of the Holocene that were so congenial to human evolution…Humanity…is acting on the planet like a force of nature, a nature that seems to be turning against organic life, as it has been known to us' (Fay 2018: 2). The Chthulucene, meanwhile, perhaps needs some explaining, in that few theorists use the term beyond Donna J. Haraway, who coined it, and because it is one of a rift of competing, alternative, or perhaps better complementary terms, such as capitalocene and plantationocene, that attempt to describe our present epoch (see Haraway 2015). However, where capitalocene and plantationocene are terms that attempt to explain how the Anthropocene is not so much a period in which man has caused great destruction to the planet, but rather a period in which (white) *capitalist* man, not least through pernicious institutions like slavery (and thus plantations), has caused great destruction to the planet, the Chthulucene attempts to envisage what comes next. That is, capitalocene, plantationocene and other 'alter-cenes' (Yusoff 2018) revise/refine our understanding of the Anthropocene, whereas the Chthulucene is Haraway's name for an era when 'human beings are not the only important actors… with all other beings able simply to react. The order is reknitted: human beings are with and of the earth, and the biotic and abiotic powers of this earth are the main story' (Haraway 2016: 55). In other words, the Chthulucene sees humanity depart from its predominant (terrestrial) position on the planet, and instead of putting itself first, it attempts to live in harmony (or to make kin) with its others, including its aquatic others, and perhaps even evolving through a symbiogenetic process into new beings or becomings, in which the human as such no longer even exists (if it ever did).

As intimated above, and as we shall explore later in more detail, the Anthropocene is defined not just by capitalist man, but also by whiteness, while the Chthulucene, in a reading of the term that takes us away from Haraway, can be defined as both black (or at the very least as non-white), indigenous, as well as queer, as we shall see in due course. What is more, as we draw upon indigenous theory as it intersects with black and queer theories, we shall also propose that the era to come might not just be the Chthulucene, but also the Autochthulucene, in that the autochthonic is working in conjunction with the other non-normative and anti-hegemonic forces that we can sense in Keaton's film, even as the latter attempts to suppress them.

And so while *The Navigator* is overtly problematic (or just plain racist) in its treatment of primitive natives who are seen here as coveting the white woman, especially via close-ups of otherwise undifferentiated and curiously black (as opposed to brown, or red) bodies that leer at her with desire, Keaton's film nonetheless stages many of the issues that highlight both the whiteness of the Anthropocene and the Blackness + Redness = Maroonness of the (Auto)Chthulucene to come – including in its deployment of tropes as seemingly unremarkable as the octopus, ink and blood, the sea, the ship, the canoe, the shoal, marriage and the submarine. In the process of establishing how these tropes in fact convey meanings that are far from contingent, we shall also be able to highlight the whiteness of various scholars and thinkers who have engaged with Keaton's film, as well as with cinema more generally, including Henri Bergson, Gilles Deleuze and Jennifer Fay. In order to advance such an argument, though, let us first focus on various of the details from the above-described sequence.

**Chapter 2**

# Killing an octopus

Rollo's killing of the octopus is one of two mediated acts of violence committed by the hero in *The Navigator* – with the second being the killing of the native with the cannon. In this way, the octopus is marked as 'other', in that it cannot be assimilated into Rollo/Keaton's worldview. Compare, for example, his killing of the octopus to how Rollo uses the lobster as a wire-cutter and the swordfish as a sword; these latter two species clearly are mapped, to humorous effect, on to the human world by being treated like tools – and in this respect both the lobster and the swordfish are anthropomorphised. While Keaton has 'a remarkable ability to convert all objects into tools to secure ends' (Trahair 2002: 586), however, such a mapping of the octopus on to the human world does not seem possible.

The reasons for Rollo/Keaton's inability to make a tool-based gag out of the octopus could be numerous, but there is one in particular that I should like to emphasise – and that is the traditional understanding of the octopus as not just a kind of alien, but, indeed, as an *intelligent* alien. This is an idea that surfaces repeatedly in cephalopod literature, with Peter Godfrey-Smith being perhaps the most prominent in recent times to suggest that

> cephalopods are an independent experiment in the evolution of large brains and complex behavior. If we can make contact with cephalopods as sentient beings, it is not because of a shared history, not because of kinship, but because evolution built minds twice over. This is probably the closest we will come to meeting an intelligent alien. **(Godfrey-Smith 2016: 9)**

That is, humans and cephalopods are not 'distant cousins', as we might say of humans and apes. Rather, our most common ancestor is, Godfrey-Smith suggests, likely a sort of worm, after which point humans and cephalopods, perhaps especially octopuses, squids and cuttlefish, independently developed eyes and brains. Setting aside speculative proposals that various cephalopods are literally aliens, in the everyday sense of coming from another planet (see Steele et al 2018), this lends to them an inhuman otherness that makes them hard to understand, and perhaps even fearful. Indeed, countless tales both literary and audiovisual describe octopuses and other tentacular creatures as fearsome threats to humanity, with one of the most (in)famous being H.P. Lovecraft's Cthulhu, to whom I shall revert shortly. The aim is not to offer a detailed analysis as to why the octopus is scary, even as it is slimy, boneless and thus what Georges Bataille might term *informe* (Bataille 1986: 31). Rather, having ascertained that it is alien, the aim is to suggest that the octopus is not and cannot be mapped on to an anthropocentric conception of the world because it also is understood as intelligent. That is, where other animals are rendered by Rollo as tools for human use, the octopus is not; and its intelligence makes it not just scary, but incomprehensible or unmappable (for the human it is not a 'living wire-cutter' or a 'living sword'). In its utter alienness and unmappability, the octopus becomes a creature with which we cannot identify.

'Identify' is a term I use in reference to Eva Hayward, who in her treatment of the invertebrate jellyfish suggests the following:

> The trouble with identification, it seems to me, is that it is a misalignment of empathy with the possibility of familiarity. Jellies are radically different from us, though not without shared histories or consequences. Identification relies on extending empathy across similarity to dissimilarity, providing the identifying human with the authority of

encounter. As such, the organism can only receive benefits of empathy if we can identify with it. This might work well for charismatic mega-fauna – dogs, horses, cats, dolphins – that we can map our bodies onto, but for organisms like jellies or coral or octopuses, the overwhelming bodily differences make identification a politics of erasure rather than empathy. **(Hayward 2012: 177)**

Put simply, then, the octopus, like the jellyfish and the coral, is simply *too different* for us to understand, and thus too different for us to identify with. Being so different, it would seem that Rollo/Keaton is happy momentarily to forego the comedy and simply to murder the beast, even if offscreen in that Rollo and the octopus are behind a rock.

Now, if Keaton's conception of animal otherness as presented in *The Navigator* amounts to his being able to identify animals only when they can be used as tools, then we might critique his powers of identification as such; Rollo (if not Keaton) does not identify with the other at all, instead acknowledging them only as they are either useful (the lobster) or something with which he can play in a *faux*-useful fashion (the swordfish). That is, Rollo can only understand tools or others reduced to tools, rather than allowing those others to exist on their own terms. When an unassimilable creature arises, here the octopus, then Rollo must destroy it.

Rollo's murder of the octopus might in some senses constitute a humourless moment in Keaton and Crisp's film – depending on one's conception of humour, to which we shall also revert. Nonetheless, Keaton and Crisp decided specifically to keep this non-gag moment within the film, even though it does not necessarily advance the plot in any way, and even though he filmed interactions with other animals before discarding them from the movie. Indeed, as Imogen Sara Smith has written in her production history/analysis of the film, Keaton had in fact shot a gag in which Rollo stuck a starfish to his chest and then pretended to 'direct' traffic/the flow of fish, as if the use of the starfish – also as a tool – had made of Rollo a sheriff. According to Smith, the gag was discarded due to a limp (invertebrate?) response from test audiences, even as Keaton had had hundreds of model fish created for the scene – which was shot under difficult circumstances at the bottom of Lake Tahoe (see Smith 2008: 124). The point to make, then, is that the killing of the octopus made the final cut of the film *over another gag* involving starfish and fish.

We shall return later to the discarded starfish, especially in light of how that same critter features in the work of Hayward. However, for the time being, it seems clear that Keaton/Crisp specifically kept the cephalocide in *The Navigator*, even as it serves no obvious comic or narrative purpose – and that they preferred to keep this moment over another moment featuring a gag. As a result, it becomes hard not to seek to read the moment for meaning, be that intentional or otherwise. For, the killing of the octopus suggests a destruction of the animal that is also always already taking place, at least metaphorically, when Rollo uses the other animals as tools (which, by virtue of being recognised only as tools, are not recognised as animals). If you will, when Keaton treats the other animals as gags, he 'gags' them in the sense of silencing their animal otherness (they are not animals, but tools); when confronted with the octopus, meanwhile, he cannot gag it, and so kills it – notably offscreen/behind the rock, since rendering it invisible as well as dead is about as 'funny' a joke as he can make of it.

Likewise with the black natives. For, it is telling that the octopus reels in Rollo at precisely the moment when the natives abduct Betsy, since this suggests a parallel between the natives and the octopus, as is perhaps most clear when later it is a native who is the victim of the film's second moment of explicit violence, namely the cannon exploding in their face/chest. In enacting flippant violence on the octopus and the black native alike, the two share kinship not simply as being on the receiving end of cruel humour, but also as being annihilated necessarily for the structural existence of the world from which they are otherwise excluded, namely the patriarchal world of the white heterosexual couple – a world from which their sacrificial exclusion is made clear by the fact that the octopus' death is not (especially?) funny (they are not even assimilated in 'gag' form; they are just killed, with the filmmakers even rejecting other gag opportunities – the starfish – in order to keep this murder in the film).

## Chapter 3

# Cthulhu rises in the 1920s

In her consideration of octopuses, Katherine Harmon Courage explains in consecutive sentences that:

> [a]ccording to Hawaiian mythology, the octopus is the only living holdover from the world's previous incarnations. Per local Gilbert Islands legend, the octopus god Na Kika is responsible for having pushed the islands up from the bottom of the sea. The strange octopus-dragon-human beast Cthulhu, created by writer H.P. Lovecraft, has appeared in popular culture for nearly a century. **(Courage 2013: 2)**

In other words, Courage creates a link immediately between indigenous Pacific islanders, octopuses and Lovecraft's Cthulhu, a link that also seems to be suggested in Keaton and Crisp's film, which further adds Blackness to the mix by (problematically) casting black actors as the natives, a decision that we shall explore in more detail in due course. For the time being, though, I wish to add that Lovecraft's Cthulhu is regularly considered to be an expression of the author's own racism and misogyny, as various writers have attested, including Haraway (see Haraway 2016: 101). Indeed, Michel Houellebecq suggests that Lovecraft's racism and misogyny developed in particular during the brief period that he spent in New York in 1925, the year after *The Navigator* was made – and 3 years before Cthulhu was unveiled to the public in 'The Call of Cthulhu', published in *Weird Tales* in 1928. In other words, Lovecraft's weird and repugnant monster functions as a cipher for his 'hatred of the "foul mongrels" of this modern Babylon [the Big Apple]' (Houellebecq 2005: 103). And these 'foul mongrels' are for Lovecraft in particular black Americans, especially as they migrated in large numbers from the South to the North in the very same 1920s. As James Snead clarifies:

> Black migration from the South to the North doubled between 1920 and 1930 as compared to the previous decade. The race riots of the early twenties (many of them in the North) still hovered in the collective memory, their recurrence an ever-present possibility. **(Snead 1994: 20)**

And if Roderick A. Ferguson similarly reports that '[w]hereas in 1910, 637,000 African Americans lived in cities in the North and the West, by 1930 that number had grown to 2,228,000', he also goes on to report how '[s]ociologists worried that African American migrants from rural beginnings were culturally unfit and morally unversed for the demands of city life' (Ferguson 2004: 19).

And so where the new urban black population might have inspired the invention of Cthulhu, a similar logic is also at work in *The Navigator*. For, given that the natives abduct Betsy as Rollo faces the Cthulhu-esque octopus, not only is the encounter with the octopus elided through the film's editing with Indigeneity, which itself is elided with Blackness through the film's casting, but the whole premise of the film is equally set in motion when Rollo sees a newly-wed African-American couple drive past the window of his sizeable mansion, which image spurs in Rollo the desire also to get married. Not only does the image in some senses refute the thoughts of contemporary sociologists, who feared that African Americans were unfit for city life (a refutation also pursued by Ferguson), but it also evokes a dual sense in which Rollo seeks to get married out of envy for the African-American couple (unable to bear their happiness, he must seek to have at least the same), which in turn bespeaks processes of theft (Rollo must take what is theirs), as well as perhaps a perceived white need to procreate in the face of reproductive competition from what W.E.B. Du Bois (2008) calls black folk.[1] As much is suggested by the cinematic construction of the moment and in Rollo's response to what he sees.

First of all, the cinematic construction of the moment: Rollo stands in his dressing gown at his window in three-quarters view, looking out of it from right to left. Cut to a street, where from right to left a car pulls into frame, decorated with flowers, tassels and two signs that read *just married*. The black driver turns to the back seat of the car, which remains on the right hand edge of the frame, before the film cuts to a two-shot of the newly-weds as seen from the perspective of the driver. Here we see the smiling bride on the left of the frame, with a white dress, white gloves and white tiara, together with her groom, who wears top hat and tails, and who opens up his arms in seeming praise before the two embrace. That the two-shot is not actually Rollo's point of view, but rather an image taken from inside the car, lends to the moment a kind of imaginary quality; that is, Rollo is projecting this happy moment as much as he is observing it from his window, which in turn suggests that he is fearful of and threatened by the happiness of the newly-weds, which he thus must have for himself, as much as he is inspired by it.

Then, in his response to this moment, we cut back to see Rollo looking momentarily at a photograph of Betsy that sits on top of his dresser, before a servant joins him and begins to select clothes for Rollo to wear. Rollo announces that he will get married that day, and orders the servant to get for him two tickets to Honolulu for his honeymoon. Rollo then walks into his enormous bathroom and descends some stairs into a bath that looks akin to what today we would call a hot tub – still in his dressing gown. In other words, the observation of the black couple causes Rollo to immerse himself in water, thereby creating a visual link with how it will be upon his descent into water from the *Navigator* when he will have to defend Betsy from the cannibalistic natives. In other words, it is the threat of Blackness, which the film will also conflate with Indigeneity, that leads Rollo to undergo a baptism/birth (immersion in water) that sees him emerge as a 'man'. More boldly put: were it not for Blackness, we can imagine Rollo remaining a single dandy, perhaps even queer. It is because of, and against, Blackness/Indigeneity, then, that white reproductive/heteronormative masculinity feels compelled to emerge, with the saving of the white woman imagined as the rationale for doing so. But really the compulsion towards white reproductive/heteronormative masculinity is married to, or an excuse for, the subjugation of Blackness and Indigeneity. That is, whiteness is born through antiblackness, as (hetero)normativity is born through murder. Honolulu did not, if you will, become a honeymoon location because of colonisation; it was colonised in order to become a honeymoon location, since colonisation justifies heterosexual marriage as much as the other way around.

Potentially we might argue that *The Navigator* and/or its makers, Buster Keaton and Donald Crisp, subtly critique Rollo, rather than sharing his perspective. But whether Keaton and Crisp have invented Rollo in order expressively through visual rhymes to lay bare and to explore his underlying racial anxiety, or whether that anxiety simply shows through because of unconscious racial bias in the filmmakers' creative process, we can still see that Blackness/Indigeneity cause Rollo to feel, or quite literally to be, 'out of his element'. This can be seen as he descends into water first in response to the presence of Blackness outside his home, and then as a means of inadvertent preparation for fighting off that Blackness. And so when Rollo kills the octopus, he in some senses is also killing Blackness and Indigeneity alike, an association that is furthered when the only other victim of violence at Rollo's hands, in addition to the octopus, is precisely a black native. As the octopoid Cthulhu/the cthulhoid octopus stands in for Blackness, so does the violence towards the octopus suggest antiblackness on the part of Rollo, as well as perhaps of Keaton more generally. In this way, even if the film were attempting to critique Rollo, whose rescue of Betsy from black natives is simply an act of his own racist imagination, a dream inspired by his unthinking immersion into the bathwater upon seeing the newly-weds earlier in the day, the filmmakers have all the same repeated that racist imaginary in staging events from Rollo's point of view – and presenting them to us as if real (Rollo does not wake up at the end to let us know that this has all been a dream; as far as the film is concerned, the events that we see actually take place).

While many studies of Keaton do not mention the role of race in his work, and while Keaton only merits passing mentions in the foundational work of both Donald Bogle (1973) and Thomas Cripps (1993) on Blackness in cinema, Keaton's treatment of race has nonetheless garnered some critical attention in recent times. Writing of *The Navigator*, for example, Susan E. Linville suggests that:

> Keaton not only perpetuates negative stereotypes of African Americans, but also...mimics the newly-wed African-American couple because he is a kind of blank, passive, privileged white boy, ignorant of and unaltered by what the film seems to imply might be more socially appropriate role models. Or...Rollo provides living proof that to be 'free, white, and twenty-one,' as an old, racist slogan went, was, in fact, to be something pretty funny. **(Linville 2007: 276)**

Meanwhile, Todd McGowan explains that a key difference between the work of Keaton and the work of Charles Chaplin is that the latter embodies exclusion, while the former 'exposes an internal excess within society' (McGowan 2016: 602). However, one of the issues with Keaton is that:

[w]hen his films show that the insider is at once an outsider, that belonging also entails a failure to belong, they sometimes have recourse to racist images in order to convey the outside. He fails to see that the racialized outsider is different from the insider, that there is a distinction between the insider's failure to belong and the situation of the outsider. That is to say, not everyone fails to belong in the same way, and Keaton creates racist images because his version of comedy does not allow him to see this fact. **(McGowan 2016: 612)**

With regard to *The Navigator*, we can see this false equivalence when the opening sequence in which Rollo sees the newly-weds would in principle create a sort of link or kinship between them: Rollo thinks that he identifies with the African-American couple (or at least the man), and that therefore he might marry. However, this kinship soon goes by the wayside when Rollo/Keaton reduces the black natives to savages, one of whom he kills with abandon, and, as far as the film is concerned, as a joke (Rollo narrowly avoids being shot by the cannon himself, a joke that gets reworked in other of Keaton's films, as we shall see). Indeed, the treatment of the black natives in *The Navigator* would seem to rehearse the same treatment of black people that James Snead identifies in the later *King Kong* (Merian C. Cooper and Ernest B. Schoedsack, USA, 1933), in that the 'whites always behave as individuals, while the blacks are always seen (except for the chief) as group phenomena. Also look at the way Africans are coded by highly obvious external clues (Afro wigs, bones, paints, etc.) that quickly signify "blackness = native"' (Snead 1994: 136). In this way, black people for Snead become 'props', as in property, or what Snead calls being 'figuratively owned by the whites' appropriating "look"; soon to be literally owned through various modes of exploitation' (Snead 1994: 19).[2]

The reduction of black people to 'props' might in some senses mirror the treatment of the lobster and the swordfish as tools, which in turn suggests an animalisation of the black figures in *The Navigator*, of the sort that we see identified by Zakiyyah Iman Jackson (2020).[3] However, while there is certainly a case to be made for the way in which slavery involves the treatment of black humans as tools, this in some senses does not get to the bottom of the racist imagination on display. For, while Orlando Patterson proposes that the slave is 'the ultimate human tool' – while also, notably, equating the slave (and thus Blackness for Western modernity) with the outside, a concept to which we shall also revert later (see Patterson 1982: 7) – and while slavery in the Americas would itself superficially suggest that black people are indeed 'tools' in the white Western imaginary, in that American slavery involved black humans working/ carrying out labour, this labour was in fact secondary to their Blackness. As much can be seen in Wilderson's point that there were no white slaves in the USA – even though there was no reason to trade only in black bodies, if trading in bodies alone were what one wanted to do. For, as Wilderson suggests, 'what Whites would have gained in economic value, they would have lost in symbolic value; and it is the latter which structures the libidinal economy of civil society' (Wilderson 2010: 15). That is, rendering humans as tools was not the point of American slavery, but rather antiblackness was (otherwise why not have white slaves?). What tool-ness black slaves in America embodied, then, was itself only a tool to structure antiblackness, which itself was premised upon a perception that Blackness was/is unassimilable, utterly other, alien.

And if in *The Navigator* the black figures function as 'props', out of which Keaton makes a gag (as well as being the engine for setting in motion the film's entire plot), their otherness is not the otherness of the lobster or the swordfish. That is, their status as props/property does not quite render them tools; their otherness is, rather, that of the octopus, an intelligent otherness not assimilable to the white world, even as the white world is built upon Blackness. And we can see how this is so through the rendition of the black figures not as bodies, but as what Hortense J. Spillers (1987) identifies as flesh.

# Chapter 4

## *Habeas viscus*

Writing about the reactions of those present at the protest carried out by the Black Panther Party against the Mulford Bill (which would forbid black Americans from bearing arms) on 2 May 1967, Kara Keeling suggests that the televised and photographed image of black, uniformed men bearing arms as they arrived at California's capital building involved 'an appearance of the black that confounded their ability to recognize him according to habit' (Keeling 2007: 74). That is, the sight of armed black men in berets, leather jackets and with guns disrupted the everyday image of black Americans, such that suddenly (these) black humans and (their) Blackness became perceptible.

Although *The Navigator* involves an image of a black couple in full wedding regalia, I might suggest that the image is so extraordinary, at least to Rollo Treadway, that he decides that he, too, must get married. And what is perhaps most surprising to Rollo is the sheer heteronormativity – and happiness – of (the image of) the black couple. For, similar to how the Black Panthers created a new image of Blackness while leaving 'undisturbed the hegemonic common-sense notion that the struggle for liberation was a decidedly masculine enterprise' (Keeling 2007: 79), so does this image of the newly-weds leave undisturbed what Keeling might also call 'the formation of the heterosexual nuclear family', which is 'the principle social arrangement through which capitalist relations were – and are – reproduced' (Keeling 2007: 92). However, where Keeling rightly critiques the underlying masculinity (if not the maleness) of the Black Panther imago, for Rollo/Keaton it is the very normativity of the heterosexual couple that is so disturbing, as if to see a black woman in a white dress and a tiara somehow upset the white supremacist order of things. This chimes with Roderick A. Ferguson's observations that several ethnographic studies published in the 1920s 'constructed African American folk culture as outside modernity', in the process '"glamorizing crudity and immorality"', in that newly-urban African Americans, unable to handle modern life, reportedly reverted to various perceived perversions that further characterised them as backward (see Ferguson 2004: 75). Expecting backwardness, it is the very heteronormativity of the couple that is shocking to Rollo. Or rather, as Ferguson might put it, the black couple is 'heterosexual but never *heteronormative*' (Ferguson 2004: 87; original emphasis), since heteronormativity was impossible for black folks by virtue of always already being outsiders to white Western modernity.

Notably, Keeling relates how Frantz Fanon, in his own experiences of watching movies, would sit in the movie theatre awaiting the appearance of 'the Negro groom'. Such a moment would, for Fanon, be overwhelming ('my heart makes my head swim'; see Fanon 2008: 107; quoted in Keeling 2007: 38). And indeed, I might suggest that the image is in a similar fashion overwhelming for Rollo – but in a manner that signally does not result in the revolution for which either the Black Panthers or Fanon strove. For, since the image of the black newly-weds goes against the typical 'Black imago' that Keeling, after Fanon, identifies as being equated with 'sin, rape, the genital, badness, ugliness, immorality, evil, and so on' (Keeling 2007: 30), Rollo feels compelled to himself get married in order to restore the status quo of heterosexual union as the preserve of whiteness. And this restoration of the status quo is signalled in the film by the way in which Rollo's pursuit of white heterosexual union involves him going on an adventure that involves black humans associated with 'tom-toms, cannibalism, intellectual deficiency, fetichism, racial defects, slave ships, and above all else, above all: "Sho' good eatin' [Y A Bon Banania]"' (Fanon 2008: 84-85;

quoted in Keeling 2007: 30). That is, after seeing a progressive black heterosexual couple (who, had they been queer, say, would have simply been an image of deviant Blackness-as-usual), Rollo/Keaton must create the circumstances in which he can construct the clichéd and detrimental image of the black and native cannibal.

I shall return later to Keeling's engagement with the work of Gilles Deleuze and Henri Bergson in her theorisations of the black image, but I draw upon her work here in order to evoke how *The Navigator* specifically rejects the Fanonian image of the 'Negro groom', and instead reconstructs the typical, racist 'Black imago' as its replacement, thereby restoring order to a white world that is otherwise threatened by black chaos. And this process of reverting to racism via the treatment of black humans as 'props' and as an undifferentiated mass with no individual features is important because it also sees the black figure deprived of the possibility of having a body. That is, rather than being a case of *habeas corpus*, the black humans in *The Navigator* constitute a cinematic case of what Alexander G. Weheliye would term *habeas viscus*, which is 'differently signified flesh…for in the world of Man, the hieroglyphics of the flesh are translated to the jargons of negativity, lack, the subhuman, and so on' (Weheliye 2014: 111).

In order to explain what Weheliye means here, it is worth explaining how in constructing the concept of *habeas viscus*, Weheliye draws extensively upon the work of Hortense J. Spillers, who proposed that rather than having a body, the black person becomes merely flesh in Western modernity, a mode of existence that, as we shall see, has resonances once again with the invertebrate mollusc octopus, as well as with the tragedies of the Middle Passage (Spillers 1987: 67). Of especial note is that for Spillers black flesh (especially black female flesh) is not gendered, but rather *ungendered*; in particular, the female slave no longer fits within the white, heterosexual gender binary of man/woman, since she no longer leads a domestic(ated) existence where she carries out prescribed gender roles, but rather, when cargo on a slave ship and when strung from a tree to be whipped, she is just flesh (Spillers 1987: 68 and 72). As we shall see, this refusal of/rejection from the hegemonic gender binary also aligns Blackness with queerness. Meanwhile, Tiffany Lethabo King offers a 'generous' reading of Spillers, based upon one mention of Indigeneity ('the New World... order, with its human sequence written in blood, represents for its African and indigenous peoples a scene of actual mutilation, dismemberment, and exile'; (Spillers 1987: 67)), to propose that Blackness and Indigeneity alike are 'the flesh that makes Europe's man the epitome of the human' (King 2021: 9). In this way, the black and indigenous body, reduced to flesh, effectively signifies nothing or carries no meaning (for this reason, one cannot attribute gender to it) – hence its existence as negativity, lack and sub-human.[1]

Furthermore, for a thinker like Sylvia Wynter, whose influence on Weheliye is also strong, Frantz Fanon serves as a point of inspiration in her theorisation of the 'sociogenic principle', whereby we live in a world where '[b]eside phylogeny and ontogeny stands sociogeny' (Fanon 2008: 4). That is, we do not live in a world that has an underlying categorisation of species ('phylogeny'), nor even a world with an underlying reality ('ontogeny'); rather, all categorisations, including that which counts as human, and all that which gets to be counted as real, are based upon social constructs (they are 'sociogenic' or 'sociogenetic'). In Wynter's work, this comes through when we understand that the human is not a distinct being according to the laws of biology (phylogeny) or physics (ontogeny), but what distinction the human has is as a result of social laws that have in fact rendered as non-human those various others, including black people, who fall outside of society, and yet whose existence as such is not just essential for that society to exist, but for humanity to exist. The very idea of the human (the human as distinct) relies upon the historical obliteration of those others who are consigned as non-human, including the black slaves upon whose backs Western modernity has been built, or, as I shall propose, whose backs were broken (and who were thus rendered, like the octopus, invertebrate) for that Western modernity to be built as such.

However, what is important for Wynter is that this exclusion of black people from the realm of the human is not just an unfortunate quirk of history or an unintended by-product of colonialism and Empire; rather, what had to be in place *before* colonialism and Empire themselves began was the belief that black folk (and other non-whites, including indigenous peoples) were inferior/inhuman, such that colonialism and Empire could take place at all. By this token, ontology/ontogeny and phylogeny are themselves constructs that follow from, or at the very least are constructed in concert with, this sociogenic principle.

If you will, it is not that racism emerges from a white supremacist reality; it is that 'reality' was white supremacist in its conception, with humans then taking this conceptual 'map' for reality itself (see, *inter alia*, Wynter 2001; Wynter 2006). By this token, '[t]he "negro" was so "Other" that he was not even considered, "since he was not imagined even to have languages worth studying, nor to partake in culture, so total was his mode of N[****]r Chaos…" with no effort made to "find the ceremonies which could wed the structural oppositions, liberating the Black from his Chaos function"' (Wynter 1984: 36-37). Or, as Frank B. Wilderson III puts it, '[b]eing can thus be thought of, in the first ontological instance, as non-n[*****]ness, and slavery then as n[*****]ness' (Wilderson 2010: 37).

To summarise, Weheliye's intervention into this Fanonian tradition of black thought is that in being cast outside of being and into the realm of non-being, the black person therefore does not have a body, but is 'merely' flesh, with Weheliye, after Spillers, proposing that flesh/fleshliness can constitute 'a site for freedom beyond the world of [white] Man' (Weheliye 2014: 125) – while black studies more generally can, citing Wynter, provide 'an aquatic outlook "far away from the continent of man"' (Weheliye 2014: 136; see also Wynter 2003: 287). However, while 'flesh embodies both more and less, but above all something other, than it does in the world of Man' (Weheliye 2014: 111), by which we mean the world of the white Man, or, after Wynter, the white world of Man (since it is the world itself that is conceived as white/through whiteness), to be 'merely' flesh is to be 'desubjectified', 'hypervisible' and 'illegible' (Weheliye 2014: 110).

The black natives in *The Navigator* are indeed these things: presented to the viewer in long shot as an undistinguished mass, they are very visible in terms of how they pose a threat to Rollo and Betsy, and yet they also are illegible, in the sense that they, like the octopus, cannot be assimilated into the white world, but rather must be eradicated from it. In this sense, after Wilderson, the black person is not a tool (as is, say, the Asian coolie, who nonetheless retains some subjectivity within the American imaginary). Nor is the black person constituted uniquely in their destruction, as happens with Native Americans, who paradoxically also achieve subjectivity in having that genocide recognised (Wilderson 2010: 9). Rather, the black person never was in the first place, meaning that black folk also cannot be destroyed. It is in this sense that they are 'flesh'; and it is in this sense that Weheliye, after Wilderson, can take philosophers like Giorgio Agamben to task for arguing that events like the Holocaust help us to understand the 'state of exception' and the concept of 'bare life', since these events present a singularly Eurocentric perspective on world history – and one that once again leaves outside the earlier black and indigenous holocausts upon which modernity was built, namely the always already exceptional and the always already sacrificed (sacri-ficed, or, in Agamben's terms, *homines sacri*) indigenous peoples and African slaves transported to the Americas during the Middle Passage (Weheliye 2014: 53-73; see also Agamben 1998; Wilderson 2010: 35-38; Byrd 2011: 185-220).[2]

We shall in due course address Wilderson's distinction between Blackness and Indigeneity, since while he argues that antiblackness alone is the structuring principle of our white supremacist modernity, I wish to suggest that anti-Indigeneity is also an ineluctable component of white supremacy, as clearly signalled by *The Navigator* in its very conflation of black and indigenous peoples (casting black actors as Pacific islanders). Sticking to the concept of flesh, however, I wish here to argue that if the black is in effect always already outside of reality and outside of humanity, we can once again understand how the image of the newly-weds constitutes for Rollo such a rude, even impossible, interruption into his everyday worldview, just as the view from within the car is impossible for him to have seen from his window. Perhaps it is for this reason that McGowan sees Keaton as an 'insider' who, as mentioned, does not really understand his own insiderness – and this 'insiderness' means that Keaton/Rollo is constituted in and as *a body*.

Peter Kravanja confirms as much when he calls his study of Keaton a 'portrait of a comic body' (Kravanja 2005), while Noël Carroll refers to Keaton as comedy *incarnate* (Carroll 2009). Lisa Trahair says that 'Keaton is a virtuoso physical performer who uses *his body* simultaneously to demonstrate the forces of the material universe, whether bounce, tension, liquidity, gravity, flight, and so forth, and, to a certain degree, to defy them' (Trahair 2007: 56; emphasis added) – meaning that Keaton, and (white) slapstick comedy more generally, involves a reaffirmation of the body, such that elsewhere Trahair suggests that 'the body of Keaton the performer…[is] another element of the technological apparatus' (Trahair 2002: 583). Meanwhile, in his classic study of cinematic comedy, Gerald Mast says that:

> Keaton's physical comedy is essentially a synthesis of malleable human flesh and Bergsonian encrusted machine. While his human brain clicks away its strategies, his body becomes a perfectly designed machine for carrying them out. Where [Mack] Sennett converts people into pure toys and Chaplin displays a limber flexibility that abhors the mechanical and inelastic, *Keaton is both machine and man at once.* **(Mast 1979: 131; emphasis added)**

Not only does Mast suggest that Keaton has a body, then, but he also suggests how this body is built upon both flesh and machine. That is, if in addition to his use of the term 'body', we consider Mast's use of the word 'flesh', especially in light of Weheliye/ Spillers, then we can see that Keaton's body, which itself is at the heart of his humour, is built upon (an appropriation of) Blackness. Put differently, Man as the white man (Keaton) is built upon flesh (Blackness) and tools (machines).

If, as discussed in the last chapter, toolness is an attempt to cope with what we might now call the 'chaos' of Blackness, it is also an attempt to harden, or to ossify, that which is soft. We shall revert to Bergson and the concepts of elasticity and the machine evoked above, but at present I should like to end this chapter by suggesting – perhaps a little too poetically for some people's liking – that what distinguishes a body from 'mere' flesh is bones, and that what makes a body white is hardness. That is, whiteness is built upon bones – solid, barely malleable structures that indeed are white in the Western imagination (while in reality being near- or off-white). In contrast, Blackness is imagined as soft, boneless, viscous/*viscus* and thus, as we shall see, invertebrate and cephalopod/octopus-like.

## Chapter 5

# The ocean as ossuary

The ocean looms large in transatlantic postcolonial and black diasporic thought. Derek Walcott, for example, gives as the title of one of his most famous poems, 'The sea is History', which refers to how the sea has 'locked up' the history/histories of those carried across the Atlantic during the Middle Passage (Walcott 1992: 364). Importantly, bones play a prominent part in Walcott's famous poem, in that the ocean floor features '[b] one soldered by coral to bone' – the remnants of 'the million and more [slaves] tossed into the Atlantic' from slave ships (Hartman 2007: 138). 'Bones ground by windmills / into marl and cornmeal', continues Walcott, 'and that was Lamentations – / that was just Lamentations; / it was not History' (Walcott 1992: 366). In other words, not only do the bones of slaves remain on the ocean floor, enmeshed into that alien species, coral, but they also have been ground down into 'marl and cornmeal', thereby falling outside of the same History that is the sea. Might it be that once the bones have gone, only flesh remains, with bodies and bones being the stuff of history, while those ground down bones are lost to history forever?[1]

Dionne Brand has at length considered bones in both a collection of poems entitled *Ossuaries* (Brand 2010), as well as in *A Map to the Door of No Return*, her prose consideration of the Middle Passage, and in which she engages directly with Walcott (see Brand 2011: 12). Indeed, in a passage from this latter text, Brand would seem to cite Walcott when she reminisces on the first time that she heard the word 'sargasso', explaining how she 'imagined multitudes, throngs, wandering the bottom of the ocean, eyeless and handless, cuffed and coffled...Then I remembered my dreams of the Sargasso, its thick tangle of bones long turned to coral and sand' (Brand 2011: 86). This passage in turn brings to mind Saidiya Hartman's own recollection of how '[t]he ocean never failed to remind me of the losses, and its roar echoed the anguish of the dead' (Hartman 2007: 32). This evocation of the ocean as echoing the anguish of the dead furthermore recalls M. NourbeSe Philip's own questioning of 'whether the sounds of those murdered Africans continue to resound and echo underwater. In the bone beds of the sea' (Philip 2008: 203). '[T]he atoms of those people who were thrown overboard are out there in the ocean even today', asserts Christina Sharpe (Sharpe 2016: 40). Before we might also add how Alexis Pauline Gumbs sees black humans as 'people who had been mistaken for an ocean' (Gumbs 2019: 335). In other words, when we consider the ocean in relation to Blackness, we cannot but think of the Middle Passage, and thus of all of the bones that remain below the surface, and where they have become part of the sea bed (turned to, or conjoined with, coral).

Perhaps inevitably these ruminations of the ocean (or, in keeping with the bony logics discussed in this chapter, perhaps the 'os-ean') bring to mind the philosophy of Édouard Glissant, who equally considers the Middle Passage to be a defining moment of modernity. Indeed, at the outset of his *Poetics of Relation*, which uses quotations from Walcott and Edward Kamau Brathwaite as its epigraphs, Glissant describes a triple abyss experienced by those twenty/thirty million Africans transported across the Atlantic during the Middle Passage. The first is the abyss of the slave ship, 'pregnant with as many dead as living under sentence of death', while the second abyss is 'the depths of the sea', which are filled with bodies weighed down by balls and chains. Finally, the third abyss is the abyss of memory, 'a reverse image of all that had been left behind, not to be regained for generations' (Glissant 2010: 6-7). These abysses thus shape the 'ordeal' that is the Middle Passage, such that Glissant elsewhere says that '[t]he land on the other side (our land [i.e. the land of the Americas and the Caribbean]) thus became for us an intolerable experience' (Glissant 1996: 38). That is, having been dispossessed of their homeland, those cast into slavery (and in the process cast into Blackness) in effect became abyssal creatures, not suited to the land but rather becoming of the sea, or oceanic. Kara Keeling suggests as much when she writes of black Americans that '[h]omelessness is our home. We carry the abyss that Édouard Glissant characterized so well. For Glissant, the Middle Passage of the transatlantic slave trade and the formation of "the new world" mark an apocalyptic catastrophe. We are forged in its wake' (Keeling 2019: 54).

However, as Keeling implies here, a paradoxical home emerges from this homelessness, or, as Glissant explains it, 'the absolute unknown, projected by the abyss and bearing into eternity the womb abyss [of the slave ship] and the infinite abyss [of the os-ean], in the end became knowledge' (Glissant 2010: 8). This new knowledge is born out of the 'new world' discovered and created in the wake of Christopher Columbus' discovery of the Americas and the transatlantic slave trade that was part of its 'civilization'. As Keeling says, '[w]hat is important for Glissant is that the Middle Passage, the foundational narrative of the Americas, which marks the founding of a "new world," framed an encounter with "the Abyss," one that signified a beginning, not through the death of a Father, but by marking the erasure of a certain spatiotemporal trajectory and its possibilities' (Keeling 2019: 187). This 'beginning' is not just the beginning of a white modernity, and thus the erasure of an alternative, black modernity (a black spatiotemporal trajectory). For, even as the Middle Passage in some senses institutes Blackness as such, as Wynter might argue and as Elizabeth DeLoughrey, using Glissant, would also seem to suggest (see DeLoughrey 2010: 703), and even if Blackness is in white modernity blighted by slavery and the violence that surrounds it, this institution is also an evolution. Or, if for Christina Sharpe we are still living *in the wake* of slavery, then in the wake of slave ships there is an *awakening*. In this way, and with reference to Wilderson, Sharpe argues that 'rather than seeking a resolution to blackness' ongoing and irresolvable abjection, one might approach Black being in the wake as a form of *consciousness*' (Sharpe 2016: 14; original emphasis). Achille Mbembe equally echoes this perspective when he argues, also in dialogue with Glissant, that silt, as a 'castoff of matter', and which is 'stolen' from water – and which thus functions as a metaphor for the black survival of the abyss, is 'a residue deposited along the banks of rivers, in the midst of archipelagos, in the depths of oceans, along valleys and at the feet of cliffs – everywhere, and especially in those arid and deserted places where, through an unexpected reversal, [it functions as a] fertilizer [that] gave birth to new forms of life, labor, and language' (Mbembe 2017: 181). If Elizabeth DeLoughrey says that 'Atlantic modernity becomes legible through the sign of heavy water, an oceanic stasis that signals the dissolution of wasted lives' (DeLoughrey 2010: 703), she is therefore only half correct. For while we cannot understand modernity without understanding Blackness and the wasted lives of unnumbered slaves, the ocean has not and never will be static (it is in this sense, after Brathwaite, 'tidalectic'), and from it emerge new and other intelligences, intelligences that are perhaps marked as other by being boneless, or by being positively flesh/*viscus*, and not just deficient by virtue of being bodiless. If slavery, at least metaphorically, broke the backs of numerous black humans (see Sharpe 2016: 78), whose bones lie also in the abyss, then what emerges from underneath the surface of white modernity is an invertebrate, black intelligence. And so when Brathwaite says in the second epigraph to *Poetics of Relation* that 'the unity is submarine,' he:

can only evoke all those Africans weighed down with ball and chain and thrown overboard whenever a slave ship was pursued by enemy vessels and felt too weak to put up a fight. *They sowed in the depths the seeds of an invisible presence*. And so transversality, and not the universal transcendence of the sublime, has come to light. It took us a long time to learn this. We are the roots of a cross-cultural relationship...We thereby live, we have the good fortune of living, this shared process of cultural mutation, this convergence that frees us from uniformity. **(Baucom 2001: 65-66; original emphasis)**

Black people are not simply always already dead, cast outside of life and being. Rather, to be black is to live otherwise, with and through an other, invertebrate intelligence, with a new consciousness. Rather than being defined by the hard whiteness of bones, which are patriarchal in their phallic nature (Western culture as defined by the 'boner'), Blackness is a soft, mollusc becoming, or what Hartman describes in an image of slave corpses washed up from the ocean as a 'human-mollusk' (Hartman 2007: 2010).[2] Provocatively, but inevitably, then, I shall suggest that Blackness constitutes an octopus – not just an other, but an intelligent other, whose intelligence is different from, if born out of a common, worm ancestor with, whiteness.

# Chapter 6

# Plasticity

Perhaps it seems fanciful, or, to use a term employed regularly by those who study tentacular and Lovecraftian creatures, *weird* to pursue further this notion of a human-mollusc, or a black octopus.[1] However, we can begin to see how this entity might be worth conceptualising when we consider what Zakiyyah Iman Jackson calls the 'plasticity' of Blackness.

Analysing Toni Morrison's *Beloved* (1987), Jackson notes that at one point, the slave Paul D, upon being made to wear a bit in his mouth, finds himself envying Mister, a rooster that lives on the Sweet Home plantation where Paul D is kept as property. Jackson reads this moment not simply as an example of 'interspecies male rivalry', but that Mister's freedom and Paul D's comparative lack of freedom highlight the way in which the latter's enslavement means that '(anti)blackness is symbolically a form of natality' (Jackson 2016: 115). In other words, Mister, whom Paul D pulled out of his shell at birth, 'reminds him of the plasticity of his manhood, or more precisely that such plasticity represents the impossibility for unqualified manhood to take hold' (Jackson 2016: 116). In the language of hardness/softness evoked above, Paul D is in effect 'boneless', his phallus 'reduced' to nothing more than a loose tentacle. This is for Jackson not simply an obvious case of emasculation, though; being born black/having natal Blackness means that he is malleable, such that, bit in mouth, he is both animal and human. '[T]he co-ordinates of the human body are changed into a different shape or form', Jackson continues,

bizarre and fantastic: human personality is made 'wild' under the weight of blackness's production as seemingly pure potentiality...Paul D [who at this point realises that he will never 'be' Paul D again, and/or that he is not human] is pointing to the way that the black body and mind are twisted and contorted in a manner indifferent to structures of form, their integrity and limits. So it is not only a body that is stolen but also the becoming of the slave: the slave's future perfect state of being. The black(ened) can only be defined as plastic: impressionable, stretchable, and misshapen to the point that the mind does not survive – it goes wild. We are well beyond alienation, exploitation, subjection, domestication, and even animalization; we can only describe such transmogrification as a form of engineering. *Slavery's technologies were not the denial of humanity but the plasticization of humanity.* **(Jackson 2016: 117; original emphasis)**

In this way, slavery constitutes 'coerced formlessness as a mode of domination and the *unheimlich* existence that is its result... the slave is the discursive-material site that must contend with the demand for seemingly infinite malleability' (Jackson 2016: 118). Shapeless, *informe*, boneless and able to fit through even the smallest of gaps, the octopus and other cephalopods are also 'infinitely malleable', or what Jackson calls *plastic*.[2] The black human and the octopus are thus entangled in their plasticity, with Calvin L. Warren saying that 'Black...is the index of formlessness...[which] serves as the precondition of the whole itself...The Negro is the interstice of metaphysics, the formless form between man and animal, property and human, whose purpose is to embody formlessness as a corporeal sign' (Warren 2018: 34-35).

*The Navigator* equally suggests this 'formless' connection in its linkages between the octopus and the black natives. While potentially malleable, however, Keaton still kills the octopus and the native; irreducible to tools, both are threatening others that must be killed. Or rather, since they were never really alive, to kill them is the only logical thing to do with them; for, their function is, in the spirit of Mbembe's necropolitics, to die (see Mbembe 2003). That is, their death *is* the tool that allows whiteness to come into being and to take up its central position in the universe. Conversely, inexhaustibly to die, or to be killed by whiteness, is precisely the 'infinite malleability' and 'plasticity' that constitutes Blackness as such. With Orlando Patterson's famous work in mind, slavery does not so much equate to 'social death'; rather, slavery *is* Blackness *is* death – an infinite, endless and ongoing death that functions as a tool for giving life to whiteness, and perhaps even to all other beings, a becoming that gives rise to being as such, as per Paul D's giving of life to Mister, only for himself to be eradicated under the bit. In this way, for Keaton to kill the octopus, as for Keaton to kill the native, *is* a gag exactly on a par with using the lobster to cut the wire and using the swordfish as a sword; for, in the eyes of white Western modernity, Blackness is life-giving (and thus natal) death. As Warren says, '[t]he Negro is invented precisely to absorb the terror of…nothing…nothing as formlessness, nothing as interruption, nothing as black, and, ultimately, nothing as the Negro' (Warren 2018: 36). Or, as Fred Moten puts it in his own (tidalectic) consideration of Blackness and/as nothingness, '[i]t's terrible to have come from nothing but the sea, which is nowhere navigable only in its constant autodislocation' (Moten 2013: 744).

In her engagement with Herman Melville's infamous scrivener, Bartleby, Kara Keeling draws upon Giorgio Agamben to suggest that this queer sort who 'would prefer not to', is a 'new creature', while also quoting Gilles Deleuze, who says of Bartleby that he is a 'new, unknown element…the mystery of a formless, nonhuman life, a *Squid*' (see Keeling 2019: 51; original emphasis).[3] Bartleby is 'squidlike' because he 'upends Western humanism's categories' (Keeling 2019: 51), being practically incomprehensible to and indescribable for the narrator, Bartleby's former employer, over the course of Melville's 1853 novella. Bartleby's perplexing bizarreness, his very indescribability (in an anti-story that contains no rollicking action, even as some might perhaps erroneously expect as much from the author of 1851's *Moby Dick; or, The Whale*) means that he is for Keeling comparable to the black American – and it is perhaps no surprise that Keeling segues from her analysis of Bartleby to an exploration of the work of Sun Ra. For, if Bartleby and the black American are both squids, and if Edward J. Steele and his colleagues argue that octopuses, squids and cuttlefish supposedly originate from beyond our own planet, and thus are in some senses literal aliens (see Steele et al 2018), then we can see how Afrofuturism further combines the infinite malleability and the alien-ness of the octopus in order to suggest that black folk like Sun Ra are from another planet.

Furthermore, when we consider the nexus of plasticity, Blackness and the cephalopod in light of the increasing technologisation of the world, then we can see clearly the slave logic involved in digital technology, computers and artificial intelligence. For, in our study of cephalopods in cinema, David H. Fleming and I point out that the octopus was at the heart of early research into artificial intelligence, with marine biologist-turned-computer programmer John Zachary Young basing his post-war research into the development of computing systems on the distributed brain of the octopus (see Brown and Fleming 2020: 10-12). The computer, or the Universal Machine as conceived by Alan Turing, is, like the black slave, also supposed to be infinitely malleable and thus able to carry out any labour so desired by its owner. The computer, as a Universal Turing Machine given material form (or, with Weheliye and Spillers in mind, 'made flesh'), and perhaps especially software (which, being soft, is also like a mollusc) is thus in some senses 'black', while the black human is always in some senses 'artificially intelligent'. Perhaps it is not surprising that the etymological roots of the word *robot* come from the Czech *robota*, meaning 'forced labour'. That is, robots are (intended as) slaves. Furthermore, robots and human slaves share the infinite malleability, or the cephalopodic qualities, of Blackness, which thus emerges as linked to, or at least echoing, the alien intelligence of the cephalopod (note also that '[i]n the medieval Muslim world "Zandj" meant slave as well as black'; see Patterson 1982: 250). When Keaton kills the octopus and the black native, casting another black body to the ocean, where their bones will join with the coral, he demonstrates the white Western construction of the black other as threat, whose forced labour, especially the labour of dying, demonstrates their plasticity. If the married couple take Blackness away from 'the *unheimlich* existence' assigned to it, and indeed, if they, like robots, become 'too human' and cross the uncanny/*unheimlich* valley, then Keaton must destroy them in order to reassert his own humanity. In this way, the black human is, as Wilderson (2010) suggests, antagonistic to American life – but we must also understand that this antagonism is itself a tool for constructing whiteness. And as the black native falls into the ocean, he forms a picture of the ongoing existence in, from and with the abyss of black folk more generally. If Blackness is an awakening, it is also, in the language of Christina Sharpe, 'in the wake', with the wake being of course the ongoing celebration of the simultaneous life and death of black people.[4]

# Chapter 7

# Black blood, white Cthulhu

How is the becoming-cephalopod of black folk not itself just another imposed form that gives expression to the infinite malleability, or plasticity, of Blackness, in addition to being yet another offensive metaphor whereby black (and indigenous) people are not granted human status, but rather are considered (the equivalent of) invertebrate animals?

With regard to the latter charge, there is indeed a sense in which *The Navigator* elides Blackness with the octopus, and in a fashion that sees the black natives reduced to non- or sub-human status. All the same, as Weheliye and Jackson appropriate out of viscosity and plasticity alike a mode of existence that gives expression to black existence, so might attempting to work positively with the cephalopod as a kind of kindred critter. With regard to the former charge, meanwhile, perhaps one can say that being itself infinitely malleable and plastic, the cephalopod (the octopus and/or the squid) has no form. Indeed, being formless or *informe*, the becoming-cephalopod of the black human is not to take on a set form, including the non-set form of the octopus itself. Rather, becoming-cephalopod is a way for us to acknowledge the formlessness of Blackness in an antiblack world, and to understand that the cephalopod and Blackness, alike in their intelligent otherness, are the *informe* and plastic flesh from which the antiblack and white world is made, or they are the non-being becoming that makes being possible.

Perhaps we can see this in the 'Blackness' of the cephalopod in *The Navigator*. For, when Rollo first interacts with the beast, the octopus as mentioned jets its ink at the film's supposedly intrepid hero. The black cloud that we see is itself formless/ *informe*, with ink being a technique and a technology that octopuses use in real life to mask their flight and/or, on occasion, to mask their non-flight as they simultaneously use their ability to change colour to impersonate the very ink that they have just squirted and to hang in their own ink cloud until their predator has gone (see Mather et al 2010: 107). The ink thus provides a screen of Blackness, with the word for ink in various Scandinavian languages being, pertinently, *blaek* or a variation thereon. Meanwhile, the Sanskrit word for ink is *kali*, which also means black. In other words, the jet of ink from the octopus belies its own *informe* Blackness. If we think that calligraphy typically is supposed to mean 'beautiful writing', from the Greek κάλλος/kallos, meaning 'beautiful', we might nonetheless rethink this etymology and consider cal(l)igraphy, or kali-graphy, to be 'writing with blackness', the inverse of white Western modernity's more common attempt to write with light, or photography. As the octopus writes its Blackness/ squirts its ink, then, Rollo comes in to write with light, and in the process we understand that Keaton's cinematic project – written in light – is once again founded upon a prior 'writing in black.' Perhaps it is no coincidence that Keaton's film is thus made in large part in Cali-fornia, the black furnace (from the Latin *fornax*) that has become the 'spiritual' home of light-writing, or cinema.[1]

What is more, soon after the octopus has squirted its ink, Rollo kills it with his knife, and the ink is replaced/intermixed with the blood of the creature. Indistinguishable to the camera and to the eye of the viewer, Blackness and blood become one, with cali-graphy thus becoming not just writing with darkness, but also writing with (maroon?) blood, that viscous/*viscus* substance that bespeaks *informe* flesh. Writing with light, or cinema, now becomes built upon the spilling of black blood, and it is telling that moments after the killing of the octopus, a similar cloud is spewed forth by the cannon when it fires at the black native. Rather than a black cloud of ink, though, the cannon jets out a white cloud of smoke. The visual rhyme of the two clouds creates a link between these two moments of violence, but the distinction between the black ink and the white smoke also betokens a shift from the octopus spilling black blood and ink as victim to the cannon belching white smoke as (tool for the) aggressor.

Meanwhile, California, the USA and Western modernity more generally are built upon the spilling of the same, salty black blood that also has mixed once again with the salty sea water from which it sprang. Or, as Alexis Pauline Gumbs puts it, 'out of the ocean came life as we know it. life as we be it. the salt in our veins. the who we are the who we are not. we have not yet seen the bottom of it, the depth of mourning that birthed us here. and it was. well, it was. what it was' (Gumbs 2018: 109).

And yet, if my reading of *The Navigator* seems to be heading towards a 'simple' suggestion that the octopus and the black are monstrous others alike, and that the cruel blood-letting carried out by Rollo of both the octopus and the native is simply racist, then I would like to bring in further nuances. For while Rollo kills the octopus, it is not the only tentacled creature in the *mise-en-scène* of the film. Indeed, I have already mentioned how Rollo pulls on his oxygen pipes to discover that they have come loose during Betsy's abduction. Bearing in mind this image of the loose pipes extending from his body, I would argue that while Rollo stands in contradistinction to the octopus, his appearance at this point in fact gives to Rollo himself the appearance of a tentacular monster. That is, while I have been equating the octopus with Blackness, it is neither the octopus nor Blackness that is monstrous, but Rollo himself. In an inversion of Lovecraft's notion that the cephalopodic (and black) monster Cthulhu will rise up to destroy the white world, it is in fact whiteness that is the real, world-destroying monster – with the supposed monstrosity of Blackness thus being a projection of whiteness' own destructive and cruel tendencies.

The monstrous nature of Rollo is made clear when, still in the guise of a tentacular sea monster, he emerges from the ocean – only to scare the natives away from Betsy. When we consider that this sequence reputedly takes place not in the Atlantic but the Pacific, then we might propose that the Pacific islanders whom Rollo encounters take Rollo not just for a monster, but for the very octopus god, Na Kika, whom earlier we noted is thought to have created various Pacific islands by pushing them up from the bottom of the ocean. What I wish to suggest, though, is not that Rollo emerges as a white god to these natives, who, after all, do soon pursue him back to the *Navigator*, but that the ambition of whiteness is to position itself as a kind of 'god' in relation to an 'inferior' Blackness and Indigeneity. This emergence of the 'god', Na Kika, or perhaps even Cthulhu, does indeed signal, then, the end of the world for those black natives, just as the discovery of the Americas, as the supposed beginning of modernity and the instituting moment of the Anthropocene, was apocalyptic for indigenous peoples throughout the Americas and for the Africans forced to migrate to these continents via the Middle Passage. If Lovecraft projected Blackness on to his Cthulhu, *The Navigator* (inadvertently) suggests that Cthulhu is white.

Halfway through *The Navigator* (some 10 minutes before the ship runs aground in terms of running time), we see Rollo and Betsy trying to get some sleep in one of the lounges on the ship. However, the rocking of the boat causes a door latch to catch the switch of a gramophone, which sets the record player in motion. The record in question is 'Asleep in the Deep', an 1897 song written by Arthur J. Lamb and composed by Henry W. Petrie, and which was recorded by Wilfred Glenn for the Victor Talking Machine Company in 1913. The film cuts between shots of Rollo and Betsy, decked in sailors' uniforms, trying to get to sleep on chairs, and shots of the record player, over which are imposed lyrics from the song: 'Danger is near thee...Many brave hearts are asleep in the Deep…BEWARE.' Since they do not know where this sound is coming from, Rollo and Betsy take fright and go up on deck to sleep there. Betsy nearly falls overboard on top of a rolling deckchair, before it starts to rain, and the couple retreat indoors, where Rollo memorably shuffles and mashes up a soggy deck of cards, the fragments of which he then proceeds to deal.

There are various details of the song that are worth highlighting. Firstly, given that the song is about '[m]any brave hearts asleep in the deep', one cannot but consider how the lyrics evoke those souls tossed overboard during the Middle Passage. Indeed, that Rollo and Betsy hear the song *as if coming from nowhere*, which is why they stay awake, take fright and head on deck, lends secondly to the song a ghostly presence. In the words of M. NourbeSe Philip, this song is, like that poet's *Zong!*, 'hauntological; it is a work of haunting, a wake of sorts, where the spectres of the undead make themselves present… Our entrance to the past is through memory – either oral or written. And water. In this case salt water. Sea water' (Philip 2008: 201). That is, the waves of the water and the soundwaves of the song suggest an echoing Blackness that wakes, or at least keeps awake, Rollo and Betsy.

Thirdly, since *The Navigator* is a silent film, of course no one actually hears the song. Indeed, even if musical accompaniment referenced the song during screenings of the movie at the time of its initial release, the musical accompaniment likely would not have played the specific Victor record of Glenn's version of the Lamb and Petrie song. In other words, the song doubly haunts the film, since it only exists as lyrics superimposed over the record player itself. Or, if Rollo and Betsy are scared by the disembodied voice that is Wilfred Glenn singing 'Asleep in the Deep', then the film in fact 'dis-voices' the already-disembodied Glenn, lending to the film a fantastic quality as music as a whole becomes a ghostly presence in the film.

Fourthly, is the fact that the lyrics appear as superimposed text, such that the song becomes a sort of ink or blood that seeps on to the movie's screen – and it is not so much the actual music, then, that frightens Rollo and Betsy as it is the text itself. Indeed, text is revealed within *The Navigator* to be unreliable, as when a sign that should say Pier 12 is partially covered such that it says Pier 2, which leads Rollo to embark the *Navigator* instead of the cruise ship bound for Honolulu. Furthermore, the film opens with six white men sat around a table plotting to scupper the *Navigator*, which has been sold to their enemy in a war supposedly taking place between 'two small countries far across the sea'. Surrounded by books and papers, these men set in motion the film's plot by casting off the *Navigator* that night, but not before Betsy's father (Frederick Vroom) has to return to the ship that he has sold in order, in his own words, 'to get some papers'. This leads him to be kidnapped by the foreign spies, and for Betsy to wander herself on to the *Navigator* in search of him – such that she ends up on board with Rollo when the ship is cast adrift. What is more, when we first see the shipping magnate, he is holding a piece of paper in his hand, something that Betsy also is doing when Rollo first turns up to propose to her shortly afterwards. In other words, intrigue and *realpolitik* would seem to belong to literate societies, but with text not helping to settle issues so much as creating them. In this way, the text that we see onscreen, be it via superimpositions or intertitles, in some senses comes to signify the blood/ink that is spilled for the purposes of creating the white, literate world. Furthermore, 'Asleep in the Deep', understood now as 'the song of Rollo', gives expression to the haunting presence of Blackness, even as *The Navigator* is not a slave ship on the Atlantic but, as we shall see later, a war ship of sorts on the Pacific – and even as we do not actually hear the song, but just are haunted by its lyrics.[2]

## Chapter 8

# Unity is (a) submarine

*The Navigator* was shot on the *USAT Buford*, a ship that had served in the Spanish-American War of 1898, and which in 1919 had carried to the Russian Federation 249 political radicals and other 'undesirable aliens', including Emma Goldman and Alexander Berkman. While not a historical slave ship, then, the *Buford* was nonetheless implicated in the history of a nation to and from which were transported bodies (or rather flesh) that, in both cases (kidnapping and deportation), were considered outsiders both to American society and to what Ferguson calls its 'liberal capitalist economic and social formations' (Ferguson 2004: 2).

Goldman described her experience of the journey as being like a prisoner, 'cooped up in dark, damp quarters, wretchedly fed, all of us in complete ignorance of the direction we were to take' (Goldman 2003: 2), while Berkman described the *Buford* as 'a leaky old tub repeatedly endangering our lives during the month's Odyssey...Long, long was the voyage, shameful the conditions we were forced to endure: crowded below deck, living in constant wetness and foul air, fed on the poorest rations' (Berkman 1976: 11). These accounts are partially reminiscent of that of Olaudah Equiano, who of the Middle Passage described how '[t]he stench of the hold while we were on the coast was so intolerably loathsome, that it was dangerous to remain there for any time,' and that once 'the whole ship's cargo were confined together, it became absolutely pestilential' (Equiano 2018: 41; see also Gillespie 2016: 130). The aim here is not to equate these two passages the one with the other; rather, it is to suggest that the *Buford* carries its own memories and air of confinement and transportation/

transplantation – and that this later transportation in the name of creating an America free of radicals is haunted by the earlier Middle Passage that took place in the name of creating a white America. In turn, both haunt *The Navigator*.

Furthermore, Ferguson considers the growing black middle-classes of the 1920s to be under pressure to 'make themselves, as well as queer and working-class blacks, available for surveillance and [to] do so in the name of recognition and normativity' (Ferguson 2004: 76). That is, black Americans had to display their 'normativity' in order to shake off the unruly image (the Black imago) that they otherwise had in mainstream American society. In relation to this surveillance of black America, Simone Browne also suggests that the slave ship itself functioned as a kind of Panopticon responsible for creating specific types of subject through permanent surveillance (see Browne 2015: 24). In this way, we can see how the *Buford*, implicated as it is in an anti-communist history (and thus a second anti-Red history, beyond that of anti-Indigeneity?) of surveillance and control, is also linked to an antiblack history of racial surveillance and control.

There are various details that Equiano describes, and yet which were not endured by Goldman and Berkman, including spending the journey in one's own filth (Equiano confesses to thinking that 'many of the inhabitants of the deep [were] much more happy than myself. I envied them [i.e. the dead] the freedom they enjoyed, and so often wished I could change my condition for theirs'; Equiano 2018: 41). However, one detail I would like to mention is what Equiano describes as 'the galling of the chains' (Equiano 2018: 41).[1] I mention this because, as per various references above to balls and chains around the ankles of slaves who then were drowned, so does the phrase 'ball and chain' colloquially mean (typically) a man's wife. Again, the idea is not to equate heterosexual marriage with murder during the Middle Passage. However, the very false equation between the ball and chain around the ankle of a slave and the ball and chain around the ankle of a married (white?) man nonetheless does allow us to consider how both heterosexual coupling and the slave ship function(ed) as forms of surveillance, as Ferguson and Browne between them suggest.[2]

Rollo spies the newly-weds from his window, while the spies that seek to sink the *Navigator* also observe the ship from their window. Surveillance thus plays a key role in Keaton's film, with the final arrival of the submarine confirming as much. For, as Cormac Deane has argued, the submarine has been a staple trope of the 'cinematic techno-thriller' since around the time that *The Navigator* was made, with the slightly later *Mare Nostrum* (Rex Ingram, USA, 1926) functioning for Deane as an early example of this genre.[3] Deane traces a genealogy of 'control rooms' from films like *Mare Nostrum* through to contemporary drone movies, suggesting that they have been central in naturalising, or what Deane terms 'grammatizing', the systems of *command and control* that lie at the heart of modernity (Deane 2015: 3-4). For Deane, '[g]rammatization is the process by which language, gestures and bodies become rendered informationally by mechanical and industrial processes', including both cinema and the control room (Deane 2015: 5). That is, modern technologies produce a 'grammar' that both is extrapolated from humans (humans as a source of data), and which we as humans adopt both in terms of what we say and in terms of what we do and how we do it, with this process in some senses producing, therefore, a mechanised human.

Now, as we shall see, much of Keaton's comedy derives from his refusal to be entirely mechanised, even as he is built upon both flesh and machine, as identified earlier, as well as from his way of using machines in manners for which they are not intended. However, the point that I wish to make at present is that as the submarine control room leads to the total surveillance of the drone era, whereby all of our words and gestures are recorded and thus in some senses controlled, so were these logistics of war already at work even before the submarine – in the form of the ship, which not only deported radicals like Goldman and Berkman, but which more importantly forcibly controlled the bodies of slaves in the Middle Passage via what Stefano Harney and Fred Moten call logistics. They argue that logistics 'wants to dispense with the subject altogether' (Harney and Moten 2013: 87), before suggesting that:

[m]odern logistics is founded with the first great movement of commodities, the ones that could speak. It was founded in the Atlantic slave trade, founded against the Atlantic slave. Breaking from the plundering accumulation of armies to the primitive accumulation of capital, modern logistics was marked, branded, seared with the transportation of the commodity labor that was not, and ever after would not be, no matter who was in that hold or containerized in that ship. From the motley crew who followed in the red wakes of these slave ships, to the prisoners shipped to the settler colonies, to the mass migrations of industrialisation in the Americas, to the indentured slaves from India, China, and Java, to the trucks and boats leading north across the Mediterranean or the Rio Grande, to one-way tickets from the Philippines to the Gulf States or Bangladesh to Singapore, logistics was always the transport of slavery, not 'free' labor. Logistics remains, as ever, the transport of objects that is held in the movement of things. And the transport of things remains, as ever, logistics' unrealizable ambition. **(Harney and Moten 2013: 92)**

In other words, logistics and the shipping not of people-as-subjects but of people-reduced-to-objects, of people who fall outside of being, goes hand in hand with surveillance and control, and that Deane does not dig back further than the submarine in his 'media archaeology' suggests that his is only a white archaeology (like a movie archaeologist, Deane only looks at bones?). For, even a cursory look at how Hortense J. Spillers (1987) invokes the same term, 'grammar', to discuss the role of slave ships and the Middle Passage in creating the black slave, demonstrates how the system of control against which Deane would seem to rail in fact relies upon an earlier, occulted and 'naturalized' racial 'grammar' that neither Deane nor Keaton calls into question – including especially the 'ungendering' of the black human that we discussed earlier. If Deane therefore appeals to how the prominence of the control room is intensified in the era of the 'war on terror' (Deane 2015: 22), then he misses the war on Blackness, or the antiblackness, as well as the anti-Indigeneity, that precedes it, and which continues to rage. As Harney and Moten suggest, 'we [black folk] remain in the hold [of the slave ship]' (Harney and Moten 2013: 94).[4] And when Deane points to how the control room involves a 'dizzying *mise en abyme*' (Deane 2015: 26), as we see screens embedded within screens in contemporary control rooms, he misses how this also is based upon a literal *mise en abyme*, or a placement in the abyss, of Blackness.[5]

When the submarine emerges at the end of *The Navigator*, we might believe that we are witnessing a *deus ex machina* ending, whereby the submarine saves Rollo and Betsy from 'out of the [deep] blue [sea]'. However, the presence of the submarine would really suggest that it has been surveilling Rollo and his escapades for some time. In this way, the submarine does indeed come to fulfil its function à la Deane as a further technology of surveillance. Furthermore, that the *Navigator* has been sold by Betsy's father to one side in a war between two non-US countries would also suggest that the submarine is keeping tabs on the *Navigator* as a ship involved in that conflict. Or, in fact, the submarine was surveilling the Pacific islanders all along, since they constitute a threat to whiteness and national security. As Audre Lorde says of a possibly independent Grenada, an island to whose shores we shall return, '[w]hat a bad example, a dangerous precedent, an independent Grenada would be for the peoples of Color in the Caribbean, in Central America, for those of us here in the United States' (Lorde 1984: 23; see also Rogers 2018: 176).

If the 'war on terror' therefore sees surveillance being deployed in many non-American 'theatres of operations', then so, too, is the 'war' taking place in Keaton and Crisp's film one that has American meddling and surveillance at its heart. That it intervenes when Rollo and Betsy are under threat from black natives would also suggest that American interests, be they domestic or foreign, always have antiblackness at their heart. The emerging submarine, then, echoes the emerging Rollo: white America, with its tentacles spread into every other nation, is a figurative Cthulhu, a white beast that casts Blackness and Indigeneity alike as others that must always be destroyed. If Glissant draws upon Edward Kamau Brathwaite to posit that the 'unity is sub-marine', then the submarine here demonstrates the American goal of creating a unitary world whereby *e pluribus unum* is built upon sending black people into the abyss, and whereby difference is not so much tolerated as characterized as deviance and thus destroyed (see Ferguson 2004: 111). That is, Keaton and Crisp's film (pre-)appropriates Brathwaite's dictum, but it does so by eradicating difference, casting it out as deviance, and making the submarine *qua* control room a white-only space.

Maybe as much is also intimated in the uncredited casting as the film's Cannibal King of Noble Johnson, who in the 1910s was a black character actor at Lubin and Universal. For Johnson was one of the founders in 1916 of the Lincoln Motion Picture Company, considered the first African-American film studio to produce movies committed to 'countering existing portrayals of blacks with images of respectability, prosperity, and morality' (Gaines 2005: 34; see also Robinson 2007: 233ff.). Indeed, 'Lincoln's goal was not only to make "respectable" race films but also to open up work and investment opportunities for Blacks in the growing field of motion picture production' (Stewart 2005: 203). However, while the Lincoln films included 'three of the most highly acclaimed and widely distributed Black-produced race films of the silent era' (Stewart 2005: 203) – namely *The Realization of a Negro's Ambition* (Harry A. Gant, 1916), *The Law of Nature* (Harry A. Gant, 1917) and *The Trooper of Troop K* (Harry A. Gant, USA, 1917) – it was still uncertain as to whether Johnson 'was more attractive to Black audiences in Universal and Lubin films or in Lincoln productions' (Stewart 2005: 209). That is, while Johnson was a popular performer among black audiences, he still funded his Lincoln work through his appearances in Lubin and Universal films, where he played a litany of stereotypical characters, including various native and cannibal kings in white films like *Love Aflame* (James Vincent and Raymond Wells, USA, 1917), *Drums of Fate* (Charles Maigne, USA, 1923) and *Little Robinson Crusoe* (Edward F. Cline, USA, 1924). This latter role followed his performance 2 years earlier as Friday in Robert F. Hill's *Adventures of Robinson Crusoe* (USA, 1922), with his turn in *The Navigator* preceding his performances as Uncle Tom in *Topsy and Eva* (Del Lord, USA, 1927), as the cannibal Queequeg in *Moby Dick* (Lloyd Bacon, USA, 1930), and as the native chief, mentioned above by James Snead, in *King Kong*. Importantly, Johnson had had a role (also uncredited) in Stuart Paton's *20,000 Leagues Under the Sea* (USA, 1916), proclaimed as the 'the first submarine photoplay ever filmed'. In other words, as a star text, Johnson brings with him racist associations between Blackness, cannibalism, the ocean and the submarine. And yet, in spite of his success as a 'cross-over' performer Johnson's work at Lincoln had ended by 1921, and he does not appear in the credits for *The Navigator*. In other words, *The Navigator* as a film, and the film industry more generally, negates Johnson's black identity for the purposes of constructing whiteness. And having played such a key role in this and other films, as well as being a major, if almost forgotten, figure of African-American cinema, that he disappeared into obscurity only bespeaks the construction of white cinema on black labour.

More curious still is that Johnson was listed on his death certificate as white (Gaines 2005: 38), a seeming erasure of his black identity that further belies the antiblackness of the medium of cinema and white Western modernity, or the Anthropocene, as a whole. Johnson was paradoxically 'visible' when understood as black, but only when he was surveilled in a series of racist roles; his 'genuine' black roles, meanwhile, have all but disappeared – with 'only a few feet' of a film called *By Right of Birth* (Harry A. Gant, USA, 1921) remaining of all of the Lincoln films (Gaines 2005: 37).[6] By becoming 'white', Johnson paradoxically disappeared, but he also was no longer under surveillance, and, given his repeated refusals to discuss his career, including with his estranged brother and business partner George, it would seem that he sought for this specifically to be the case. If film stars famously embody certain contradictions, as Richard Dyer (1979) so clearly acknowledged, then Blackness and cinema seem to have an equally contradictory relationship; black stardom in white cinema functions as a form of surveillance, casting a (sur)veil over Blackness, while black stardom in black cinema remains to some extent invisible, equally (sur)veiled (or screened or gagged) from view (see also Gaines 2005: 41).

# Chapter 9

# Black + Red = Maroon

One reason for casting black actors as Pacific islanders might be because the darker skin of African descendants contrasts more clearly with the white skin of Keaton/Rollo and McGuire/Betsy, meaning that they stand out as 'other' in a more concerted fashion than if the natives had been played by, say, Native Americans, whose skin, when recorded by the cinematograph, would potentially become 'white passing', or at least not 'other' enough, thereby confusing viewers who might believe that they were seeing 'civilised' whites in a struggle against 'uncivilised' whites. In this way, the binaristic black and white logic of cinema trumps the reality of skin tones, with *The Navigator* using black skin to connote 'threat' and 'savagery' in a simplistic and perfidious fashion, even as this renders actual indigenous peoples invisible – while also leaving intact the damaging associations between Indigeneity and both 'savageness' and 'primitiveness', as identified by Jodi A. Byrd, among others (Byrd 2011: 63). But while we might attribute this conflation of Blackness and Indigeneity to a combination of laziness and the racial-ideological shortcomings of both a technology (cinema) and its users (both filmmakers and viewers), it is perhaps more important to understand that the 'equivalency' of racialisation and colonisation, here carried out visually through the conflation of Blackness and Indigeneity, is, as Byrd writes elsewhere, 'after all, a tool of colonialism' (Byrd 2014: 178). For, this equivalency/ conflation perpetuates the 'historical aphasia of the conquest of indigenous peoples' (Byrd 2011: xxvi).

If above I posited the potentially weird or unsettling formula of black + red = maroon, then I did so in a bid to create a framework that does not involve such aphasia (and which, in its shifting colours, is a bit like the chromatophoric camouflage of the octopus?). For while *The Navigator* seemingly conflates diasporic Africans with Pacific islanders, there is a danger in conflating Blackness with Indigeneity, even if here I shall work towards proposing a positive alliance between the two. For, the process of racialisation that leads to black slavery is not necessarily the same as the process of settler colonialism that sees indigenous peoples exterminated, as scholars like Patrick Wolfe have noted. Indeed, the logic of settler colonialism is for the latter 'the logic of elimination', involving, among other things, 'the summary liquidation of Indigenous people' (Wolfe 2006: 387-390). Racialisation, meanwhile, especially when manifested in slavery, involves in principle not elimination, but the preservation of the body for the purposes of labour (Wolfe 2016: 2).

As we have seen, though, such a view is limited in that antiblackness involves the preservation not of the body, but of flesh; what is more, while in some senses indestructible, Blackness, as flesh, is nonetheless permanently undergoing elimination at the hands of white supremacy (and in this sense is in a kind of hell). Now, Wolfe tentatively recognises that as much happens to black Americans after the abolition of slavery, since '[o]n emancipation, Blacks became surplus to some requirements and, to that extent, more like Indians. Thus it is highly significant that the barbarities of lynching and the Jim Crow reign of terror should be a post-emancipation phenomenon' (Wolfe 2006: 404). Nonetheless, Wolfe cannot help but add that '[a]s valuable commodities, slaves had only been destroyed *in extremis*. Even after slavery, Black people continue to have value as a source of super-cheap labour... so their dispensability was tempered' (Wolfe 2006: 404) – a perspective for which Wolfe is taken to task by, *inter alia*, Robin D.G. Kelley, who goes so far as to say that Wolfe's refusal to recognise antiblackness as a 'process of elimination' in and of itself contributes to that process (Kelley 2017: 268).

While both black and indigenous communities face elimination, though, there are nonetheless differences between Blackness and Indigeneity, as can be most visibly seen in the divergent policies of blood surrounding them. Indeed, Wolfe explains that 'whereas race for black people became an indelible trait that would survive any amount of admixture, race for Indians became an inherently descending quantity that was terminally susceptible to dilution' (Wolfe 2001: 887). That is, in a white supremacist system to have even a minimal amount of black blood renders one black, while to have even a minimal amount of non-'Indian' blood destroys one's claims to Indigeneity – a divergent set of policies that no doubt inform Wolfe's belief that it is Indigeneity that is to be destroyed (one stops being indigenous if one is not of a fully indigenous lineage), and not Blackness (one is always black even if one has only a distant black relative), even as that very set of policies might affirm the opposite (Indigeneity is preserved in a pure form, while Blackness is itself diluted into non-existence/ meaninglessness).

All the same, in the face of mutual elimination, both Indigeneity and Blackness can and do lay respective claim to being *the* structuring other of white Western modernity. Indigenous scholars like Byrd, for example, find proof of this in how the American Empire persists 'through the reproduction of Indianness that exists alongside racializing discourses that slip through the thresholds of whiteness and blackness, inclusion and exclusion, internal and external, that are the necessary conditions of settler colonial sovereignty' (Byrd 2001: 27). That is, 'Indianness' gets forgotten, and thus doubly eliminated, amid discourses of Blackness and whiteness, which forgetting is key to ongoing settler colonialism. And for his part, Frank B. Wilderson III argues, after Ronald Judy, that the Indian is regularly considered in the white Western imaginary as rational and civil, with 'the two most frequently cited acts of abomination held against Indians, cannibalism…and sacrifice[,]…[being] viewed…as no more than singular temporary aberrations of reason and so not evidence of true irrationality'. However, 'when cannibalism is blackened it is considered to be a genetic predisposition rather than a "temporary aberration of reason"' (Wilderson 2010: 47; see also Judy 1993: 80-81), and thus proof that the black is the true outsider to white Western modernity.

At times, these competing claims even lead to loggerheads, as per Wilderson's searing analysis of Native American films, especially *Skins* (Chris Eyre, USA, 2002), about which Wilderson argues that while 'White supremacy, the press of civil society, constitutes the greatest threat to the project of a restored sovereign [indigenous] ontology, they [Native American films] make an emotional argument that Blackness also threatens this restorative project' (Wilderson 2010: 221). This argument finds an unexpected echo in Byrd, who contends that for diasporic black people, whom Byrd refers to after Edward Kamau Brathwaite (1973) as *arrivants*, to adopt indigenous values as part of their resistance against white hegemony would 'affectively appropriate…Indianness to reconcile the violent exclusions they experience at the hands of empire' (Byrd 2014: 180). That is, for black folks to effectively 'become indigenous' – but on a land to which they signally are not indigenous – is further to impose settler colonialism on the 'Indian', since the latter still has to live with the arrivant when, in the language of Bartleby, they would prefer not to. Similarly, for the arrivant, this process involves what Jared Sexton identifies as a '*re-indigenization*' (since the African diaspora was of course once indigenous to Africa), but nonetheless a re-indigenisation that is not their own (Sexton 2016: 588, original emphasis). If the aim, then, is for black and indigenous peoples alike to achieve sovereignty, then this seems impossible, especially if sovereignty is conceived in the singular (a shared sovereignty as opposed to numerous sovereignties; see Trask 2004: 14).

As William S. Willis remarked back in 1963, it was important for white people historically to maintain 'social distance between Indians and Negroes', at times even encouraging them to murder each other (see Willis 1963: 176). For, by doing this, whites managed to keep their supreme position in the racial hierarchy. Indeed, this led to certain historical confrontations that cannot easily be forgotten, if at all, such as black folk being enlisted by whites (here, the French) to fight against the Chickasaw (Willis 1963: 167), and Cherokees taking black humans as slaves (King 2019: 50). In the competing claims for black and indigenous victimhood, we might perversely see a continuation of this colonial policy of division and conquest, although we might note that scholars like Kelley (2017) and Iyko Day (2015) do seek to reconcile the potentially conflicting black and indigenous positions, while Lisa Lowe expands this argument out further, in particular to include the Asian 'coolie' in a globalised system of 'distinct yet connected racial logics' (Lowe 2015: 8).

As Lowe seeks 'relation across differences rather than equivalence' (Lowe 2015: 11), there have also been moments of historical alliance between black and indigenous peoples, most notably the alliance between Natives and Africans in Seminole to fight against US forces in the nineteenth century (see Philip: 1997: 12). Looking beyond the USA, we might also consider how in Brazil 'maroon colonies were called *quilombos*, the most famous of which is Palmares, where generations of Africans, Indigenous and mixed-race peoples lived side by side, grew crops, raised their children and fought off several Portuguese military campaigns aimed at wiping them out' (Amadahy and Lawrence 2009: 133).[1] That is, if maroonage is thought typically to involve escaped slaves (and thus constitutes a 'black' phenomenon; indeed, Native Americans were often engaged to track down maroons; see Willis 1963: 165), I wish to argue here, against its etymology but in line with its constitution as a colour, that 'maroon' can offer to us a positive conceptual example of black and red coalition.[2]

In order to achieve what Joy James (2013) would thus call a 'maroon philosophy', though, or Kelley's 'freedom dream' of a revolution crafted by 'Maroon poets' (Kelley 2002: 195), we perhaps need to move away from white concepts such as sovereignty, as well as the notion of land, and to go, as Fred Moten says, 'in search of marronage' (Moten 2013: 743). Indeed, Sexton attributes to Moten the possibility that sovereignty might itself be the problem in resolving the tensions around Blackness and Indigeneity (Sexton 2016: 593), regardless of whether it is used in the singular or plural (sovereignties, as opposed to sovereignty). For, in being a Western concept, to achieve sovereignty 'from' the settler colonial state would thus always already be something supposedly 'permitted' by the same, and thus not 'sovereignty' at all. That is, it would involve white society recognising as equal non-white groups, which would mean that the recognition would be done on the terms of the white society (okay, we now choose to recognise you), which in and of itself undermines the difference/sovereignty of the group(s) being recognised (why should I effectively exist only when I am recognised by the white?). Indeed, the impossibility of this situation leads to the Afropessimism of Sexton and Wilderson, as well as to the indigenous rejection of the politics of recognition as 'colonial' by Glen Sean Coulthard (2014).

If we are to move away from sovereignty, though, perhaps we must also move away from the land, a concept to which sovereignty, especially as it pertains to settler colonialism, is tied. Indeed, settler colonialism involves the clearing of the native from the land, before then claiming that land as one's own, thereby introducing/enforcing the concept of land as possession. As Mishuana Goeman explains, land is understood from the indigenous perspective as 'more than property or territory' (Goeman 2015: 72), with the native possessed by, rather than possessing, the land (Goeman 2015: 80).[3] Nonetheless, land remains 'necessary to all our survival for generations' (Goeman 2015: 74) – and thus becomes almost inseparable from indigenous thought.[4]

The aim here is not to abandon the land entirely and to carry out a potentially suicidal leap into the ocean, even as such 'revolutionary suicides' can entail 'the falling away of the fleshly body toward collectively carrying on in dignity' (Rogers 2018: 198; see also Newton 1973). All the same, in contrast to the role played by land in indigenous thought, we might note, as does Tiffany Lethabo King, the numerous 'oceanic and water metaphors…[that] theorize Black life, aesthetics, and decolonial politics' (King 2019: 4; for an example, see Walcott 2021, writing in the esteemed journal *liquid blackness*, no less). Indeed, as King goes on to say,

> [l]iquidity as a totalizing metaphor for Blackness is not just an ethical problem for depictions of Black life and the Black radical (and political) imagination – it also effaces the generative conceptual problem of Blackness. For instance, what happens – or needs to happen conceptually – when Black diasporic people, aesthetics, and politics land and encounter Native peoples' cosmologies and resistance to conquest? In an attempt to register this shift, the shoal disrupts the nautical and oceanic coherence of Blackness as only liquid and enables other modes of thinking about Blackness that opens up other kinds of potentialities, materialities, and forms. **(King 2019: 8)**

If a maroon philosophy that allies Blackness with Indigeneity seeks to move away from the land, it also seeks not to be lost at sea, and it is in the liminal space of the shoal, the shallow waters that combine both land and sea (rather than pitting them against each other), that we can begin potentially to find the (black + red =) maroon. Indeed, for King, '[j]ust as Black and Indigenous life, struggle, and joy are forged off the shoreline in the space of the shoal, so must the new worlds we desire and make for one another' (King 2019: 209). And if the shoal is a 'danger to navigation', then the shoal can unsettle the settler colonialism/white supremacy at work in *The Navigator*.

King draws upon Vicente M. Diaz and Alice Te Punga Somerville to posit 'water as connected with the currents rather than water as that which divides continents, islands, and land', before arguing that:

> the historical and ongoing violence that separated the land and the ocean – and, more importantly, Indigenous people – from the water is of utmost importance. Coastal Indigenous peoples were removed from the life-giving space of the water through military force and transformed into combatants pushed to the edge of the map. **(King 2019: 94)**

That is, for King, the terrestrial nature of Indigeneity is a result of a divorce from the water, the relationship with which Diaz nevertheless reclaims, especially in his suggestion that it was '[o]n outrigger canoes, with sophisticated maritime technologies and knowledge...[that] Austronesian seafarers would fan out and settle roughly four fifths of the globe's southern oceanic hemisphere' (Diaz 2015: 93), a process that took place 'millennia before Europeans ventured from sight of their shores' (Diaz 2015: 97). Meanwhile, indigenous scholar Jack D. Forbes explains how Christopher Columbus writes about meeting with Native Americans in Galway in or around 1477, some 15 years before his 'discovery' of the 'New World', with this encounter being for Columbus clear evidence that he could and should sail west to the Indies. That is, Americans discovered Europe at least some time, if not long before, Europeans discovered

America (see Forbes 2011).

In *The Navigator*, we see the relationship between indigenous peoples and the water alive and well through the canoes that they use to reach the titular ship. While the film denigrates the canoes as a 'primitive' technology, in that it is from a sinking canoe that Rollo and Betsy are rescued by the submarine, they nevertheless serve as reminders that, as Diaz puts it, 'no island is an island'. That is, the film's Pacific island supposedly untouched by civilisation, degenerate in its cannibalism, technologically backward with its flimsy and sinking canoes, and where Indigeneity is conflated with Blackness, is what Diaz calls a 'necessary political fiction' that helps 'continental thinking' to justify its perceived superiority (Diaz 2015: 101). What the continental Rollo refuses to accept, and what *The Navigator* refuses to depict, is that those native islanders have in fact been using water to travel for longer than continental people have had ships – suggesting not their isolation or backwardness, which are imposed upon them along with 'constant surveillance...colonizers, militaries, anthropologists, filmmakers, and tourists' (DeLoughrey 2019: 170), but their progressive interconnectedness with the world. The continental in this sense creates the island in order to justify itself, but really it is the island that creates the continent.[5]

Our maroon philosophy is not about a retreat into some mythical past. As it brings together land and sea, the red and the black, it must also tidalectically combine both past and present in order to create a future. However, it does not seek recognition from, or sovereignty/sovereignties within, white Western modernity. Russell Maroon Shoatz, who is one of the key maroon philosophers identified by Joy James (see James 2013: 130), reminds us that

> [m]aroons *differed* from the runaway slaves who tried to blend-in or fully integrate themselves within the otherwise

'free' societies. And that's where the true distinction lies between maroons and the other fugitives! Whether the maroons term their communities quilombos, ladeiras, palenques, cumbes, Nanny Town, Trelawny Town, or one of the scores of other designations we know of, they all were clear on the fact that direct integration into the surrounding oppressive settler colonial communities was something they did not desire. **(Shoatz 2013; original emphasis)**

That is, maroonage creates a space and a time outside of white Western modernity, different to it, evolved from the human that inhabits it. The shoal of *The Navigator*, where the octopus roams, is where we can begin tidalectically to think this maroon existence. As already mentioned, the Black Chthulucene is therefore (tidily?) also an Autochthulucene, where black studies and autochthonous thought unite.

# Chapter 10

# White face, Black hole

Their first morning aboard *The Navigator*, Rollo sits in an empty dining hall awaiting some breakfast. When it does not come, he wanders the boat in search of human company. Descending a ladder, he has his back to Betsy, who leaves the frame just as Rollo turns around – meaning that he does not see her. Rollo smokes a cigarette and discards the butt, which Betsy finds. Aware that she is not alone, she calls out to see who is there, and then wanders around the deck. Having heard her call, Rollo also wanders the deck, the two just missing each other as Betsy turns a corner right at the moment when Rollo arrives on the same part of the deck. This goes on for two laps of the ship, split into four shots, as Rollo and Betsy both walk faster and faster to try to catch up with whoever else might be there. Betsy enters a doorway and goes through the middle of the ship, going down a flight of stairs just as Rollo enters the same doorway. The film cuts to a wide shot looking back at the superstructure from the bow of the ship: Betsy appears on a lower deck as Rollo walks along an upper deck. They cross sides, before each zigzags their way up and down the ship, crossing the decks but never quite finding each other. This particular sequence involves a 30-second shot in which a static camera observes Betsy and Rollo in long shot as they keep missing each other, going up or down a ladder at precisely the moment that the other arrives on the same deck as them.

I include this relatively lengthy description because while I have argued above that the submarine and the ship both function as surveillance technologies within the context of white Western modernity, this particular shot, in which the viewer can see so much more than the characters, who are trying to but cannot see each other, demonstrates clearly how cinema itself functions as a surveillance technology, and how it is cinema that is, or aspires to be, panoptic. And if the Pantopicon is, as I have been arguing after various scholars, a white technology used to construct and to entrap/imprison Blackness and Indigeneity, then cinema might also be such a white technology, as I began to suggest earlier via the brief foray into the career of Noble Johnson.

Alan Bilton has, among others, pointed out that Keaton's work is self-conscious, foregrounding how 'the movie camera is itself a machine' (Bilton 2006: 487; see also Kerr 1980: 130). Being conscious of cinema as a machine, Keaton is perhaps also aware that cinema is a machine that in certain respects springs from and helps to produce whiteness. That is, after Richard Dyer's landmark critique of film stock and lighting systems as having been calibrated to capture white skin (see Dyer 1997), cinema reaffirms whiteness – something that Keaton makes clear when he employs what Linville, in relation to *The Navigator*, calls 'emphatic white face' (Linville 2007: 274). Drawn from the clown traditions through which Keaton emerged, Linville contends that Keaton is a 'whiteface clown' (Linville 2007: 272), who in *The Navigator* is, as mentioned, 'a kind of blank, passive, privileged white boy', and that the '[p]roblematic racist images of dark-skinned savages thus contribute to a mise-en-scène for white male caricature and accomplishment' (Linville 2007: 276).

Now, Linville does acknowledge that Keaton effectively adopts blackface in films where he gets covered in mud, paint and perhaps coal, as happens, for example, in *Neighbors* (Eddie Cline and Buster Keaton, USA, 1920). For Linville, this 'denotes the doubling of Irish-American and African-American identities' (Linville 2007: 279), a point to which we shall revert later. Furthermore, we can relate how Linville's argument that the whiteness of Keaton's make-up also involves a 'stone face' effect, such that the hardness of whiteness could thus be contrasted with the softness (mollusc-like nature) of Blackness (Linville 2007: 273). However, for the time being, I wish to suggest that the self-consciousness of the medium, including the self-conscious panopticism of the medium, is linked to a relatively self-conscious construction of whiteness in *The Navigator*. More than this, I also wish to suggest that the film cannot but convey how this whiteness is, once again, built upon Blackness.

One of the most celebrated images from *The Navigator* does not actually feature in the film. It depicts Rollo/Keaton in sailor costume and pork pie hat sitting in a funnel on the titular ship, his hands clasped together on his lap as his legs hang down. His eyes are downcast, a characteristically forlorn look across his white, stoney face. Keaton in particular stands out against the black hole that surrounds him and that is the darkness of the funnel. While this image does not feature in the film, it nonetheless plays an important role in the life of *The Navigator*, being one of the first images even today to come up alongside the film when one looks for it on Google. Furthermore, it is accompanied by two related 'black hole' shots in the film itself. The first is when Rollo, in similar but not the same framing, falls backward into one of the ship's funnels – this time wearing top hat and tails, shortly following the 30-second 'Panopticon' shot that I described above. In a static long shot, Rollo climbs up some steps, presumably to see if he can spot Betsy (whom he does not know for sure to be aboard the ship at this point in time). From this vantage point, he turns to the camera and looks out for shipmates, only for his top hat to be swept from his head and down the funnel, with Rollo himself then falling backwards into it. Rollo drops on to and splits in twain a plank, on which Betsy also sits. Rollo and Betsy gather themselves and recognise each other, with Rollo immediately proposing to Betsy, who turns him down. She is hungry and they go get something to eat.

Meanwhile, the second 'black hole' shot takes place shortly before the record of 'Asleep in the Deep' begins to play, and which features Rollo taking fright at the portrait of an angry, white sea captain (in fact, co-director Donald Crisp) who appears in the porthole of his cabin. The image appears because Betsy, having discovered the image in her own cabin, attempts to throw it overboard, only for its wire to catch on the side of the *Navigator*, and for the image thus to dangle back and forth over the porthole to Rollo's cabin.

These three images, two taken from the film itself and the other a major 'paratext' for the film, all feature white faces highlighted against black backgrounds, or more specifically against black holes. I wish to suggest, then, that these images each stage the construction of whiteness at the expense of Blackness, in that whiteness is made visible not exactly through the invisibility of Blackness – for we can, after all, see the darkness within the frame of each shot. Rather, whiteness is made visible through the use and treatment of Blackness as if it were invisible, or nothing.

The concept of the black hole in black studies dates back to at least Houston A. Baker Jr., who used it in relation to the work of Richard Wright, whose literary œuvre he reckoned as '[i]nvisible, massive in its energies, erasing old law, nullifying time and space in its singularity' (Baker Jr. 1984: 151). It is taken up next by Michele Wallace, who in her consideration of black female sexuality, reminds us both that 'black holes in space are full, not empty,' and that 'black holes may give access to other dimensions' (Wallace 2016: 556-558). Evelynn Hammonds then uses the concept as a means to consider how black female sexuality has what she terms a 'different geometry' from 'more visible sexualities' (Hammonds 2004: 310). But as the invisible black hole affects the visible star, so do the visible and the invisible not function as opposites, or even in parallel with each other. Rather, they are in 'dynamic relation' with each other, or what we might term, after Karen Barad (2007), entangled.

Hammonds hands the baton to Rizvana Bradley, who pits the black hole against the 'black (w)hole', a term introduced by Hammonds, and which helps to convey the plenitude of the black hole, otherwise thought erroneously to be empty. For Bradley, 'black w/holeness' possesses a 'performative potentiality' through which it can express 'the empty fulfilment or fulfilled emptiness of black female dispossession', or the process whereby black women were during slavery regularly dispossessed of their children (Bradley 2016: P13). In generating new life, the black mother is clearly 'whole', but in not being recognised, and in not being allowed to be a mother, she also is 'nothing'. Black femininity is, therefore, a 'destabilizing, vernacular force' (Bradley 2016: P14), perhaps not unlike a black hole that is both negative and yet, perhaps, generative of all that exists.[1]

Finally, Zakiyyah Iman Jackson, drawing precisely on Barad, proposes that rather than being caught between negativity and generativity, or between life and death, the black woman is an example of superposition, 'which stresses virtuality and indeterminacy rather than teleological passage or "in-betweenness"' (Jackson 2018: 645).[2] Failing by virtue of this complexity to fit into the normative categories of white modernity is what leads Jackson once again to posit the plasticity of the black, who is in fact 'blackened', or rendered as black by white modernity:

New World slavery established a field of demand that tyrannically presumed, as if by will alone, that the black(ened) via their relational proximity to black femininity in their humanity could function as infinitely malleable lexical and biological matter, at once sub/super/human. What appear as alternating, or serialized, discrete modes of (mis)recognition – sub/super/humanization or privation/superfluity – are

> in practice varying dimensions of racializing demand that
> the black(ened) be all at once, a simultaneous actualization
> of seemingly discontinuous and incompatible virtualities.
> **(Jackson 2018: 636)**

In other words, the way in which Blackness is both negative/
absent/nothing/dead, and yet whose death is necessary for
whiteness to exist, is not an accident, even if it appears so (or,
rather, is made to appear so). For, rather, these contradictions
are necessary for whiteness, encapsulated by Jackson as New
World slavery, to exist. If you will, Blackness does not function
as a tool for us to understand the difference between the human
(heteropatriarchally white, straight and masculine) and the non-
human (that which lies outside of heteropatriarchy, or which
functions as its tools). Put differently, that which is considered
human is not that which is white in contradistinction to that
which is black (or, at least, that which is 'human' is not *just*
that). Rather, that which is black is *difference itself*. What this
means is that Blackness is never separate from white humanity
(they are entangled); furthermore, it means that whiteness is
always appropriating its own difference from the Blackness that
it renders as different. Blackness, thus, is a difference generator
that brings the white into existence while simultaneously
being dispossessed of its own generation of difference (black
mothers are dispossessed of their own children, and made to
raise white children). Blackness is in this way everywhere and
nowhere (superposition), giving access to other dimensions
in its generativity, but which generativity is stolen from it by
the whiteness that it also produces. The black hole, then, is
generative of whiteness, as the three 'black hole' images from *The
Navigator* would seem to suggest, with the fact that each of these
three examples features one of the film's two directors, Keaton
and Crisp, equally suggesting a kind of self-consciousness in
this process.

When Spillers writes of 'the "flesh" as a primary narrative, then we mean its seared, divided, ripped-apartness, riveted to the ship's hole, fallen or "escaped" overboard' (Spillers 1987: 67). The white faces of Rollo/Keaton and Crisp, contrasted against the black holes that surround them, thus come into existence as a result of the Middle Passage, which cannot but be expressed in the darkness of the funnel and/or porthole. When Rollo falls through the funnel and effectively into Betsy's arms, we also see how the black hole functions as a wormhole, trans*porting Rollo into 'new' (if really normative) dimensions – towards a heterosexual coupling – that allow him to 'live' and/or to prove his existence as such. While Baker Jr. refers to the black hole in relation to a 'vernacular theory' (as per the title of his study), then we derive from 'vernacular' a worm-like tentacle that is inscribed etymologically into the term, in that it not only comes from the Etruscan *verna*, meaning a 'home-born slave or native', but also carries echoes from, or is haunted by, the *ver*, which is French for worm, and which also means a line of poetry (as in a 'verse'), which itself comes from the ProtoIndoEuropean root **wer-*, meaning to turn or to bend. Blackness as vernacular is therefore a wormhole through the black hole, appropriated here by Keaton/Rollo for the purposes of white heterosexual coupling.

Finally, in *The Navigator*'s third instance of a 'black hole', Rollo is scared that the angry captain's face is that of a ghost, meaning that the black hole does indeed offer to us here an evocation of the spirit of those 'asleep in the deep', but which *The Navigator* of course can neither name nor depict directly (hence it is the face of Crisp that we see). Or, at least, *The Navigator* cannot in effect show Blackness in a human(istic) fashion, as instead we see the cannon kill the one native, who falls overboard.[3] Blackness is other, with black women perhaps especially overlooked by the film in its quest to construct, and for us to see, the white face – a topic to which we shall revert in due course. For now, though, perhaps it is no surprise that it is Audre Lorde whom Roderick A. Ferguson cites at length when he suggests that difference is cast out as deviance by white mainstream society, as we saw in Chapter 8 (see Ferguson 2004: 111). For it is perhaps inevitably black feminist discourse as it intersects with queerness, traces of which we can find in Spillers, Wallace, Hammonds, Bradley and Jackson, that allows us to comprehend the meaning of these images.

# Chapter 11

# Queer trans*port through the wormhole

If the black bride sets in motion Rollo's decision to get married, black women do indeed seem generative of white desire in *The Navigator*, but the black woman is all the same forsaken for the purposes of a white coupledom that is insincere at best (since Rollo does not seem to have any genuine interest in Betsy, at least not before they are stranded together on the *Navigator*). However, while the quasi-absent black female thus functions as a black hole that produces whiteness, I shall here propose that Keaton and Crisp's film both draws upon and negates a queer potential that also has within it a queer logic that we can draw from trans* theory. And we can do this by returning to the moment, excised from Keaton's film, involving the starfish.

Eva Hayward has drawn repeatedly upon the starfish in her theoretical work in order to give expression to transsexual existence, which here I shall explore under the umbrella term trans*, where the star/* evokes precisely the critter (that is, the starfish) in question (see Hayward 2008a; 2008b).[1] Hayward in particular draws upon Antony and the Johnsons' 2000 song 'Cripple and the Starfish' in order to suggest that to be transsexual is to experience not just a cut (which might be fetishized as the literal cut of a surgeon, as per the dominant logic that ties sexual identity to genitalia), but also to create a new identity from that experience. As the limb, or the ray, of a starfish grows back, so does the (surgeon's) cut become generative of a new being; as Hayward says, '[t]he cut is possibility...my cut is not passive – its very substance (materially and affectively) is generative and plays a significant role in my ongoing materialisation' (Hayward 2008a: 255, original emphasis). In particular, Hayward takes care to suggest that

'Antony's starfish rays may not just be stand-ins for penis = finger, but interventions in phallus = vision' (Hayward 2008b: 70). By this, Hayward means that the myth of disembodied vision, or at least of 'objective' and controlling vision, is linked to the 'phallic', and as such is key to patriarchal society. Indeed, this can be seen in the very principles of surveillance that we discussed earlier: patriarchal society involves the development of a controlling gaze, which also for Hayward plays a key role in differentiating species and distinguishing human from animal (as well as differentiating between sexes within species). Rather than lament the loss of the finger/the loss of the penis as a 'loss of vision', though, Antony's song suggests, for Hayward, the development of a new way of being, whereby one does not see but *feels* (in the hold?), and which is a world not of distal vision, but of entangled connection – a 'sensate ontology' that involves 'zoomorphic, *re*-morphic, and *trans*-morphic subjects' (Hayward 2008b: 82). Since the human is now connected with rather than separated from the starfish ('trans-morphism'), there is at work, therefore, a trans, or trans*, logic that is not necessarily particular to, but which all the same is emphasised in, the transsexual. As Hayward concludes: 't]his is what my being transsexual knows about being a starfish' (Hayward 2008b: 82).

With regard to *The Navigator*, Keaton was, as mentioned, to take the starfish in the cut scene and apply it to his chest as if it were a sheriff's badge, before directing fish traffic. Notably, then, Keaton was to take the starfish and subjugate it in a quite literal sense to the law; it would be used as a symbol to confer upon Rollo a certain kind of 'natural' authority that perhaps even the fishes would understand and follow. If Antony refuses the starfish as penis in order to develop a *different* trans-species ontology, Keaton would seem to reaffirm the starfish as phallus – a trope that is in keeping with his other relations with animals, whereby they are subjugated to a tool-being that deprives them of their animality – with the possible exception of the octopus, but the murder of which might well be an expression of its very (non-)tool-existence, as suggested above. However, as we know, the starfish sequence was *cut* from Keaton and Crisp's film and now only exists in a parallel universe or version of the film, and to which parallel uni-ver-se/ver-sion we would only be able to travel via a wormhole (or *ver*-hole).

That said, while the cutting of the scene reaffirms the anthropocentric nature of Keaton's film, I discuss it not simply to present a 'what if' argument about the film. Indeed, since Keaton's treatment of the starfish would not differ in any philosophically substantial manner from his treatment of other animals and of black people, it would simply function as a means of 'hammering' home (tool pun intended) the same point that I have already made at some length. Rather, I mention this because while Keaton cuts the starfish and keeps the octopus, he nonetheless also cuts the octopus open with his knife, a moment that is signalled by a cut from the octopus, visible through a glass plate, to the octopus, invisible, or only partially visible, behind a rock.

The aim is not to conflate starfish and octopus and to suggest that Keaton somehow enacts a kind of metaphorical violence towards transsexuals, even as such a case might conceivably be made. Nor is it to suggest that in killing the octopus behind a rock, Keaton in fact hides how he does not kill an octopus at all – in keeping with the tradition that no animals supposedly are or do get killed in the making of fiction feature films. That is, the aim is not to suggest that Keaton saves the octopus via the cut, while Rollo kills it mercilessly with his knife – albeit that this also could plausibly be argued. Rather, the aim in discussing these two cuts – the cutting of the starfish from the film and the cutting of the octopus within the film – is to suggest that both work according to a capitalist logic that pertains not just to the content of *The Navigator*, but also to the form of the film, and perhaps to cinema itself as a whole.

For, as Eliza Steinbock has argued, in language that at least implicitly recalls the logic of the surveillance control room, '*cinema*, with its system of editing cuts', is a kind of 'operation theatre' that also functions as an 'aesthetic regime' (Steinbock 2012: 161-162). Keaton gets rid of the starfish sequence for commercial reasons (audiences didn't like it), and he retains the octopus killing since the logic of capital also suggests that it must die, because without usefulness as a tool, the octopus is in effect dead already. And while the underwater sequence of *The Navigator* has the potential to involve the sorts of 'shimmering' images that Steinbock in her wider work considers to be redolent of a trans aesthetics of change and becoming (see Steinbock 2019), what Keaton's cinema really does, with its logic of surveillance, is to instigate a heteronormative and white logic, as is made clear by the narrative union of Rollo and Betsy. Nonetheless, *The Navigator* does involve the transformation of Rollo from singleton to coupled, and so what takes place in the film, and perhaps in cinema more widely, is the subjugation of the trans* logic of cinema, whereby anything could happen (meaning that cinema is, like Blackness and like the octopus, plastic), and yet whereby the most predictable and white thing happens: heteronormative union. Without the potential that cinema clearly possesses for radical transformation, though, the white heteronormative union and narrative resolution (or cinema as a narrative form *tout court*) would not be possible.

If for Gilles Deleuze, the cinema of the time-image is created in part through 'irrational cuts', then this is because when a film cuts from one image to another in an unpredictable, or 'irrational', fashion, then it creates (new) links between those things that we see in the images either side of the cut. For Deleuze, the 'relinkage' that takes place through an irrational cut involves 'thought', which for Deleuze is a:

power which has not always existed, is born from an outside more distant than any external world, and, as power which does not yet exist, confronts an inside, an unthinkable or unthought, deeper than any internal world…there is…this thought outside itself and this un-thought within thought. **(Deleuze 2005: 266)**

This can be compared to a 'rational' cut, whereby what we see from one image to the next is what we'd expect to see, as per the rules of continuity editing, a type of cinema that Deleuze refers to as the movement-image, to which we shall revert.

With regard to the present argument, the irrational cut of the time-image coincides with the trans aesthetics that Steinbock promotes. However, the rational cut equally is emblematic of the 'operation theatre' that Steinbock describes, in that rational cuts in effect reinforce (the predictable, white and heteronormative) narrative. Indeed, that the cuts/editing of *The Navigator* are subjugated to/for a commercial logic (the starfish is cut from the film) suggests that Keaton forgoes in many respects the irrational, and instead prefers a rational approach to filmmaking.

This argument can and must be nuanced, in that part of Keaton's comedy is that his films at times supposedly surprise us, as he makes use of a lobster to cut some wires, for example. We shall consider Keaton's relationship with narrative in more detail later when we turn our attention to the unthinking whiteness of the film-philosophy of Gilles Deleuze, but for present purposes, I should like simply to assert that while such 'irrational' use of the lobster might indeed help us to 'rethink' this and all lobsters, there is all the same a tool-based logic at work here, based on the relatively obvious semblance between a lobster's claws and human clippers (we might compare this use of the lobster to Salvador Dalí's rather more surprising *Lobster Telephone*, from 1936, in which the link between the critter and the human technology seems far more oblique). This tool-based logic is in addition to the commercial logic that Keaton clearly follows when he excises the starfish. And so, for all of Keaton's genius as a filmmaker, this actually-quite-logical approach to objects, animals and indeed to film form that he adopts is itself conventional (Deleuze defines Keaton as a maker of 'action-image' cinema, of the sort that most clearly characterises Hollywood and the American ethos more generally), and, at least in the instance of *The Navigator*, it is heteronormative and white.

Nonetheless, just because Keaton in effect eschews the creative potential of cinema to rewire our brains (to make us think) in a non-white and/or non-capitalist/non-patriarchal (non-cinematic?) fashion, cinema always carries the potential to be irrational, not to be narrative and not to be white. This in some senses we have already gleaned from the identification of the 'black holes' that allow the white face to come into being. But here I would like to push the argument further and say that while cinema is perhaps built upon black holes, each cut is also a wormhole.

In accordance with the formula in physics that ER = EPR, Einstein-Rosen (ER) bridges that connect distant points in space-time (wormholes) are equivalent to quantum entangled particles, and which are referred to as Einstein-Podolsky-Rosen (EPR) pairs. The latter are also thought to involve 'spooky action at a distance', Albert Einstein's description of how information between entangled particles would have to travel faster than the speed of light in order for their actions to be simultaneous – which in principle would contravene Einstein's understanding that nothing can travel faster than the speed of light, even though such 'spooky action at a distance' has been proven mathematically to be true. Not only is there a simultaneously racial and hauntological logic at work in Einstein's thinking ('spook' as both ghost and racist slang for a black person), but more particularly, wormholes are theorised as being the heat that black holes slowly give off and which typically is called Hawking radiation, after Stephen Hawking. In effect, for physicists like Juan Maldacena and Leonard Susskind, every wormhole is a tentacle of Hawking radiation verting out of a black hole and re-entering space-time as we know it at a point completely different from where it entered the black hole (see Maldacena and Susskind 2013). In this way, wormholes via black holes potentially connect together each and every point in space-time.

To return to the perhaps less rarefied realm of cinema, if cuts in effect offer up 'bridges' between distant points in space-time, each cut in cinema constitutes a kind of wormhole, even if a cut in fact only takes us to an adjoining point in space-time. That is, from the perspective of quantum entanglement, here and now is entangled with four billion years ago on the far side of Alpha Centauri; but then, so is here and now entangled with here-plus-one-metre and now-plus-one-second. Cinema may well, according to an anthropocentric (and capitalist/patriarchal) logic dispense most of the time with showing us the former in order more regularly to show us the latter – thereby making for films that are much easier to comprehend and follow (but which do not challenge us to think very much). However, even if cinema cuts from here and now to here-and-a-bit and now-and-a-bit, the cut would still take us from the one to the other via a wormhole, which here I wish to relate to the entangled and tentacular logic of the asterisk * (which is indeed described as having a 'sticky tentacularity' by Eva Hayward and Jami Weinstein 2015: 196), such that there is a trans* potential in every wormhole/cut. And, of equal importance is that each wormhole functions via a black hole. That is, every cut involves/ is a trans*ition, but, as we shall see, the trans* aspect of cinema's wormholes is once again built upon a prior blackness.

If the potential is there for radical trans*itions in any cut, and thus in any film, it is only according to a capitalist/patriarchal, heteronormative and white logic that so many cuts in cinema are subjugated to the logic of narrative progression and the commercial imperative, which themselves emerge as deeply intertwined. In effect, cinema can vert across worlds and verses, such that it presents to us a multiverse (multi-worm-holes). But most of the time cinema somewhat unimaginatively, unpoetically and/or unthinkingly gives us a logic of a single world, or what we have characterised as the American logic of *e pluribus unum*, a unitary world that is built upon the destruction of other worlds, including that of the slaves trans*ported or trans*planted from Africa to America during the Middle Passage.

We have here a seeming contradiction. I am suggesting that cinema can trans*port or trans*plant us, and that to do so might involve realising the radical potential of cinema to demonstrate the entangled nature of our multiverse (a logic in which different vers-ions of *The Navigator*, for example, one including the starfish, share equal ontological status with the supposedly single version of the film that we have today). However, I am also suggesting that this unitary world, or this 'finished' version of the film, are built precisely upon trans*port and trans*plantation. So, if *The Navigator* is in effect built upon wormholes as much as a more radical film might be, then how does Keaton's film also 'deny' this logic? Put differently, Keaton might try to eradicate difference, as well as the potential for cinema to be other and tentacularly to connect completely different spaces and times (Keaton kills the octopus and cuts the starfish), but, even if he kills it, he also reveals difference in doing so. By this token, cinema is not white, but black *and* white (and many other colours). Or, in the language of Deleuze, every movement-image is a time-image (and perhaps vice versa), provided that we look at them correctly (see also Brown and Martin-Jones 2012).

However, while this in some senses may be the case – that cinema inescapably conveys both a black and a trans* logic, even when it is telling us heteropatriarchal stories via conventional narrative – the latter conventions all the same constitute not so much a version of Blackness as an *inversion* of Blackness, as we shall see presently.

In her consideration of the starfish, Hayward makes reference to *fingeryeyes*, a term that she adopts to demonstrate how becoming-starfish involves a move away from the would-be objective and controlling vision of the normative, white human (the logic of surveillance). And, in a subsequent essay, Hayward elaborates upon the term, describing coral and other species as 'inverts', or 'critters without backbones', who themselves mirror 'the sort [of people] who transpose gender roles' (Hayward 2010: 589). In the process, Hayward creates a link between invertebrates and trans people broadly defined (Hayward 2010: 589), such that the starfish and the octopus alike can now also be read as connoting trans*ness, even if *avant la lettre*.

Meanwhile, Sylvia Wynter, in a consideration of the work of Édouard Glissant, discusses how:

the construct of N[*****] as well as that of the non-European native now [following the rise of the new discourse of evolutionary biology, in the wake of Charles Darwin's Origin of Species in 1859] came to serve as the *inversion* of the divinely instituted realm of the supernatural and therefore as the extrasocial source, 'beyond the reach of the human desire and temptation,' since both N[*****] and native were now projected as being generically, if no longer divinely, predetermined to be a mode of Lack defining an ostensibly evolutionarily determined mode of 'normal' human being, Man. **(Wynter 1989: 642; emphasis added)**

I have added emphasis here to the word 'inversion' in order to highlight how Blackness is constructed in the white Western and modern imagination as the inversion of whiteness, a kind of inverted creature, perhaps with no backbone.

In her consideration of the concept of negativity in relation to Blackness in film and media, Racquel J. Gates furthermore points out that '[t]he concept of negativity derives first from the idea of a photonegative...in which a positive image is considered normal (or, in the case of the media, normative) and a negative image is *the complete inversion* of that image' (Gates 2018: 17, emphasis added). In other words, while Gates wrestles progressive potential from the negative, much as Weheliye, Jackson and Moten respectively find potential in the flesh, plasticity and the paraontic, the inversion that Hayward attributes to trans* culture is also always already there in black(ened) culture; and while men might invert women and vice versa, Wynter might also argue that no inversion is so powerfully incorporated into white Western thought as the inversion of black and white. More than this, the logic of inversion is a photographic (and by extension cinematographic) logic, as Jonathan Beller argues (see Beller 2018: 100).[2] While it is thus as a result of 'photographic' and 'cinematographic' thought that Blackness becomes (entrenched as) an inversion of whiteness (rather than, say, Blackness and whiteness as simply being continuous), it is also as a result of this logic that Blackness in particular takes on the qualities of *negativity*, as is implied in terms like *negro*, *negritude* and the n-word.

If Keaton's cinema entails cutting, then, it is a cutting that involves violence and excision, rather than, say, cutting(s) that can be replanted in order to grow anew. That is, the language of cinema involving cutting and shooting is not only a language of violence; it is also a horticultural and generative language that sees new life grow, or at the very least that allows life to continue (for a similar argument about 'budding cinema', see Eastwood 2015). To continue with this potential 'plant' logic of cinema, the Middle Passage may involve the trans*portation and, more particularly, the trans*plantation of Africans to the New World, where in spite of the perils of the plantation and slavery, black(ened) life comes into (some sort of) being. However, rather than going trans*versally through wormholes into multiverses, the dominant and dominating logic of white Western modernity simply *inverts* Blackness, casting it as negative (as *not* being) – and so in Keaton's cinema, cutting takes on this violent and antiblack function.[3]

Furthermore, if we have arrived at this 'wormhole' logic via trans* theory, especially Hayward's theory of the starfish, it is worth reminding ourselves that the trans* logic of becoming also only ever follows from the 'plasticisation' of Blackness. When Susan Stryker writes in her germinal trans essay 'My Words to Victor Frankenstein' that 'I suck for air – and find only more water. My lungs are full of water… This water annihilates me… I will learn to breathe water,' she is in some senses drawing unconsciously on the fleshy and marine logic of the Middle Passage that we established earlier (see Stryker 1994: 247). And if as theorists like Ferguson and others have suggested that Blackness was always already queer, in that Blackness was itself a 'perversion' and/or 'never *heteronormative*' (see Ferguson 2004: 87, original emphasis), then in some senses Blackness has also always possessed a trans* logic, or, at least, Blackness has like trans* always been based upon the cut, or being cut out of white, heteronormative reality. C. Riley Snorton argues, for example, how the black character of Phillip DeVine was cut from the otherwise landmark trans film *Boys Don't Cry* (Kimberly Peirce, USA, 1999), meaning that while the film can celebrate, or at least explore violence towards, white trans identities, it can only do so by itself doing violence to a black identity; as Snorton puts it, 'antitrans violence is also and always already an articulation of anti-blackness' (Snorton 2017: 185; for more on how trans feminism has been 'whitened', see, for example, Skidmore 2011; Krell 2017). L.H. Stallings, meanwhile, similarly explores how 'race, not gender…[might be] the definer of a particular sexuality', in that interracial sex would not historically have been remarkable or problematic to mainstream society were it not considered a 'perversion', as the case of *Loving v. Virginia* would help to signify (see Stallings 2015: 99-102). Blackness in this sense 'transcends' gender, since if for a white person to desire a black person is always a 'perversion' (illegalised interracial love, as per the Lovings), then regardless of whether it is in a nominally hetero- or homosexual fashion, Blackness in effect falls outside of gender, an argument also made by Marquis Bey (see Bey 2017).

For Jasbir K. Puar, the very fact that 'race' can sometimes denote colour (the black race, the white race), while at other times denoting speciation (the human race), would suggest that *'becoming trans...*[is] a capacitation of race, of racial ontologies, that informs the functioning of geo- and biopolitical control' (Puar 2015: 64). Indeed, when we think à la Wynter about how 'Man' is constructed as white through the othering of the black (or what Jackson might call the blackening of the other), then Blackness does indeed always already fall outside of the human (that Blackness is a race suggests that it is not part of the 'human' race), which in turn means that it has no gender, since gender is a facet of 'human' existence. As Bey summarises Puar's argument, an upshot of this is that 'value is extracted from (trans*) bodies of color in order to produce transgender whiteness,' in that if mainstream society now recognises white transgender people as human, then this is because Blackness is still not part of the human race (see Bey 2017: 287). Since Blackness falls outside of the human, Blackness also falls outside of the binarisms that structure human society (male/female, straight/gay), and as such Blackness possesses a trans* logic. More than this, though, is that Blackness is what allows binaristic 'human' thinking to exist as such, including that paradoxical thinking that is binaristically non-binaristic and which is mainstream (i.e. white) trans* life. As micha cárdenas says, if the appearance of Laverne Cox on the cover of *Time* magazine constitutes 'a historic moment indicating a widespread acceptance of transgender people, and the event was made possible by a black trans woman, a trans woman of color', then it is curious that 'in the following month four trans women of color were murdered' (cárdenas 2015). Not only does Cox's Blackness thus function as a 'plastic' tool for legitimating a certain kind of trans identity, but for cárdenas, the ongoing killing of trans women of colour points to the ongoing 'necropolitical' logic whereby Blackness is always already associated with death, and therefore can be killed 'with impunity' in an extension of the logic of the plantation and the colony (cárdenas 2015). While the starfish sequence in *The Navigator* would suggest the potential for trans*plantation, its excision, together with the death of the octopus and the killing of the native (as 'non-human'), would suggest that Keaton adheres not to a trans*, and certainly not to a black, logic, but rather to a plain old 'plantation' logic (*e pluribus unum* as the degradation of soil via monoculture).

Since this logic coincides with a photographic and cinematographic logic of 'inversion' and applied negativity – such that the issue is not so much that the non-white human is 'blackened', as per Jackson, but that the non-white is 'negativised' – then Keaton's film is not alone in possessing a racial/racist logic, since it is cinema as a whole that becomes an antiblack medium. In the spirit of Richard Dyer, cinema may be a technology that has a photo-graphic base, in that it 'writes with light', but this process is itself premised upon darkness, which is peddled to us as antithetical to, or an inversion of, light, but which in fact is generative of it. In this way, the light show that is cinema is inseparable from Blackness, even as it necessarily both uses and destroys Blackness in order to exist as such. And this turn to 'cinema as a (black) w/hole' that also is in a trans* fashion made up of wormholes, or what we might call 'cinema itself', allows us now to consider not just Keaton's film, but also what Keaton's film has meant within the history of cinema, or how film theorists and film-philosophers have understood his work, including *The Navigator* very specifically.

## Chapter 12

# The Black Irish?

In the previous chapter I suggested that Keaton subjugates the wormhole/multiversal/ black/trans* potential of cinema to the logic of narrative. However, scholars of Keaton's cinema have in many ways correctly identified that his films, as well as slapstick and comic cinema more broadly, have a shaky relationship with narrative. Lisa Trahair summarises both the historical and theoretical analyses in her own Deleuzian consideration of Keaton, which work will allow us in turn to consider the whiteness of Deleuze and the philosopher who was so influential on his thought, namely Henri Bergson. Before we reach that point, though, we shall presently turn to how Keaton draws upon Irish and Irish-American comic traditions, which themselves are entangled with African-American comic traditions. We shall do this in order to give a fuller account of Keaton's racial politics, as well as to work our way towards a critique of the whiteness of film criticism, film theory and/or film-philosophy more generally.

Trahair notes that as Keaton turned away from shorts and towards full-length feature films, he began to work with other directors (such as Donald Crisp), since these other directors helped Keaton to develop storylines. While we might surmise from this, as does Trahair, that Keaton was less interested in coherent narratives and that he was more interested in series of (often improvised) gags, he nonetheless 'subordinated' the comic to narrative, with that subordination being driven by the turn from making two-reelers to features, a turn that was driven by commercial imperatives as narrative cinema came to be the dominant (commercial) form of the medium (Trahair 2004), replete as it was with expected running times that in turn allowed for optimal numbers of film screenings per day based upon projected and actual numbers of bums on seats and how much those audience members expected to get/would stay to watch based on the price of their ticket (in effect, more money was to be made charging audiences a larger sum to watch a feature than a smaller sum to watch shorts). The shift to narrative was, according to Trahair, not straightforward for Keaton, with *Three Ages* (Buster Keaton and Eddie Cline, USA, 1923) being a film that switches between three different storylines (in a parody of D.W. Griffith's *Intolerance*, USA, 1916) in such a nonlinear fashion that a) Keaton was clearly not immediately adept at single, linear storylines that lasted six or more reels (or roughly an hour of screen time), and b) Keaton may well have been making cinema at this stage in his career that was more akin to the 'wormhole' aesthetic, and which concomitantly was 'less patriarchal' than I have here been arguing with regard to *The Navigator*.[1]

As Trahair reminds us, the relationship between comedy and narrative is not necessarily clear and has been the subject of much scholarly debate, with David Bordwell, as well as Steve Neale and Frank Krutnik, for example, arguing that 'in the relationship between narrative and the comic the abandonment of causal motivation is more or less a generic convention' (Trahair 2004; see also Bordwell 1982: 2; Neale and Krutnik 1990: 30), while Tom Gunning proposes that 'mechanical causality [is] the crux of the relationship between cinematic comedy and the operational aesthetic' (Trahair 2004; see also Gunning 1995). As an extension of his well-known work on the 'cinema of attraction' (Gunning 1986), the 'operational aesthetic' is for Gunning linked to the audience's attraction to the cinematograph itself, in that it involves characters (and the audience) being/becoming fascinated by how machines work, including the machine of cinema, with comedy being produced in particular from moments when machines do not work, or when they do not work as intended. If comic films, including Keaton's, are structured around machines and their operations, this diminishes the strictly narrative causality, or the agency, that the characters might have, thereby downplaying the importance of 'narrative' *per se* in Keaton's films.

We can find the '*operational* aesthetic' at work in *The Navigator*, not least through the structuring device of a ship that is set adrift. The functioning of the ship, and of the devices on board the ship, from gramophones to playing cards to mini-cannons to kitchen utensils (to which we shall revert), do indeed provide the structural 'bones' of the film as much as does the drive towards the would-be union of Rollo and Betsy. Furthermore, we can find 'queer' and 'trans*' components dotted throughout Keaton's work if we choose to look for it – from what Trahair (2007: 59) refers to as the 'Cinderfella' that Keaton plays in *My Wife's Relations* (Eddie Cline and 'Buster' Keaton, USA, 1922) through to the 'pansy outfits' that the younger Willie is forced by his overbearing father not to wear in *Steamboat Bill, Jr*. Indeed, at a stretch, we might even contend that when he is mistaken for a black man as a result of having a muddy face in *Neighbors*, Keaton even engages in a kind of racial consciousness that involves him being/becoming black. In other words, it may well be that I am extrapolating too much from a single example, *The Navigator*, about Keaton's credentials as a strictly white, and by extension, patriarchal filmmaker who in effect does capital's bidding.

With regard to *Neighbors*, however, Susan E. Linville suggests that while the way in which Keaton-in-blackface is mistaken for a criminal offers us a 'commentary on the police practice of racial profiling', the film nonetheless involves 'repugnant racist stereotyping' (Linville 2007: 277). Linville also points to how nineteenth-century minstrelsy 'navigated among masculinity, blackface and Irish ethnicity', with such blackface performances supposedly having as their primary target a mimicking and/or subversion of expectations of masculinity. This is thought to be born out of the frequent status as 'victims of ridicule and prejudice' of Irish immigrants (Linville 2007: 270), a group to which Keaton's family reputedly belonged, or at least was perceived to belong. In some senses, then, blackface carries both an *anti*-patriarchal heritage and an expression of kinship or identification between black people and the Irish. Indeed, quoting Michael Hechter, Cedric J. Robinson writes that:

English colonisation of Ireland claimed to involve reforming the Irish, but in fact involved slaughtering them, a 'formula… repeated in the treatment of the Indians in the New World… We also find the same indictments being brought against the Indians, and later the blacks, in the New World that had been brought against the Irish. It was argued that the Indians were an unsettled people who did not make proper use of their land and thus could be justly deprived of it by the more enterprising English. Both Indians and blacks, like the Irish, were accused of being idle, lazy, dirty, and licentious, but few serious efforts were made to draw any of them from their supposed state of degeneracy' **(Robinson 1983: 80; see also Hechter 1975: 72-73)**

Given that Keaton's father, Joe, claimed that the family was Irish, while his sister, Louise, 'steadfastly maintained that the family's roots were Native American', we might argue that Keaton embodies cross-racial/non-white kinship owing to shared historical persecution – even though biographer Marion Meade claims that the Keatons moved to the USA from England (see Linville 2007: 271).

If accepted, such an 'outsider' position for Keaton would also fit in with Noel Ignatiev's argument that the Irish only became 'white' within the American imaginary over time (see Ignatiev 1995), meaning that Keaton carries a legacy of non-whiteness, a non-whiteness that has also been understood as queer if we recall E. Patrick Johnson's contention that both African Americans and the Irish were linked by the term *quare*. That is, the Irish, like black Americans, possessed a (perverted) sexuality of their own, which in turn meant that they did not fit into normative gender binaries – at least in the popular perception (see Johnson 2005).

This shared 'quareness' of the Irish and African Americans (which is not to mention Native Americans, were we to take seriously the claims of Keaton's sister) has been further noted by both Mel Y. Chen and Kyla Wazana Tompkins, with the former arguing for the way in which queerness does not always apply simply to non-normative sexuality alone, but also to non-normative race and class (Chen 2012: 59). Tompkins, meanwhile, suggests that the term becomes an example of 'white sovereign entrepreneurial terror, a free-market production of white disinhibition that is experienced as white freedom but is deployed as a kind of terrorising vulgarity against non-white and especially black citizenship' (Tompkins 2017: 75). That is, queerness can be empowering for whites, but is used to oppress black people, a distinction that can be seen as fitting into Ignatiev's history of the Irish in America, who 'became white' over time, but in an accelerated fashion from the 1850s onwards, when many Irishmen joined the police – and thus could carry out state-authorised brutality towards other non-white groups, especially black folk (with the use of police uniforms to legitimise antiblack violence being still very much in practice today). Indeed, the role of Irish police officers enacting violence towards African Americans in order to acquire and/ or to stage their whiteness fits in with Tompkins' contention that 'the methodologies of queer-of-color critique…investigate the recurring historical and, indeed, theatrical production of a whiteness that, I argue, returns again and again to do violence to nonwhite peoples' (Tompkins 2017: 65).

In this way, as Todd McGowan summarises, 'Keaton uses blackface…to show how he is a lacking figure who requires the excess of blackface in order to fit in. But what the act of putting on blackface fails to see is that it inherently mocks those who are genuinely excluded' (McGowan 2016: 613). That is, Keaton's cinema may well have queer/quare and historically non-white elements (Keaton as Irish; Keaton as Native American; Keaton as blackened), and it may well have non-narrative elements that are befitting both his roots in 'Irish' performance practices and the fact that he is working with slapstick and comedy more broadly. Keaton's cinema in general, and *The Navigator* in particular, might thus have what José Esteban Muñoz might define as 'utopian' elements, in that Keaton seeks 'a blueprint for alternative modes of being in the world' (much like the Afrofuturist work of people like Sun Ra; see Muñoz 2009: 172).[2] However, as *The Navigator* also hopefully makes clear, Keaton ultimately stages whiteness, heteronormativity and patriarchal values, not least in his recursion to narrative.

# Chapter 13

# White Deleuze

While various scholars of course find much of value in Keaton's work, the aim here is to show that when read through the combined lenses of posthumanism (especially cephalopodic thought) and critical race theory (as drawn primarily from black and indigenous studies), *The Navigator* in fact demonstrates a clear white supremacist, antiblack and anti-indigenous logic. The aim is not necessarily to have Keaton thrown on to the scrapheap of film history, as various scholars seek to achieve with, say, D.W. Griffith (whom Keaton did, after all, parody, as mentioned). However, to demonstrate the 'whiteness', or, better, the antiblackness of Keaton's work can help to convey both the 'whiteness', and thus the antiblackness, of the medium, perhaps especially in its narrative iterations, while also helping us to pick out the whiteness, and by extension the antiblackness, of much film criticism and/or film-philosophy. Indeed, Gates not only points out that 'whiteness functions invisibly in media,' but that 'whiteness [also] occupies a similar default position in *scholarship* on the media' (Gates 2018: 27; original emphasis). And it is in bringing out this unthinking and/or invisible whiteness that we might navigate from the white Anthropocene and towards the Black Chthulucene (or the Maroon Autochthulucene), a journey that we can undertake not just through a consideration of Keaton's film, but also through theoretical and/or philosophical considerations thereof.

The recursion to narrative that I described at the end of the last chapter is matched by what Trahair, via Gilles Deleuze, identifies in Keaton's work as a recursion *of* narrative. As Trahair points out, where Deleuze uses the terms *fonctions récurrentes* and *séries récurrentes* in his original text, the English-language version of *Cinema 1: The Movement-Image* translates these as 'recurrent functions' and 'recurrent series' (see Deleuze 1997: 173-177). For Trahair, however, these translations miss the notion of *recursion* that also is implied in Deleuze's language, and which stems from mathematics (Trahair 2004). Simply put, recursion is a kind of tautological explanation that leads to... recursion (or as the joke goes: 'to understand recursion, you must understand recursion'). So, for example, when in *The Navigator* Rollo seeks to cook an egg in a huge pot that would otherwise serve hundreds of passengers aboard the ship, he creates 'an ingenious system' made up of 'pulleys, wires and levers' (Deleuze 1997: 176). As Deleuze explains, these pulleys, wires and levers form a series, and '[e]ach element of the series is such that it has no function, no relationship to the goal, but acquires one in relation to another element which itself has no function or relation' (Deleuze 1997: 177). That is, each pulley, wire and lever does not really help to boil the egg, but each pulley, wire and lever does help to trigger the next pulley, wire and/or lever, and so from this structure emerges what Deleuze calls 'large geometrical structures' and 'great trajectories' (Deleuze 1997: 177).

Much of Keaton's work, then, addresses issues of scale, whereby the tiny and the massive come into relation with each other, as per the image of Rollo/Keaton trying to tow the giant *Navigator* in a tiny rowing boat. Furthermore, while Deleuze uses the term geometrical, this also lends to Keaton's work a 'fractal' component, whereby patterns repeat across scales in a recursive fashion (with the tautological-causal aspects of recursion being embedded in a speculative etymology, in that to recur might not only mean to 'run backwards', as per the Latin *re*/again + *currere*/to run, but also to ask the question why (*cur*) over and over again: why does the lever turn? because the wire turns it. why does the wire turn it? because the pulley pulls it, and so on, *curiosity recurring*). And this fractal component also brings to mind the famous examples of chaos theory, such as the butterfly beating its wings in Argentina being quasi-causal of the cyclone in Mississippi: the butterfly beats its wings, which causes the leaf to shimmer, which causes a shift in shade that causes the worm to surface, which causes the sparrow to attempt to eat it, which causes the owl to hunt the sparrow, which causes the other birds to take flight, which produces a gust strong enough to force a cold front to come into contact with a warm front, which friction sets off a mini-storm, that in turn works its way up the coast of the Americas until a cyclone rips through the American South (this is my own example, but for more, see Gleick 1998). In some senses, then, we can see a kind of 'wormhole' logic at work in Keaton's cinema – in that all of space and time would seem to be interconnected. And perhaps it is for this reason that Deleuze defines Keaton's work as 'anarchistic-machinic', as opposed to Chaplin, who is for Deleuze a 'communist-humanist' (Deleuze 1997: 176). We shall be reverting to Keaton's connection with the weather imminently. However, for the time being, I wish to suggest that while Keaton's 'smallness' in his treatment of scale leads to what Deleuze calls 'minoration' in his work, in that a huge ship is now home to only two people (and thus is 'minored'), Keaton's films, especially *The Navigator*, betray a white supremacist logic that Deleuze fails to grasp.

For Deleuze, Keaton's cinema is, unlike Chaplin's, concerned with machines and not tools (Deleuze 1997: 175). That I take issue with this might be clear from the earlier discussion that Keaton uses the lobster and the swordfish as, precisely, tools, and not machines. Nonetheless, while animals and perhaps black others do function as tools in Keaton's world, the emphasis on machines is surely just. With reference to *The General*, Deleuze says that:

> the girl who feeds the train's boiler with little pieces of
> wood is behaving [not only] in a clumsy and inept way...but

she also brings to realisation Keaton's dream of taking the biggest machine in the world and making it work with the tiniest elements, thus converting it for the use of each one of us, making it the property of everyone. **(Deleuze 1997: 176)**

While this might sound like a fine democratic vision, we know that the same does not hold of the *Navigator*, which Keaton may wrest from the possession of a warring nation, but which all the same is not the property of the natives who otherwise board it. Deleuze compares Keaton's cinema to Dada, suggesting that 'Keaton makes machines his most precious ally because his character invents them and becomes part of them, machines "without a mother" like those of [Francis] Picabia' (Deleuze 1997: 175). That is, for Keaton, machines spontaneously emerge and/or, in some senses, 'birth' themselves (if they do not have a mother). Deleuze returns to this image of birth when he says that Keaton's 'two essential forms of the gag', which are the trajectory-gag (effectively chases comprised of many components, as in *Three Ages* where Keaton in the ancient Rome section 'escapes from a dungeon, seizes a shield, runs up a staircase, grabs a lance, jumps on to a horse' etc; see Deleuze 1997: 174) and the machine-gag, are 'two aspects of a same reality, a machine which produces man "without a mother," or the man of the future' (Deleuze 1997: 177). In other words, Keaton would for Deleuze in effect 'birth himself', finally bringing 'man' into being – the ultimate expression of self-realisation, even as Keaton's characters, including Rollo Treadway, grapple with a multiverse that is far larger than them. That is, in Keaton's cinema, do we not get an expression of the American mythos of *e pluribus unum*, or Manifest Destiny, and is it not precisely for this reason that Deleuze categorises Keaton's cinema as an example of the action-image/movement-image, the classical American cinema *par excellence*?

Read through the combined lenses of posthumanism and

critical race theory, though, do we not also get a sense that Keaton's 'motherless' birth involves the extermination of the other in a bid to create a world just for himself? Is the self-birthing that Keaton attempts to stage, then, not also a 'birth of a nation', meaning that *Three Ages* functions not just as a parody of Griffith, but also as the expression of a (white) affinity with him? Of course, Johnnie Gray, whom Keaton plays in *The General*, is fighting for the South. And even if Keaton focuses less on tools and more on machines, *The Navigator* would suggest that the (sacrificial) tools for the creation of the American machine ([narrative] cinema itself?) are the animal other and Blackness/Indigeneity, or more simply expressed as Blackness and Indigeneity in various different guises, while also conflated. Keaton's characters seek utopia; but it is a white utopia that excludes the other, even as Keaton's world is indeed threatened by the weather.

But this foray into Deleuze's work is not simply for the purposes of reaffirming Keaton's whiteness, but also to draw out the whiteness in the film-philosophy of the Frenchman. For while Keaton's cinema might indeed aim to 'birth' both the 'man of the future' and/or itself, it is also a birth that in *The Navigator* constitutes for Deleuze 'the finest metaphor in the history of cinema' (Deleuze 2005: 155) – even if Deleuze's enthusiasm needs some qualification. For, the moment from *The Navigator* that Deleuze praises is a moment that he slightly misremembers. Deleuze describes it as follows:

> the hero in the life-jacket, strangled, dying, drowning in his life-jacket, is going to be awkwardly saved by the girl. She takes him between her legs to make sure of a grip and finally manages to open the jacket by cutting it, whereupon a flood of water escapes from it. Never has an image rendered so well the violent metaphor of giving birth, by caesarean section and explosion of the amniotic sac. **(Deleuze 2005: 155-156)**

What actually happens in the film, though, is that as Betsy tries to pull Rollo up a collapsed gangplank on to the *Navigator*, after riding on him away from the natives on the shore, it is Rollo himself who cuts open the costume, water thereby gushing forth from it. They continue to climb as the film cuts to the chief of the natives sending his tribesmen in pursuit of the white couple, before we cut back to Betsy and Rollo reaching the main deck of the ship. Betsy awkwardly helps Rollo on to a stepladder, from which he then hangs upside down, as mentioned earlier. There are several cuts as water continues to pour from Rollo's diving suit and as Betsy reacts in astonishment, before sitting next to him on the deck at the foot of the stepladder. She begins to help him get out of the suit as we cut back to a long shot of the shore to see the natives readying their canoes to give chase, before we cut back to the *Navigator*, where Betsy now does indeed stand above Rollo on the stepladder, tugging at the suit, from which Rollo emerges, before he lugs it over to the left-hand side of the frame where he and Betsy sit. Cut to the natives arriving at the ship in their canoes...

In fairness to Deleuze, he was writing in a period before easy access to movies, and he wrote from a remarkably good memory given the number of films that he mentions in his *Cinema* books. What is more, while he is 'off' with regard to a couple of details – for example, it is Rollo who cuts his own suit open and not Betsy – he nonetheless offers a plausible reading of the moment. Rollo cuts his own amniotic sac, but it is with Betsy's help that he is indeed 'born'. And his birth, of course, corresponds to his killing of the octopus, his rescue of Betsy from the islanders, and the murder that he is about to commit with the cannon. In other words, the 'finest metaphor in the history of cinema' that Deleuze praises is also that of a 'birth' born out of racial violence and violence towards animals, as well as violence towards women if we consider the Caesarian also to be a technique/ technology that 'wrests control of childbearing from the hands of women/community and into [the] mechanized hands of the hospital/patriarchy; [it] also leads Black women to have higher mortality rates in birth' (Rogers 2021).

Notably, Deleuze discusses this moment in *Cinema 2* à propos of metaphors, and the possibility that cinema can create metaphors. For Deleuze, cinema can certainly create metaphors, sometimes across cuts and, in the instance of *The Navigator*, sometimes within a single shot (or so says Deleuze; the moment in question in fact functions across several cuts, albeit that they are either employed to reframe otherwise continuous action, or they are used to show to us the impending attack of the natives). For Deleuze, cinema's capacity for metaphor is linked to its ability to create concepts, and thus to provide an image of thought, something that he sees as being linked to the time-image, broadly defined. However, while the moment of 'birthing' has a metaphorical meaning alongside its literal depiction of Rollo getting out of the diving suit with Betsy's help, what are we to make of the octopus moment, or indeed the natives?

When Rollo uses the lobster as a pair of cutters, and when he uses the swordfish as a sword, *The Navigator* is both literal and metaphorical at the same time. Keaton/Rollo in effect stages a metaphor as if it were literal, in that a lobster is not literally (and therefore is only metaphorically) a pair of cutters, but here is used literally as a pair of cutters. A swordfish is not literally a sword, even though 'sword' is in the name that anglophone (and other) humans give to it; however, in *The Navigator*, it, too, is used literally as a sword. While the example of the swordfish potentially points to how all language is in some degree metaphorical, in that signifier does not match signified (a swordfish is not literally a sword-fish), both moments nonetheless involve clear conflations of the representational (lobster, swordfish) and the metaphorical (cutters, sword). In this way, these examples conform to Akira Mizuta Lippit's famous concept of the *animetaphor*, whereby:

> [o]ne might posit provisionally that the animal functions
> not only as an exemplary metaphor but, within the scope of
> rhetorical language, as an originary metaphor. One finds a
> fantastic transversality at work between the animal and the
> metaphor – the animal is already a metaphor, the metaphor
> an animal. Together they transport to language, breathe into
> language, the vitality of another life, another expression:
> animal and metaphor, a metaphor made flesh, a living
> metaphor that is by definition not a metaphor, antimetaphor
> – 'animetaphor.' The animetaphor may also be seen as the
> unconscious of language, of logos. **(Lippit 2000: 165)**

The lobster and the swordfish are both animal (i.e. not metaphor)
and metaphor, and the swordfish in particular brings out the
way in which animetaphors are indeed 'the unconscious of
language', in that language shapes our understanding of the
critter as much as we understand the critter 'for itself' (were it
called a nozzlefish instead of a swordfish, the joke would not
work so well). In this sense, as Lippit goes on to say, by way of
Jacques Derrida, '*Logos* is a *zoon*. An animal that is born, grows,
belongs to *phusis*' (Lippit 2000: 165); that is, language is itself
an animal that has a physical reality, not least in the sense that
it shapes our understanding of reality, and what, therefore, we
consider to be real (by this token, we 'live by' metaphors; see
Lakoff and Johnson 2003). Indeed, Keaton makes jokes out of
precisely this matter, thereby making us conscious of how the
animal is a metaphor that, for Lippit, helps humans to define
themselves as precisely human.

With regard to the octopus in *The Navigator*, it is in some
senses also an animetaphor, especially as it 'returns like a meal
that cannot be digested, a dream that cannot be forgotten, an
other that cannot be sublated' (Lippit 2000: 165; see also Barker

2018: 29). However, Keaton cannot make the joke out of the octopus that he does the other creatures, including the starfish; or, if he does make a gag, it is by killing the animal, which may thus also function as a metaphor of otherness, the outside of the human, and in this sense akin to Blackness. But, to follow Henri Bergson's famous definition of comedy as *du mécanique plaqué sur du vivant*, or the mechanical encrusted on the living, where language becomes the machine/the mechanical that is 'encrusted' on to the living for the lobster and the swordfish, the octopus defies the mechanical, not least because it is soft and 'plastic'. Perhaps it is Rollo/Keaton who encrusts himself on to the octopus and the natives; but in this sense, we come to understand that Keaton/Rollo is the mechanical, the machine... and that the octopus and the native alike are the only living things that we see – and which paradoxically must be killed for this very reason, in that they challenge the anthropocentric, read white, worldview that Keaton is at pains to create as he births himself as the man of the future. All contradictions to this solipsistic worldview must be removed. And so the octopus is in this sense the limit of metaphor; but so, crucially, are the black natives, as well as the newly-weds, who emerge not only as 'animals' in the Keaton mythos, but also as perhaps the structureless but structuring others upon whom not just whiteness but also animality, language, metaphor, cinema, 'life' and 'man' are founded. Indeed, Blackness is itself therefore a metaphor that we live by, in that it is a term used to classify untold numbers of humans, none of whom is literally black, and yet whose 'Blackness' has been a central conceit in the creation of a white Western modernity.

Various philosophers have taken Deleuze to task for not being engaged enough in politics, including Peter Hallward (2006), Gayatri Chakravorty Spivak (1994) and Slavoj Žižek (2004). With specific regard to film, scholars like Laura U. Marks (2000), David Martin-Jones (2011) and Matthew

Holtmeier (2019) have also tried both implicitly and explicitly to demonstrate the Eurocentrism of Deleuze's thought, and thus to try to expand his ideas into a more 'global' view of cinema. This is a task also undertaken by Patricia Pisters, who argues in a direct refutation of Hallward and Spivak that Deleuze's (film-)philosophy is indeed 'political', as can especially be seen when it is applied to the work of Palestinian filmmaker Elia Suleiman (see Pisters 2012: 243-270). What distinguishes the present consideration of Keaton from the work of these writers, though, is that it seeks not necessarily to demonstrate that Deleuze's philosophy is devoid of political engagement, or that it is limited by its 'Eurocentrism'. The aim is, indeed, not to rehabilitate Deleuze as a 'political' thinker of cinema or the world in general, a project undertaken with reference to Palestine by Kathryn Medien (2019). While Deleuze does in his *Cinema* books deal with a handful of filmmakers of colour, including Charles Burnett, Robert Gardner, Haile Gerima, Charles Lane and Ousmane Sembène, and while Deleuze does engage more generally with black thinkers like activist-prison-writer George Jackson (for more on Jackson's role in Deleuze's philosophy, see Koerner 2011), his film-philosophy nonetheless remains white – even as Martin-Jones has in more recent work (at least indirectly) critiqued the Frenchman's film-philosophy from the perspective of the Anthropocene, which he (correctly) identifies as the result primarily of European colonialism, but without engaging with how that colonialism was/is in particular raced, and thus without engaging in how antiblackness plays a key role in bringing about said Anthropocene (see Martin-Jones 2018).

While I shall in due course return to various of these scholars in order to discuss the ecological aspects of Keaton's cinema, the aim here is quite simply to demonstrate, or at least to indicate, the limiting *whiteness* of Deleuze's thought. As much can be seen in the central role that the European Holocaust plays in his thinking; as per the argument against Agamben above, to see the European Holocaust as the structuring event of modernity, or in Deleuze's case as the event that makes the movement-image unthinkable and which calls forth the time-image, is to overlook the prior holocausts that allowed modernity to come into being at all, based as that modernity is upon ongoing antiblackness and anti-Indigeneity.

In his consideration of black American cinema, Deleuze briefly and somewhat enigmatically quotes *Cahiers du Cinéma* critic Yann Lardeau in stating that 'the specificity of black cinema is now defined by a new form, "the struggle that must bear on the medium itself"' (Deleuze 2005: 220). That is, in the work of Burnett et al, Deleuze finds a sort of self-consciousness that is about expressing a 'minor' existence not just in terms of content, but also in terms of form.

Notably, Deleuze spends longer discussing white filmmakers who engage with issues of race than he does with black filmmakers. For example, Deleuze identifies how Jean Rouch, Pierre Perrault, Shirley Clarke and John Cassavetes 'become other' by working with subjects and/or actors of colour, in the process reflecting in differing ways Arthur Rimbaud's famous claim that 'I is another', with the poet going on to say that, 'I am of inferior race for all eternity…I am a beast, a negro…' (Deleuze 2005: 153). Furthermore, the 'negro' is used to demonstrate in this section Deleuze's notion of the 'powers of the false', whereby films/filmmakers do not present to us a truth, but rather expose how all claims to truth are indeed false (much like how the 'minor' filmmakers mentioned above demonstrate how the truth claims of cinema itself are often false, even as cinema itself might like language produce 'metaphors we live by', or help to shape what Kara Keeling calls our 'common sense'; see Keeling 2007; see also Beller 2006). From Rimbaud again, Deleuze defines the merchant, the magistrate, the general and the emperor as all forgers – in the sense that they all claim to present to us 'the truth'. But Deleuze via Rimbaud also calls all of these people 'negroes', thereby associating the truth claims of these powerful characters with Blackness.

Deleuze in particular focuses on Clarke's *Portrait of Jason* (USA, 1967), in which the title subject, a *raconteur par excellence*, would seem to take on/perform many different roles for the camera, with Deleuze remarking that it is 'as if the white camera had slid into the great black forger; the "I is another" of Shirley Clarke consists in this: that the film that she wanted to make about herself became the one she made about Jason' (Deleuze 2005: 154). For Deleuze, a film like *Portrait of Jason* 'productively' uses Blackness (as well as queerness) as a 'power of the false', in which what is true and what is not true become confused, thereby pushing the film's viewer towards thought. If in thinking we ourselves change, then a film like *Portrait of Jason* presents to us an image of time, since it does not reaffirm to us what we already know, thereby keeping everything the same, but instead it makes us wonder that we do not know, that there may not be such a thing as knowledge, knowing or truth, and that it is the false, then, that brings about this moment/this experience of change and thus of time.

For all that we might presently find much productive argumentation in the *Cinema* books, though, it seems clear that Deleuze assumes both a white filmmaker ('the white camera') and a white viewer. Meanwhile, to use Rimbaud to produce the 'negro' as a forger, who in one paragraph is conflated with the charlatanism of the merchant, the magistrate, the general and the emperor, and who in the next paragraph is also the unreliable, but hardly empowered, subject of Clarke's film, only muddies Deleuze's waters. And the confusion that a close reading of Deleuze produces in terms of race is not here in and of itself a 'productive' 'power of the false'; it is, rather, an abstraction, or in Zakiyyah Iman Jackson's language, a plasticisation of the black in order ostensibly to create a 'future' for the white subject, in that the white can now benefit from said 'negro' by finding their 'falseness' philosophically illuminating.

Perhaps it comes as no surprise, then, that Keeling describes Deleuze as 'notorious for having little or nothing innovative to say about race' (Keeling 2007: 5), even as Keeling draws upon Deleuze and Henri Bergson in her own analyses of cinema. Keeling pays special attention to the notion of affect/affection as it works through these two thinkers, with Deleuze adapting in his first *Cinema* book Bergson's notion of affection as elaborated in *Matter and Memory* (2004). Affection is in effect what happens in between seeing something and responding to it through an action, with the cinema of the movement-image charting this progression in sequences composed of what Deleuze calls perception-images, affection-images and action-images. As Deleuze says of the middle of these three, '*[t]he affection-image is the close-up, and the close-up is the face...*' (Deleuze 1997: 87; original emphasis). And if, as we have already seen, *The Navigator* focuses at times quite specifically on what, with reference to another of his films, we might call Keaton's *Paleface* (Buster Keaton and Eddie Cline, USA, 1922), then we can see how the affection-image is itself important for the construction of whiteness, in particular the white face.[1] Indeed, Deleuze proceeds in his analysis of the affection-image to explain how the face belongs to the individual, but that at times filmmakers (Deleuze's examples are Griffith and Sergei M. Eisenstein) show various faces in order to give a single identity to a group, and/ or to show how an individual reflects the feelings, or affects, of a collective, or what Deleuze refers to as the dividual (Deleuze 1997: 92; see also Deamer 2016: 82-84). Given that the 'collective' in *The Navigator* is the black natives, who function as antagonists to Rollo's hero (who function as a means for Rollo to become a hero), then it seems clear that, as per our analysis earlier of black holes, Blackness here functions as a means of highlighting the whiteness of the affection-image, of the face and of the close-up, in a fashion akin to Richard Dyer's excoriating analysis of the history of cinema as one created technologically by and for white/pale skin (see Dyer 1997: 122-140).[2] More than this, when we consider that Deleuze proceeds to argue how the affection-image is born out of the 'any-space-whatever', or what David Deamer describes as 'pure backgrounds' (see Deamer 2016: 84), then we can see how Blackness in *The Navigator* functions as 'pure background', and that Blackness loses all specificity, in the sense that it becomes 'whatever'. If Rollo's self-birthing is indeed the 'finest metaphor in the history of cinema', then once again we can see that it comes at the expense of an undifferentiated and black background that itself has no 'face' since it exists neither for itself, nor for Rollo/Keaton to represent it, but for it to justify Rollo/Keaton's face, or faciality.

In his rejection of the afore-mentioned politics of recognition, Glen Sean Coulthard draws upon Frantz Fanon to discuss how the master, at least in the context of (settler) colonialism, does not really recognise the slave, contrary to G.W.F. Hegel's contention that mutual recognition is at the root of the master-slave relationship. Indeed, 'the "master" – that is, the colonial state and state society – does not require recognition from the previously self-determining communities upon which its territorial, economic and social infrastructure is constituted. What it needs is land, labor, and resources' (Coulthard 2014: 40). Indeed, the very fungibility of the slave demonstrates their lack of recognition, their lack of a face – and it is, we might suggest, precisely in this refusal to acknowledge the faciality of the non-white other that the white 'master' claims faciality for themselves. It is also for this reason that Jodi A. Byrd argues, after Judith Butler, that the native is not grievable, since it does not have a face; in order for one to grieve the other, it must be 'faceable' (Byrd 2011: 37). With no face, the other can simply be destroyed, since they effectively do not exist.

To return to Deleuze, the affection-image becomes important

not just in movement-image cinema, but also in the cinema of the time-image, since in the latter actions break down and while characters perceive and are affected by what they see, they do not continue into carrying out heroic deeds, instead being stuck in moments of nothing other than affection. As per Deleuze's treatment of the negro in relation both to minor cinema and to the powers of the false above, though, we might surmise that not only is the affection-image based upon a background Blackness – a sort of any-human-whatever, or a plastic human – but that the time-image as a whole is in some senses not just white, but also antiblack, involving the construction of whiteness based upon the exploitation and the destruction of Blackness.

Perhaps the 'unthinking antiblackness' of Deleuze can be found via a final example, namely his consideration of ships, which comes during his discussion of 'crystals of time' in *Cinema* 2. Crystals of time are time-images in the sense that they simultaneously show to us, create a circuit between, or even confuse, both the actual and the virtual, as, for example, when a character in a film is bent on committing a crime: outwardly, we may not be able to know their intentions (the actual), but inwardly they are potentially plotting murder (the virtual) – a situation not wholly dissimilar to the 'powers of the false' example whereby we cannot tell if what we are seeing is true or not. Kon Ichikawa's *Yukinojô henge/An Actor's Revenge* (Japan, 1963) serves as one of Deleuze's examples, with the latter remarking explicitly on the film's 'marvellous black backgrounds' (Deleuze 2005: 72). Deleuze then contends that the ship constitutes a crystal image that combines the actual and the virtual, in effect because there is the section of the ship above water that we can see (the actual) and the part of the ship that is below water, and which we cannot see (the virtual). 'It too is a track, a circuit,' says Deleuze. He continues:

[i]t is as if, as in [J.M.W.] Turner's paintings, splitting in two

is not an accident, but a power which is part of the ship. It is Herman Melville who, in his novels, fixed this structure for all time. Seed impregnating the sea, the ship is caught between its two crystalline faces: a limpid face which is the ship from above, where everything should be visible, according to order; an opaque face which is the ship from below, and which occurs underwater, the black face of the engine-room stokers. But it is as if the limpid face actualises a kind of theatre or dramaturgy which takes hold of the passengers themselves, whilst the virtual passes into the opaque face, and is actualised in turn in the settling of scores between engineers, in the demonic perversity of a boatswain, in a captain's obsession, in the secret revenge of insurgent blacks. **(Deleuze 2005: 72-73)**

It is unclear to which Turner paintings Deleuze is referring, although the former is of course famous for his *Slavers Throwing overboard the Dead and Dying – Typhoon coming on* (1840), which is commonly referred to as *The Slave Ship*. In that painting, the ship struggles against the waves in the background while in the foreground we see a black leg and some black hands emerging from beneath the surface of the water, as well as the chains that bind them, as in particular a group of fish seem to set about eating the slave whose leg juts above the surface. In this painting, then, it is the ship itself that is 'actual', while the dead and dying slaves are 'virtual'. More than simply haunting the image, though, Turner carefully stages the ship in the background, with the slaves being buried among the waves in the foreground. This 'reversal' means that the 'actual' ship does indeed become 'virtual', while the 'virtual' slaves become actual – thereby rendering the work 'a powerful protest against the direction and moral tone of English politics' (Gilroy 1996: 14).

However, while the image might thus offer to us a crystalline image that invites us to question the moral values of England in 1840, it does not constitute the 'revenge of insurgent blacks', or even an insight into the working conditions of 'black face… engine-room stokers'. In other words, while Deleuze makes a nod to the slave mutiny that Melville depicted in *Benito Cereno*, Turner rather demonstrates the murder of slaves by casting them overboard. Furthermore, since the mutiny in Melville's novella is ultimately unsuccessful, with the slave leader Babo being sentenced to death upon reaching Lima, then we might suggest that while the revolt does upend the hierarchy of white and black, the novella ultimately sees hierarchy reaffirmed, as suggested above (see Chapter 6, Note 3), regardless of Melville's supposedly uncertain and contested views on the matter. All the same, Deleuze casts the black figures into the virtual realm, thereby denying in some senses the lived experience of slavery and in particular of the Middle Passage, while also demonstrating how the 'black' virtual realm is, like 'plastic', a world of possibilities, for sure, but which possibilities rarely come true, as slaves are drowned and mutinies suppressed.[3]

Furthermore, when read on to *The Navigator*, Deleuze's analysis of the ship might be useful in terms of helping us to think of marine life as 'virtual', since we see it under the surface, while the logic of 'everything being visible' above the surface of the water does chime with the surveillance logic that we have already identified in the film. Nonetheless, as an abandoned space, with only two passengers who ultimately are united (notably underwater), with Rollo proving his masculinity against the 'insurgent blacks' from the island, it would seem that becoming white and/or becoming heteronormative are the order of the day, with the 'virtual blacks' functioning as a means to allow this hegemonic vision to come to fruition, rather than in any way challenging it. The finest metaphor in the history of cinema, then, comes in a film that uses first the octopus and then the black other in order to construct whiteness. If Deleuze has already been charged with Eurocentrism, then he might also be charged with unthinking whiteness, which is in effect to charge Deleuze with antiblackness, a charge that might in turn be levelled at the scores of film-philosophical texts on which Deleuze has been and continues to be so deeply influential.

# Chapter 14

# White Bergson

While in *The Navigator* we do not see any engine stokers, or Keaton, in black face, we have already seen that such make-up techniques were not beyond the comedian. We also noted, at least in passing, the influence on Deleuze of Henri Bergson, with whose thoughts on cinema we shall not be engaging in the present discussion, but whose theory of comedy, as devised in *Laughter: An Essay on the Meaning of the Comic* (Bergson 2005), is often deployed in scholarly considerations of the work of Buster Keaton, and which therefore applies, of course, to *The Navigator*. In particular we should like to focus not only on Bergson's famous dictum that comedy is derived from *du mécanique plaqué sur du vivant*, or the mechanical encrusted on to the living, but also on Bergson's own brief but salient comments on Blackness.

For, in *Laughter*, Bergson discusses disguise as playing a key role in humour, functioning, if you will, as the *mécanique* that gets encrusted on to the *vivant*. And from the disguise as a source of amusement, Bergson continues to the blemish. As follows:

[w]hy do we laugh at a head of hair which has changed from dark to blond? What is there comic about a rubicund nose? And why does one laugh at a negro? The question would appear to be an embarrassing one, for it has been asked by successive psychologists such as [Ewald] Hecker, [Emil] Kraepelin and [Theodor] Lipps, and all have given different replies. And yet I rather fancy the correct answer was suggested to me one day in the street by an ordinary cabby, who applied the expression 'unwashed' to the negro fare he was driving. Unwashed! Does not this mean that a black face, in our imagination, is one daubed over with

ink or soot? If so, then a red nose can only be one which has received a coating of vermilion. And so we see that the notion of disguise has passed on something of its comic quality to instances in which there is actually no disguise, though there might be...although the black or red colour is indeed inherent in the skin, we look upon it as artificially laid on, because it surprises us. **(Bergson 2005: 20)**

Aside from making some class-based jibes at Bergson for receiving philosophical instruction from the opinionated and stereotypically racist cabby, there is much to pick apart here, including that Bergson clearly imagines his reader to be white, as implied by his use of the first-person plural (our/us), and the fact that he finds *funny* the accusation by the cabby of the 'negro fare' being 'unwashed'. For Bergson has not only internalised an association between Blackness and dirt, but also a sense that the expression of this association is comic. When Bergson later writes that the comic is 'dependent on the manners or ideas, or, to put it bluntly, on the prejudices, of a society' (Bergson 2005: 68), he inadvertently exposes the racist nature of (his) French society in 1900, when the book was first published.

Bergson continues by arguing that we cannot have any emotional affinity with the object of laughter; '[d]epict some fault, however trifling, in such a way as to arouse sympathy, fear, or pity; the mischief is done, it is impossible for us to laugh' (Bergson 2005: 68). If, however, our emotions are not affected, then we can laugh – with Bergson saying that 'as a general rule...it is the faults of others that make us laugh' (Bergson 2005: 68). It is not the aim here to say that Bergson is basically describing what many today might call bullying; nor is it strictly to say that Bergson is wrong, in that, at the very least, many people do still today laugh at the faults of others, at least from time to time (there are still bullies, with perhaps most people capable of and indeed engaging in bullying at different points in their lives). However, it is to say that for Bergson to laugh at the negro means that by Bergson's own reckoning he has no emotional connection with the negro, and that the negro necessarily does not affect him (thereby exposing perhaps the whiteness of affection as a mechanism), while he also considers the negro to be 'faulty', or 'unwashed', for no other reason than for being a negro.

We shall return to how the negro is funny for Bergson because their dirtiness is in fact 'artificial'. But for the time being it is worth charting how this definition of humour maps almost directly on to Frantz Fanon's definition of racism as elaborated in *Black Skin, White Masks*. For the cabby's 'unwashed' comment is something of an inversion of Fanon's famous anecdote about being hailed by a child:

> 'Look, a Negro!' It was an external stimulus that flicked over me as I passed by. I made a tight smile.
> 'Look, a Negro!' It was true. It amused me.
> 'Look, a Negro!' The circle was drawing a bit tighter. I made no secret of my amusement.
> 'Mama, see the Negro! I'm frightened!' Frightened! Frightened! Now they were beginning to be afraid of me. I made up my mind to laugh myself to tears, but laughter had become impossible.
> I could no longer laugh, because I already knew that there were legends, stories, history, and above all *historicity*. **(Fanon 2008: 84; original emphasis)**

To contend that the passage affirms Bergson in its claim that fear makes laughter impossible would be a misreading. For, by the time Fanon comes to realise that the child can only see him as a purveyor of a history of 'tom-toms, cannibalism, intellectual deficiency, fetichism, racial defects, slave ships and…"Sho' good eatin,'" as cited earlier, we come ourselves to realise that the child's fear and Bergson's laughter are in effect two sides of the same coin, or the positive and negative versions of the photographic image: both insist upon the inferiority of the black man, who is 'by nature' at fault (for having no face, which makes of him a source of both fear and laughter). Indeed, the association between Blackness and dirt recurs several times in *Black Skin, White Masks*, including in both chapters on interracial relationships (Fanon 2008: 35; 56), and at the outset of the fifth chapter, 'The Fact of Blackness', where Fanon calls back to the above episode by opening it with the words: '"Dirty n[*****]!" Or simply, "Look, a Negro!"

The evocation of dirt may well evoke Mary Douglas' well-known understanding that in the Western imagination dirt is 'matter out of place' (see Douglas 2001), meaning by extension that the black person is also always 'out of place' and thus by turns both a source of humour (Bergson) and fear (Fanon).[1] But, as Bergson has mentioned, the supposed source of humour is not that the negro's face *is* dirty, but that to the white observer it looks dirty when it is not. Or, with our analysis of the affection-image from the last chapter in mind, the black person to the white does not seem to/does not have a face. In some senses, the humour that the negro supposedly sparks does not follow the earlier examples in Bergson's text. For, if Bergson in effect finds funny the ruddy nose or hairs that have changed colour, then these are genuine 'blemishes' (the term is mine), rather than the Blackness of the negro, which is not a blemish at all but, as Bergson acknowledges, 'inherent in the skin'.

I imagine that a close analysis of the genetic expression of skin tones would be able to disprove Bergson's claims to 'inherence', and, by extension, inheritance, in that there is a history of white-passing black folk whose 'Blackness' thus would be as much imposed as inherent; that is, they, like all black people, are *not* inherently 'black', but, as per Zakiyyah Iman Jackson's argument, *blackened*. All the same, if we take

Bergson at his word, then he in fact contradicts his own reasoning, and exposes his own antiblack logic, in suggesting that Blackness is in effect a blemish, or a fault. More in keeping with Bergson's own logic would be the use of blackface by whites, especially if their faces were blackened by accident/not by design, as happens with Keaton's character in *Neighbors*. It is not that Bergson would not or does not find blackface funny; but more telling is the idea that Keaton certainly finds blackface funny, or hopes that his viewers do, and that this humour also depends on the perception that Blackness is a fault or blemish, as subsequently is revealed to be the case when Keaton gets hauled in by the cops *for being black*. Not only is it 'correct', then, for whites to find blackface and black faces funny, but this system of comedy in fact reaffirms white supremacy, or is white supremacist in design. Indeed, by this token, we might reason that 'comedy' is a tool for constructing and maintaining whiteness, and from such a perspective, blackface *is* funny. In this way, the whiteness of Keaton's humour is arguably revealed by Steve McQueen, who with his short experimental film, *Deadpan* (UK, 1997), stages one of Keaton's most famous gags from *Steamboat Bill, Jr.* – involving a house collapsing on to a man (Keaton in the original; McQueen in the 'remake') who miraculously survives by standing exactly where the empty space of a doorway creates a gap in the falling façade. Where in Keaton the sequence is funny, in McQueen, the moment seems deadly serious, or at least is, as the title suggests, *deadpan*.

We shall revert to *Deadpan* later, but for the time being we might evoke once again Fanon, who in his chapter on 'The Man of Color and the White Woman' in *Black Skin, White Masks* works through René Maran's novel *Un homme pareil aux autres* (1947) arguing that the black man desires the white woman so as to become white, a desire that we might add is reinforced by, if not inculcated in, the cinema, but which desire is punished if acted upon, as we see in *The Navigator* when the natives, like Gus, played by Walter Long in blackface in *Birth of a Nation* (D.W. Griffith, USA, 1915), are condemned for their desire of/for the white woman. That the natives in *The Navigator* are 'primitive' and, indeed, pre-cinematic (in that these characters would not have seen movies in the fictional world of the film) functions as a trope to disavow how the desire for whiteness is constructed in and through the cinema, since instead it is proposed as 'natural' (even without the influence of modernity and film, these black natives still prize the white woman above all other things).

However, for Fanon, it is important to realise that '[i]n no way should my color be regarded as a flaw' (Fanon 2008: 59), or *an act*, as David Marriott implies when he argues that the 'guilty freedom' that the black man feels in fucking the blonde white woman 'is more than matched by what she symbolizes: a just future to come where being black is no longer acting, where being black is an expenditure without loss' (Marriott 2007: 63). Marriott points out how the chapter in *Black Skin, White Masks* in some senses charts Fanon's own feelings about his relationship with his white wife, Josie, and that the composition of *Black Skin, White Masks*, which Fanon dictated to her, is itself 'part of that struggle for recognition, that wish to be loved, driving the black man' (Marriott 2007: 64). Indeed, Fanon would himself show the internalisation, and thus in some respects an acceptance of, 'white' logic when late in *Black Skin, White Masks* he writes that 'when one is dirty one is black – whether one is thinking of physical dirtiness or of moral dirtiness' (Fanon 2008: 146). That is, an inversion has taken place, whereby Blackness is no longer dirty, but dirtiness is rather black. For Fanon to measure dirtiness as black would, if dirt is indeed a 'flaw', mean that dirt-as-flaw is 'black', and that Blackness thus is in some senses inescapably a 'flaw'. By this upsetting token, there is seemingly no escape from the acting that Marriott evokes in relation to Blackness, or, in the language of Fanon, masks. With the affection-image again in mind, Fanon has internalised the white notion that he does not have a face, even as his 'white mask' belies the fact that whites only come to have faces because they obliterate the face of the non-white other. That is, all faces are masks (*personae*).

Now, if for Fanon the black person finds themself wearing a white mask in order to try to fit into white society, be that by choice or by imposition, then there are several levels of irony to pick apart. For, if the negro that the cabby and/or the child sees is in fact wearing a 'white mask' to try to 'cover over' or hide their Blackness, then potentially what the former finds funny and the latter frightening is not Blackness, but a mask of whiteness (like a ghost?). In such a scenario, what the Bergsonian thinker sees is a black man wearing a white mask, which they correctly identify as a disguise; what the disguise hides, though, is twofold: firstly, another mask, that of Blackness, which the white has imposed upon the black, but which the white believes to be 'inherent'; and secondly, that the white's own face is also a mask. That is, the non-white human is *blackened* through the imposition of this black mask, meaning that both the joke and the fear are not just projections on to the black figure of their own facelessness, but are in fact constituted by the white (and internalised by the black person, sometimes even as they actively refute as much, as Fanon seems to demonstrate), rather than anything at all to do with the black person's 'inherent' qualities. In this sense, race becomes, along with faces/faciality, what Wendy Hui Kyong Chun and Beth Coleman, among others, identify as a *technology*, in that race (as well as faciality) is not only a 'tool of subjugation' (Chun 2009: 10), but also a means for organising the entirety of white, Western modernity (see also Coleman 2009).

If we can understand a technology to be a machine, then in some senses Blackness is precisely *du mécanique plaqué sur du vivant* (and the imposition/creation of Blackness is in some senses risible, but at the expense of the fearful/laughing white, and not at the expense of the black person, as Bergson suspects, unless the black person is indeed complicit in their own subjugation, or mechanisation). Similarly, blackface is also *du mécanique plaqué sur du vivant*, with the upshot being that it is not whiteness or Blackness that is *vivant*, but that race – all races, as well as all faces – are *du mécanique*, or technologies; to be given a race is to have to act, as Marriott says, or as Fanon says, quoting Claude Nordey, it involves trying to 'elevate himself to the white man's level...[t]o elevate himself in the range of colors to which he attributes a kind of hierarchy' (Fanon 2008: 60). The issue is, however, that whiteness is rendered invisible (*du vivant*), such that its own *mécanique*-ness is not recognised (whiteness is assumed to have a face, something living/natural, rather than to be a persona, or mask; in fact, Bersgon's dictum is a lie, in that there is no *vivant*, but *mécanique* all the way down), and the 'hierarchy' of races (and faces) is thus accepted as natural. As Fanon says, 'another solution [beyond accepting this hierarchy of races/faces] is possible,' but '[i]t implies a restructuring of the world' (Fanon 2008: 60), as well as an overhaul of the centrality of the face in so-called humanistic thought. And if Keaton, with his Bergsonian construction of whiteness via humour, is emblematic of cinema, then maybe cinema must also be restructured if one is to get out of the racial hierarchies that are an endemic part of white, Western, capitalist modernity.

Or, put differently, while a sharp analysis can reveal race as a technology that gets encrusted upon an otherwise soft, mollusc-like entity (an octopus, which is eyes without a face?), the Keaton mythos relies upon Bergson as Bergson intended, and not as he has been deconstructed here (an argument recently put forward, but problematically without reference to race, by Paul Flaig [2021], who does not see Bergson's humour as in any way cruel). That is, in *Neighbors* and in *The Navigator* alike, as well as in *The Paleface*, Blackness (and 'Redness') are indeed machines that are placed over whiteness – in order to construct whiteness as such (in order to construct whiteness and faciality as 'alive'/*vivant*). In *The Navigator*, the black natives are thus used for Rollo to become the hero, as mentioned. However, we might in the next section push further with our deconstruction in order to examine how it is perhaps cinema itself that helps to constitute the racial and facial hierarchies that Fanon identifies and otherwise seeks to reject, even if he still goes to the cinema in search of himself as the groom, perhaps even as Rollo Treadway.

# Chapter 15

# The Keaton economy

Scholars of Keaton regularly mention Bergson in their analyses of the filmmaker. To give the first of three examples, Noël Carroll attests that Keaton and Bergson share a sense that 'the most undesirable behaviour is that which is rote, habituated, or routinised, that is, *mechanical* in the most negative sense' (Carroll 2009: 45; original emphasis). Focusing primarily on *The General*, Carroll suggests that adaptability, as the 'major feature of intelligence' (Carroll 2009: 46), is what allows Keaton's characters to overcome their difficulties, a notion that Bergson shares, and which for both is derived from their awareness and understanding of evolutionary theory.

Lisa Trahair, meanwhile, argues that 'the mechanical imitation of organic narrative that we see in Keaton's work can doubtless be understood in terms of Bergson's conceptualization of the comic as *la mécanisation de la vie*, but I argue...that the comic lays bare the mechanics of narrative ordering' (Trahair 2007: 85). That is, Trahair acknowledges the applicability of Bergson's theories to Keaton, but she also believes that the seeming lack of narrative structure in Keaton's films means that he consciously and conscientiously evades/avoids 'mechanical' narrative filmmaking, instead revelling in what, after Georges Bataille, Trahair terms the 'general economy'. As opposed to the 'restricted economy', which is the world of control, discourse, structure and sense, the general economy is the world beyond these things – unstructured, uncontrollable, perhaps in some sense linked to Bataille's notion of the *informe*, or that which has no form (see Bataille 1986: 31). For Trahair, 'what constitutes the comic is the disruption of discourse', the restricted economy, or what Trahair also equates to cinematic narrative; 'to put it another way, the subjection of meaning to a certain nonmeaning. In this sense, the comic is essentially transgressive...The comic is not nonsense as such, but the relation of meaning to nonsense' (Trahair 2007: 32-33).

It is noteworthy that Trahair does not disagree with Carroll so much as believe that 'his analysis...contains the comic by inscribing it within...his functional instrumental interpretation of the Keaton character's behavior' (Trahair 2007: 88). For Trahair, the comic is not, or should not be, 'contained', and, as an expression of the general rather than the restricted economy, it should take on what she refers to as 'sovereignty'. Where for Carroll, adaptability is simply a sign of intelligence, which means that Keaton's characters are 'stupid' when they are inflexible and 'smart' when they themselves are adaptable, for Trahair Keaton's characters are both at once, with the body of the actor sometimes eluding the control of the character (and the body of the character eluding the control of the actor), thereby reaffirming their sovereignty – even in the face of their own 'restricted economy', or attempts to regulate and control themselves. Linking this to a tradition of 'comic doubling', whereby we as viewers simultaneously see the comic performer and the character that they play (or, as I have phrased it regularly throughout this analysis, Rollo/Keaton), Trahair goes on to discuss that objects in Keaton's comedies also convey the general economy. She writes:

[i]nstead of considering the way that the Keaton character manipulates objects to his own ends, putting them to work by a kind of mastery, Keaton's actions toward objects, comprehended as specific articulations of comic performance...must be seen as an effect of those objects' own transformational capability, their metamorphosability. This interpretation of Keaton's character's behavior and his relation to objects displaces the conventional emphasis on

the psychological development of Keaton's character (as subject) from idiot to expert – which has to date been the predominant interpretation [including by Carroll] – toward the pure sovereignty of the objects he encounters. The nature of these encounters with objects in turn reflects his own sovereignty. **(Trahair 2007: 92)**

Trahair is writing in particular relation to *Sherlock Jr.*, and perhaps it goes without saying that the intended 'progressive' meaning of her words shifts when we consider them in relation to *The Navigator*, a shift that we nonetheless shall chart below.

However, first let us call upon Todd McGowan, who in his work on silent comedy says that, '[t]he train or the ship or whatever type of technological device in a Keaton film is never simply a machine under human control. It is always a machine that seems to have a subjectivity of its own. The machine is funny because, like the subject, it constantly exceeds itself' (McGowan 2016: 614). This analysis recalls the 'operational aesthetic' identified above by Gunning and Trahair, and whereby Keaton's cinema is defined by an interest in machines, including machines when they go wrong, or, for McGowan, when they assert their own 'subjectivity' and/or 'exceed themselves'.

The arguments of both McGowan and Trahair are useful, because they would suggest that at least some of the comedy in Keaton's work is derived not from *du mécanique* being *plaqué sur du vivant*, but in fact from the opposite: comedy emerges when the *mécanique* demonstrates that it itself is *vivant*, or in Trahair's Bataillean language, *sovereign*. That said, working back through Trahair's argument, it seems clear that while in *The Navigator* Rollo adapts, or metamorphoses, the lobster and the swordfish, that it is Keaton doing/imposing the metamorphosis would suggest that these 'objects' in fact lack sovereignty, except for that which Rollo/Keaton attributes to them. In this sense, sovereignty is not only a white construct, but it can only ever exist for whiteness, as per the argument made in Chapter 9.

What is more, if Rollo kills the octopus, which in its invertebrate formlessness and its ability to change colour is specifically (and paradoxically) the one 'object' that can and does metamorphose and thus exhibit sovereignty, then it would seem that Rollo/Keaton does not so much tap into the general economy as actively participate in restricting it himself. Similarly, if the newly-weds have had the sovereignty (read: gumption) to get married, and if the black natives have likewise had the sovereignty (read: temerity) to kidnap Betsy and to storm the *Navigator*, then Rollo/Keaton likewise responds by re-imposing, or at least attempting to re-impose, the restricted economy of whiteness and by killing the otherwise 'plastic' black native.

Tracking back into Carroll's reading, then, we can see that Rollo in *The Navigator* is adaptable, as we see him progress from being a relatively useless seaman to at least being able, via the *séries récurrentes* that he develops, to boil an egg in the ship's kitchen. Quite how adaptable Rollo is compared to the Keaton characters in other films is up for debate, in that the submarine *deus ex machina* ending suggests that Rollo might otherwise have drowned with Betsy at sea – but Keaton's characters always ride their luck to some extent, even if they are adaptable. However, we might make a distinction between Keaton/Rollo's adaptability and the plasticity that via Zakiyyah Iman Jackson we have seen applied to Blackness. That is, while Keaton/Rollo is adaptable, this does not make him 'black', especially as his 'adaptation' from a naïve rich kid into…a still-naïve rich guy who now has a woman on his arm is indeed built upon his rescue of that woman from black native men, and his murder of one of their number, which is played out in the film for laughs.

What Carroll brings to the discussion, however, is his placing of Keaton's adaptability within discourses of evolution, in that Keaton 'grew to maturity and prospered in a culture that derived many of its key metaphors from evolution' (Carroll 2009: 46-47), and that the development of adaptability as a theme in his work came about 'through a process of osmosis facilitated by the broad publicity of evolutionary notions and idioms in American society' (Carroll 2009: 48).

The reason why this part of Carroll's argument is important is because the concept of evolution leads us inevitably to confront man's relationship with 'his' environment. Evolutionary thinking is, for Carroll, reflected in Keaton's cinema. And yet, if *The Navigator* is anything to go by, then 'evolution' consists in the 'progress' of the white man away from the black man. That is, evolution in this instance (if not more generally) becomes a discourse used to justify and to naturalise the 'superiority' of whiteness over Blackness (even as whiteness is so naturalised as not to be remarked upon; the only races worth remarking upon, of course for their inferiority, are non-white races, perhaps especially Blackness as a result of the photographic logic of white Western modernity that we discussed earlier as occulting 'Redness', which is not to mention other races and ethnicities). Furthermore, if evolution is natural, then the 'evolutionary' logic of the intelligent/adaptable Keaton in principle grounds his character in nature, a trait that we shall look at imminently in more detail. However, most urgent to press home presently is how if Keaton's cinema, with *The Navigator* functioning as its figurehead, is about the construction of white masculinity at the expense of Blackness and Indigeneity, and if it is white masculinity that has brought about the destruction of the planet's environment such that we live in a renewed era of mass extinctions, the terminal point of which might be a planet that is unsustainable for human and many other forms of life (if not life itself?), then the supposed 'evolutionary' and, by extension, ecological aspects of Keaton's work are deeply problematised.

In short, Keaton's characters, including perhaps Rollo, show themselves to be part of and adaptable to a (black/blackened) nature that is often 'hostile'. And yet, that very adaptability to nature, in that it leads to the construction of the white man as the *summum* of human existence (or, in the spirit of Fanon, Spillers, Wynter and others, it leads to the construction of the human as white/as such), is also what destroys nature, in that it entails, or is at the heart of, the Anthropocene, the epoch in which (white, capitalist) mankind does untold damage to the planet. Evolution, the thing that is supposed to ground humans in a natural world, is here precisely that which destroys the natural world as the white man emerges from nature and adapts to it, while at the same time adapting it, such that it is destroyed.

We might contend that if machines 'learn' in Keaton's universe, such that they become 'sovereign' (Trahair) or 'exceed themselves' (McGowan), then machines adapt and evolve in Keaton's universe as much as the white man. That is, evolution would seem not to be limited simply to Rollo/Keaton in *The Navigator*, but, rather, the whole universe expresses a sort of 'intelligence', as per the thinking of Bergson in *Matter and Memory* (2004), with cinema itself also a sort of intelligent machine, as argued by the likes of Jean Epstein (2014; see also Reeh-Peters 2018). However, Keaton's use of animals as tools and his destruction of those too-clearly-intelligent others (the octopus, the black man) would suggest that Keaton does not simply adapt to, but that he does indeed also adapt the world – and this treatment of others as tools (and/or as plastic), redolent of Anthropocene thinking in which the whole world is in effect a tool for (white) humans, is a key distinction that perhaps Carroll overlooks. For all that Rollo is adaptable, he also *adapts*, or changes, or mutilates, or murders – especially that which, like the soft-bodied and metamorphosing octopus, is *adaptation incarnate*. Keaton's worldview in *The Navigator* is not one of a general economy of adaptation/evolution; it is one of an economy/evolution that wilfully is restricted to the white man.

That the natives in *The Navigator* are dehumanised and elided with a threatening nature (the octopus) only demonstrates the raced dimension of this restricted and economic understanding of evolution: the white man emerges from a black nature and then annihilates it, with 'evolution' becoming not the reason for white dominance/domination, but the excuse. And given that native and nature alike relate to birth, in that the Latin term *natura* means birth, from *nat-*/born, then Deleuze's supposed 'finest metaphor' of Rollo/Keaton 'birthing himself', thereby denying his provenance from a 'natural' (black?) mother, is precisely about the white man mythologising his own white advent as simultaneously 'natural' and supernatural, in that the white man is perhaps in the world but not of the world, fundamentally separate from and superior to it, meaning that he can treat it as he sees fit, destroying countless lives and worlds in the name of Manifest Destiny. Perhaps we might read the theatrical release of *The Navigator* on Columbus Day in 1924 (Monday 13 October) as tapping into the white psyche of American identity (see Meade 1997: 151); the logic of white supremacy at work in *The Navigator* is the same as what led Columbus to set in motion the invention of the Americas via his fortuitous 'discovery' (that, as mentioned, might have been brought to him by Native Americans who had already made their way to Galway).

In transcending birth/by effectively birthing himself, Keaton/Rollo possesses some of the qualities of the trans* person, who likewise 'creates' themself as much as they are 'born into' the world. However, where the trans* person is (always?) a queer force that in many respects undermines the separation of the white man from the world, the 'self-birthing' of the white man is carried out precisely for the purposes of such a separation, even as, paradoxically, the black other is also cast out of nature, deemed monstrous and alien, as we shall imminently see. Small wonder that Rollo kills the octopus and the black man, while Keaton excises the starfish from his film; such vitalism of a more general, *informe*, black and octopoid economy runs against his need to restrict the economy to whiteness, which results eventually in the white economy destroying the planet.

While Keaton's work should for Trahair be about the general economy, then, it is in fact about the creation of a white economy. And if, as Trahair says after Gunning, Keaton's cinema of the 'operational aesthetic' is reflective of cinema as a machine itself, then we can see that cinema also plays a role in constituting not the general economy, but the restricted and white economy, with 'comedy' being the practice of dehumanising and exploitative cruelty towards others and the planet in general, or, as Calvin L. Warren says of the work of nineteenth-century caricaturist Edward W. Clay, comedy is 'terroristic...it is a pernicious instrument of antiblackness' (Warren 2018: 162).

Trahair defends Keaton when she suggests that he struggles against the economic mandates of commercial cinema (struggling with narrative, since he prefers the unstructured freedom of just cataloguing gags). But as we have seen, where Trahair believes that Keaton gestures at narrative really to defy it, perhaps the opposite is the case; Keaton gestures at comedy to really restrict economy within whiteness. Whiteness thus becomes machinic, with Blackness being *vivant*, even as Blackness is cast by whiteness as death. It is whiteness that is death and Blackness life; but given that Blackness is cast out of life by whiteness, Blackness therefore must transcend life, becoming trans*, becoming superhuman, becoming not just life/ *vie*, but super-/sur-life, *survie*. Blackness becomes survival, or, to put Blackness into relation with Indigeneity, it becomes what Anishinaabe scholar and writer Gerald Vizenor calls, combining survival with resistance, *survivance* – 'an active repudiation of dominance, tragedy, and victimry' (Vizenor 1998: 15; see also Byrd 2011: 81).

Furthermore, the birth of the white man is, as per D.W. Griffith, the birth of the nation, in that the nation, too, is linked to the idea of birth. As Wynter says, drawing upon the vitalist language of Bergson, 'the State became a service function of the new regulatory activity of the economic life…in which the Indo-European [read: white] mode of human being was canonized… as the expression of the most perfect "organic" realization of that biogenetic élan vital that was the superior will/being of its peoples' (Wynter 1984: 36). In other words, evolutionary being, or emergent and adaptable life, is akin to Bergson's élan vital, which is used as a justification for the emergence of the nation as the tool for white economy, with the birth of the nation thus meaning the death of any other (black) mother that (white) humans might otherwise have. Meanwhile, black people, as slaves, undergo what Orlando Patterson refers to as 'natal alienation', each becoming 'a social non-person…a socially dead person', or what we might refer to as 'beasts of no nation' (see Patterson 1982: 5-10; see also Wilderson 2010: 50).[1]

What is more, it is perhaps not the *restriction* of economy to whiteness that is the 'problem' in Keaton's film. It is perhaps economy itself, and not just in the sense of cinema as a commercial endeavour, although that Keaton is driven by a commercial imperative does connote this association between economy/capital and whiteness. For here we can parse McGowan from Trahair, in that McGowan is, as noted previously, the only one of the three Keaton scholars that I have discussed here to consider race in the filmmaker's work, charting, as mentioned, how Keaton 'fails to see that the racialized outsider is different from the [white] insider, that there is a distinction between the insider's failure to belong and the situation of the outsider' (McGowan 2016: 612).

The important point to note here is the association of Blackness with the outside, which we shall discuss presently.

# Chapter 16

# The Black Outside

For Sylvia Wynter:

> different forms of segregating the Ultimate Chaos that was the Black – from the *apartheid* of the South to the lynchings in both North and South, to their deprivation of the vote, and confinement in an inferior secondary educational sphere, to the logic of the jobless/ghetto/drugs/crime/prison archipelagoes of today – ensured that...the "active creation" of the type of Chaos, which the dominant model needs for the replication of its own system, would continue. **(Wynter 1984: 37)**

This segregation or captivity of the black is, I shall propose, a paradoxical captivity that takes place outside, the paradox emerging because we normally think of captivity as taking place inside and/or involving the process of confinement. However, at the start of Tiago Hespanha's documentary, *Campo* (Portugal, 2018), the filmmaker explains in voiceover that the term *campo*, which means field in English, derives from the Latin *capere*, meaning to capture (with the Latin term for field also being *campus*, from which we get the idea of a camp and, indeed, a campus). In other words, a field, which generally is found outside, is a piece of captured land, or, more particularly, a tool for capturing or keeping captive a space and all that it contains.

Western modernity is from the Holocaust very familiar with how camps function as a tool for captivity, with those imprisoned in the camps not only being marked by their 'outsider' status with regard to mainstream society, but also with those in the camps spending much of their time outside. With Weheliye in mind, we might understand the plantation also to be a camp, with work in the field also meaning that Blackness begins to be associated both with captivity and the outside. This is compared to the whites who get to live inside the domestic space (the 'white house', often built by those same slaves), with the 'house slave' functioning as a (false?) promise of interiority and domesticity, and who also functions to keep the field slave in the field/outside (akin to Ignatiev's most virulently antiblack Irish, the house slave polices the field slave, maintaining them in their outsideness).

Critical race theorists regularly reflect, even if they do not remark upon, the relationship between Blackness and the outside, which stands in contrast with whiteness and interiority. Frank B. Wilderson III, for example, says of the film *Antwone Fisher* (Denzel Washington, USA, 2002) that it dreams of a world where '[t]here is no more terror. There is no more captivity... Domesticity is possible. Kinship is possible. Which is to say, culture is possible' (Wilderson 2010: 101). In terms that anticipate Kara Keeling's perception that '[h]omelessness is our home', as cited earlier, Wilderson furthermore outlines how '"Black home" is an oxymoron because this notion has no structural analogy with a notion of White or non-Black domestic space'; for the black person, there is instead 'just ongoing captivity, living in quarters on Master's estate, or, we might add, living today in a ghetto or incarcerated' (Wilderson 2010: 127). Indeed, considering Black Panther member Safiya Bukhari-Alston, who was imprisoned in isolation for 3 years and 7 months 'because she was "a threat to the security of the free world"' as a result of her activism, Wilderson says that her 'structural position threatens the security of the White domestic scene, the White home – the purest distillation of the state' (Wilderson 2010: 134). In other words, while *Antwone Fisher* might offer the promise of domesticity in its story of the rehabilitation/socialisation of a troubled young sailor (Derek Luke), this is only because captivity, from the plantation through to the prison, is the norm for black American lives. And where Wilderson describes the white home as the 'purest distillation of the state', we might add that the creation of the White House is indeed the 'birth of the nation'. By this token, if whiteness involves the construction of the home/*heim*, the black is always *unheimlich* (and as Indigeneity was in the early twentieth century theorised as *heimatlos*; see Byrd 2011: 167).

This structural opposition between whiteness/interiority and Blackness/exteriority is made clearer by Denise Ferreira da Silva, who in *Toward a Global Idea of Race* explains how interiority remains 'the distinguishing feature of [white, western] man' (Ferreira da Silva 2007: 23), and that 'interiority holds all that is necessary for the manufacturing of modern subjects' (Ferreira da Silva 2007: 34). If the modern subject is founded upon the invention of interiority, then this comes at the expense of exteriority, as exemplified for Ferreira da Silva in the philosophy of Immanuel Kant and Johan Gottfried Herder (Ferreira da Silva 2007: 58). As she goes on to argue, 'strategies of engulfment transform that which is exterior, the effects of the universal *nomos*, into products, moments, "other" manifestations of the fundamental interiority that distinguishes the *homo historicus*' (Ferreira da Silva 2007: 100). That is, interiority is what gives a history to man, which, if we recall Wynter, means white man, while the black person, who remains exterior, is without history. Or, as Jared Sexton might put it, 'Black life is not lived in the world that the world lives in, but it is lived underground, in outer space' (Sexton 2011).

Blackness, then, is not just associated with the outside of white houses, but also with the outside of the planet, as if the black were (like an octopus?) an alien. Nahum D. Chandler refers to Blackness as being 'the limit, the outside' that actually is paradoxically within the system of white supremacy/antiblackness (Chandler 2008: 386). Being without a history, the 'negro' has thus for Chandler been characterised as a 'problem for thought', in that the negro cannot rightly *be thought*. Chandler suggests that *economy* is the 'concept-metaphor' devised 'to account for a problem or problematic for those who would think the problem of the Negro as a problem for thought' (Chandler 2008: 384). That is, the negro must be accounted, surveilled, or rendered into data and economic value in order for its problematic existence otherwise to be dealt with, with Chandler noting that 'economy' is derived from '*nomos* (as rule or law)', a term that echoes Ferreira da Silva's words above, and '*oikos* (of hearth, domesticity, of the circular or diurnal)' (Chandler 2008: 384). That is, economy is the 'rule of the home', but not in the sense that one rules one's home through 'home' economics. Rather, economy means that the concept of home, alongside interiority, becomes the rule or the law; simultaneously it posits those who do not have a home as outside of the law, and who thus must be held captive, with the very outsideness of those outside of the law reinforcing the authority and power of that law. In short, the invention of interiority involves the invention of an exteriority that is measured along racial lines; Blackness is outside, meaning that Blackness does not and cannot belong to the inside; as a result, Blackness must be captured in the field, where the black human is forever held captive in order to justify the interiority of the white. In the language of Jordan Peele, Blackness must be 'got out', it must get out of the ghetto, or the 'jobless/ghetto/drugs/crime/prison archipelagoes of today' (Wynter 1984: 37). Even if sometimes it must be 'straight' outta places like Compton or Brooklyn, it is small wonder, then, that in always being 'out', Blackness is linked to queerness. Fred Moten, who himself has with Stefano Harney described 'radical homelessness' as 'the essence of blackness' (Harney and Moten 2015: 82), seems to fathom this queerness when he links black radical aesthetics to 'the desire for the outside' and to the 'outness' of black radical voices and musicians (see, for example, Moten 2003: 165-169).

The outrage, or rather the inrage, that I propose drives Rollo to get married in *The Navigator* as a result of seeing the black newly-weds from the window of his own home is precisely his being enraged at having seen something impossible: black folk with, or in the process of attaining, an *oikos*, an inside, or a home of their own. And when Akira Mizuta Lippit writes of the octopus that it is 'pathologically ("hysterically") outside' (Lippit 2005: 10), he creates a further kinship between the octopus and Blackness that we might briefly explore here. For Lippit charts the myth of Oedipus on to the octopus to create a new creature: oectopus, which like the black human is also 'a figure of deviant visuality' (Lippit 2005: 13), in that Blackness stands outside of cinema, in darkness, an inverted and 'negative' image (Harriet Jacobs in the camera obscura wormhole; see Chapter 11, Note 2). And if we read *The Navigator* psychoanalytically, then Rollo/Keaton's murder of the octopus, as well as his murder of the black native, would in some senses be an 'Oedipal' murder of the other with whom Rollo shares the world, but with whom he would prefer not to. That is, Rollo refuses/denies his birth from the octopus (his black mother?) and from the black native (his father?), in order instead to 'birth himself'. (Perhaps it is no coincidence that psychoanalyst Jacques Schnier equates fear of the octopus – and of the spider – with fear of the mother; see Schnier 1956: 23.) Rollo is himself 'outside', or rather comes originally from a world where there is no distinction between the inside and outside. But in murdering those who begat him and who continue to represent the 'outside', Rollo in turn gives birth to himself as inside, and so can fulfil his domestic destiny of copulating with the white woman, Betsy, as per McGowan's analysis above. In this way, we might add another layer to Lippit's work and propose not just the octopus and the oectopus, but the oiktopus, itself a critter whose name is designed to reference how its sacrifice, or its casting absolutely into the outside, is what allows for the white interior, home and the *oikos* to come into being.[1]

If the octopus and the black human are alike the outside that allows for the birth not just of a restricted economy, but of economy *per se* (as well as the nation and the white house), then this birth of what amounts to white capitalist modernity, or patriarchy itself, then this *oikos* that is at work in economy, is also the *oikos* that is at work in ecology. That is, contrary to the popular understanding of ecology as the study of our environment, ecology is always already the study of the fabricated inside, the *oikos*. And by being focused on the inside, ecology is incapable of addressing its constitutive outside. Ecology, in other words, always marks the separation of white man from Blackness and from the world, rather than their connection – as we shall explore in more detail in the next chapter.

**Chapter 17**

# White Anthropocene, Black Chthulucene

If Jared Sexton links Blackness to 'outer space', then Chandler also sees Blackness as 'exorbitant', with an extra-planetary dimension being conveyed in the term ex-orb-itant, or that which is from outside the spinning orb that we refer to as Earth, which is itself in principle 'home' to all humans, but which in the Anthropocene has been rendered 'home' only to the white man and not to others. No wonder it is that Kara Keeling turns her attention to Sun Ra in *Queer Times, Black Futures*, since the singer waits for us, many light years away in space, where he plays what he refers to as 'dark history' (see Keeling 2019: 53-80).

By this extraterrestrial token, perhaps it is not so much of a criticism as Peter Hallward thinks when he derides Gilles Deleuze's philosophy for being 'out of this world' (see Hallward 2006). Indeed, while I have suggested that Deleuze's film-philosophy is ultimately 'white', Michelle Koerner does, as mentioned, trace the legacy of black activist and writer George Jackson in his work, in the process highlighting passages, especially in his texts co-written with Félix Guattari, where Deleuze offers an active engagement with race (see Koerner 2011). Meanwhile, Amber Jamilla Musser traces the similarities and differences between Deleuze and Frantz Fanon, arguing that the black nonsubject that Fanon sees as being excluded from white reality is not dissimilar to Deleuze and Guattari's 'Body without Organs', which itself is outside of the restricting influence of Oedipus, which, as we noted above, is linked to what Musser terms 'whiteness and Nation' (Musser 2012: 77). Significantly, Freudian psychoanalysis, or Oedipus, for Deleuze and Guattari 'forecloses other paths of desire by repressing them or rendering them illegible. The singularity of the Oedipal circuit of desire coupled with its presumed universality is problematic because it prevents the productivity of desire, which Deleuze and Guattari understand as the mechanism that creates reality' (Musser 2012: 78). In other words, Rollo does not seek to do anything productive with either the octopus or the natives, engaging in some sort of perverse (line of) flight from the constricting forces of the restricted economy; instead, he kills them both, thus satisfying the American mythos of *e pluribus unum*, instead of embracing multiple worlds, or the many-tentacled and entangled multiverse.

All the same, Deleuze identifies something important in Keaton's cinema when he suggests that:

> [t]he hero is like a minuscule dot encompassed by an immense and catastrophic milieu, in a transformation-space [espace à transformation]: vast, changing landscapes and deformable geometric structures, rapids and waterfalls, a great ship drifting on the seas, a town swept by the cyclone, a bridge collapsing like a flattened parallelogram. (Deleuze 1997: 173)

For, in seeing how Keaton's use of *séries récurrentes* involves his characters seeming tiny in comparison to the world that surrounds them (as per the example already given of Rollo trying to pull the *Navigator* with a rowing boat), we get a sense that Keaton gives agency to the world that surrounds him, to the environment itself.

This notion that the entire world has agency might give to Keaton's films an ecological aspect, as Jennifer Fay acknowledges in her work on 'cinema in the time of the Anthropocene' (Fay 2018). Where various filmmakers entered the studio in order to control their environment, two filmmakers who remained faithful to shooting outside were D.W. Griffith and Buster Keaton. While for Fay these choices do mean that the weather ends up playing a key role in various of their films, in the case of Griffith's most notorious *Birth of a Nation*, we can see how the outside is pitted as a dangerous space, characterised by Blackness, and which threatens whiteness, especially the white woman. Now, this process is repeated in *The Navigator*, as Betsy is threatened by the natives, but for Fay the way in which the environment becomes, or reflects, an *inhospitable world* (which is the title of her book), means that the films of Keaton and Griffith alike demonstrate how 'the idea that man is master of his world' is 'an illusion' (Fay 2018: 40). In particular Keaton's characters survive or succeed by chance, and cannot dominate their environment so much as react to it, or adapt to it, as Carroll also suggests.

In her wider argument, Fay draws upon Peter Sloterdijk to propose that humans have rendered their world inhospitable, especially through the use of nuclear weapons, which emerge not so much as a way for humans to fight each other as to subdue and control the environment (see Chapter 9, Note 3). In this way, Fay implicates humanity in making the world 'inhospitable', and which inhospitability is evident in various films, including those of Keaton. Indeed, of *The Navigator*, Fay ingeniously suggests that the ending – whereby Rollo swaps one underwater breathing apparatus for another as he progresses from diving suit to submarine – conveys how the 'regular' environment of the planet, as shaped by man during the Anthropocene, is a space where the air is not breathable. In this way, the human relationship with the weather is characterised by war, in that humans are at war with their world, rather than the weather being merely a factor in otherwise all-human conflicts (see Fay 2018: 43). And, with regard to Keaton, the upshot of this war-like inhospitability between man and the environment is that Keaton is, 'not native to Earth. *In* but not *of* the world, an alien but not a guest, propelled from one cataclysm to another, Keaton tests the limits of the earth's hospitality' (Fay 2018: 55).

Perhaps it is not coincidental that Fay does not mention the racial aspects of *The Navigator*, for had she acknowledged the clear role that Blackness and Indigeneity play in the film, then she might have had to modify her argument somewhat, perhaps along these lines: Keaton *constructs* a world in which he is *in* but not *of* the world, but he only does so by simultaneously and paradoxically rendering Blackness and Indigeneity both of and outside of the world, in that Blackness and Indigeneity are clearly elided with the 'natural world' ('primitive' natives), while also becoming so antithetically alien to whiteness such that Blackness must be annihilated (there can be no synthesis of Blackness or Indigeneity, just their ongoing destruction). Fay surely on some level acknowledges the role in which whiteness is indeed constructed here as separate from the world, with this separation being, as mentioned, key to (white) man's ability, perhaps even his *need*, to do with and to that world, including its non-white inhabitants and other species, what it sees fit, i.e. to turn them into tools and/or to destroy them. Where Fay describes Keaton as alien, we might respond by saying that this is an appropriation of an exteriority, or what Sexton calls an 'outer space', that the white has in fact imposed upon the black and the native human alike, and which is very much a part of both the whitening of the white and the blackening of the black/the making 'primitive' of the native human. Keaton, as an archetypal white man, might be and in some senses is wilfully alien to the world; however, this alienation relies upon the more profound alienation of the black and the native other, as well as of the octopus.

To say, therefore, that the Anthropocene is really a white Anthropocene should hardly be surprising, with Kathryn Yusoff perhaps being the most incisive scholar to have outlined the way in which this is so, as we shall examine in more detail imminently (see Yusoff 2018). And if to study the Anthropocene is, for Donna J. Haraway, to refocus attention too much and once again on the white man, then we might follow Haraway, as well as Keaton in his use of the cthulhoid octopus, in suggesting that we reject the white Anthropocene and instead focus on the Black Chthulucene, or the Maroon Autochthulucene. And perhaps of equal importance to this process is that we recognise that the construction of the white *oikos* on a planet that whites otherwise render 'inhospitable' is indeed the construction of *economy*, literally the law of the home/house, or the house as law, or capital itself. The construction of this restricted white economy goes hand in hand, I shall suggest, with ecology, which like the Anthropocene emerges as a term that is too focused on whiteness/the white *oikos* in order truly to be progressive, or to help 'humanity' collectively to navigate from the White Anthropocene to the Black Chthulucene/the Maroon Autochthulucene.

Timothy Morton suggests that we should think about ecology and not nature, since the latter concept, at least as it is commonly used, suggests a world from which humans are separated, rather than a nature with which they are entangled. That is, for Morton, 'the idea of nature is getting in the way of properly ecological forms of culture, philosophy, politics, and art' (see Morton 2007: 1). We shall have to save for another occasion a critique of Morton's use of the term 'properly', which carries at its root ideas of cleanliness (*propre* means clean in French) and property (and thus possession and, by extension, systems of capital). And we shall refrain, therefore, on this occasion from suggesting the underlying whiteness of Morton's 'proper', clean and capitalist thought (with the improper, or dirt, being of course linked to Blackness, as Fanon has suggested above; for more on 'whiteness as property', see the classic essay by Cheryl I. Harris 1993). Rather, we might simply acknowledge for the time being how Morton, like Fay, does not particularly engage with issues of race in this work, and posit that if nature 'gets in the way' – which is precisely what it does in Keaton's films! – then so is ecology overly linked to economy, and the management of the white home, or the white house, which is an interiority set in opposition to a threatening exteriority that must otherwise be destroyed (in the proper, white world, whiteness is to have property, or to treat others as props, as Snead suggests; to be property/to be owned, is to be improper; economy sees having supersede being, which itself is antithetical to becoming).

The Anthropocene is leading to the end of the world? No. Ecological catastrophe is the end of the *white* world. As has often been pointed out by indigenous and other scholars of colour: the world of Native Americans throughout the American continent, as well as the world of countless Africans, was brought violently to an end by the colonialism and racism that drove the Anthropocene into being in the first place. Ecological catastrophe, with its focus on the *oikos*, speaks always already of what Wynter would call the over-representation of the white man.

Enter Yusoff: '[i]f the Anthropocene proclaims a sudden concern with the exposures of environmental harm to white liberal communities, it does so in the wake of histories in which these harms have been knowingly exported to black and brown communities under the rubric of civilization, progress, modernization, and capitalism' (Yusoff 2018: xiii). For Yusoff, Blackness came into being with the institution of extraction and mining in the New World (Yusoff 2018: 2), with whiteness therefore, after W.E.B. Du Bois being defined as 'the "ownership of the Earth for ever and ever"' (Yusoff 2018: 26). That is, the outside is cast as dirty and black, and the *oikos* is property that must be cleaned at all times, meaning that Blackness must be destroyed for whiteness/property/economy to exist at all, or, as Yusoff puts it, 'what allows white self-actualization (or comfort) is slavery' (Yusoff 2018: 80).

But beyond being linked to a non-human creature (Cthulhu) by a notoriously racist author (Lovecraft), what does conceptualising the Black Chthulucene really achieve? Perhaps I am engaged simply in a semantic battle to enforce the usage of a term that ultimately changes nothing – except perhaps to function as a tool to cement my own career. However, I would propose that if we live by metaphors and language, then to try to shift the terms that we use to think about these issues can indeed lead ultimately to changing the way that we live. That being said, I am not sure there is much hope for 'saving' the planet as is, and certainly not for ecological or Anthropocenic thinking to do so, since both are, as should by now be clear, white in conception, white in execution, and therefore will perpetuate the destruction of the planet and of those cast outside of whiteness. It is, I would suggest, too late; or, even if it is not quite yet too late and humans can find the means to perpetuate white supremacy for centuries or even millennia, be that by using alternative fuels, by colonising outer space (in yet another act of black appropriation), or by learning to breathe underwater, as the black octopus has had to do in order to live *in the wake* (see also Gumbs 2019: 338), this will only be a temporary reprieve from the inevitable. It is only the end of white supremacy and antiblackness that can give to humans a chance. If only 'the human' as such were not founded upon said antiblackness and anti-Indigeneity. That is, if 'human being in the world is, and should be, sheer criminality' (Harney and Moten 2013: 141), then humans as such (humans as white) cannot become non-white without giving up their very humanity. We must find a way for the planet-destroying, genocidal and psychopathic white human to survive? Fuck the human.

Indeed, it is small wonder, then, that we can find traces in Afropessimistic thought of just wanting to let the whole white house burn down, and for new life to emerge from the muddy biochar that remains. Let Cthulhu come and destroy white human life. Blackness has already learned to live in a broken-backed and thus invertebrate fashion. Blackness has, as Toni Morrison writes at the end of *Beloved*, resigned itself to leaving no trace and to being eroded by the same weather against which

Keaton and Griffith toil so hard.

'The rest is weather...Just weather' (Morrison 2004: 324). Weather as the only 'true' justice – blowing down the houses, even if Keaton fantasises in *Steamboat Bill, Jr.* of surviving its collapse by some cinematic miracle. The seasons will take everything away and the white man will fade, replaced not just by the seasons, but also by the black daughters and sons of the sea (the sea-sons) who have been inhabiting the oceanic ossuary since the Middle Passage, the Anthropocene, capital, whiteness and Blackness came into being. It is strange how the killing of an octopus and then a black native can say so much.

**Chapter 18**

# Submerged Sycorax

In telling the tale of a white man arriving on the shores of an island where he encounters cannibals, *The Navigator* bears some loose resemblance to William Shakespeare's *The Tempest* (1610-1611), in which the shipwrecked Prospero and his daughter Miranda enslave the dark-skinned Caliban, before the former tries to reinstate himself as the Duke of Milan through the use of magic – and the help of the spirit Ariel, with whom he seeks to control nothing less than the weather (which is also to control time, given that in French *le temps* means both the weather and time). In order to achieve this, Prospero and Ariel provoke a storm that causes a second shipwreck, bringing to the shores of the island Prospero's brother, Antonio, who usurped him, and Antonio's ally, Alonso, the King of Naples. Among Antonio and Alonso's group are Trinculo and Stephano, the king's jester and butler respectively, who find Caliban under a cloak on the beach.

The discovery of Caliban prompts in Trinculo the following monologue:

> What have we here? a man or a fish? dead or alive? A fish: he smells like a fish; a very ancient and fish-like smell; a kind of not of the newest Poor-John. A strange fish! Were I in England now, as once I was, and had but this fish painted, not a holiday fool there but would give a piece of silver: there would this monster make a man; any strange beast there makes a man: when they will not give a doit to relieve a lame beggar, they will lazy out ten to see a dead Indian. Legged like a man and his fins like arms! Warm o' my troth! I do now let loose my opinion; hold it no longer: this is no fish, but an islander, that hath lately suffered by a thunderbolt. **(Shakespeare 1993)**

In discovering a dark-skinned native who smells like a fish, and yet who has legs and arms, Trinculo would seem in some respects to be describing Caliban as an octopus, something reaffirmed by Prospero's description of Caliban as 'not honour'd with / A human shape' (Shakespeare 1993) – as if he foreshadowed, even, the mutant 'octopus' babies born in the wake of Pacific island nuclear tests (see Chapter 9, Note 3). What is more, Trinculo's comparison of Caliban to a 'dead Indian', to see whom Englishmen would pay ten doits (or five farthings, which is just over a penny), lends to him not only a sense of already being 'dead', or rather somewhere between 'dead and alive', but also an insight into how white Westerners consider non-white others to be spectacular objects (for a similar analysis of this passage, see Byrd 2011: 55ff).

If the parallel treatment of natives between *The Tempest* and *The Navigator* were not clear, it should be noted that Prospero reports in Act I Scene II how Caliban attempted to attack and rape Miranda. As Barbara Fuchs argues, 'Caliban's attack on Prospero's daughter once more genders the colonizing impulse; here it is the defense of the European woman that justifies the repression of the non-European' (Fuchs 1997: 61), with Sylvia Wynter adding that 'on the New World island, as the only woman, Miranda and her mode of physiognomic being, defined by the philogenically "idealized" features of straight hair and thin lips is canonized as the "rational" object of desire' (Wynter 1990: 360). In other words, *The Navigator* and *The Tempest* alike make of the white woman the stake of colonisation and conquest – a process that not only is antiblack and anti-indigenous, but which also assists in ensuring 'subordination and deference from white women in exchange for their protection' (with Robin D.G. Kelley going on to identify how 'chivalry…was about the protection of white women as property in order to maintain the purity of the race'; see Kelley 2002: 42).

French psychologist O. Mannoni wrote in 1956 that

Prospero's relationship with Ariel and Caliban was akin to that of the coloniser and the colonised (Mannoni 1990). Furthermore, *The Tempest* has been contextualised as giving expression in the early seventeenth century to the longstanding colonisation of Ireland, 'England's first plantation' ahead of Virginia, as well as to the relatively new colonisation by various nations of the Americas (see Fuchs 1997). With such readings in mind, it is perhaps unsurprising that the character of Ariel was taken by Uruguayan writer José Enrique Rodó in 1900 in order romantically to define Latin American existence as that of the magical island spirit (see Rodó 1988), while Cuban poet Roberto Fernández Retamar rejected Rodó's position, instead proposing that Caliban, as opposed to Ariel, was the figure whose otherness was to be embraced in the struggle against Western hegemony (Retamar 1989). Indeed, Retamar is one of a slew of writers to have adopted Caliban as a figurehead in their anti-colonial works, with key contributors to this discourse being Aimé Césaire (2002 [1969]) and George Lamming (2016 [1971]).

For Jodi A. Byrd, Caliban thus becomes 'simultaneously African, Irish, Carib, Arawak, Jewish, and Other…a cacophonous textualization that does not traffic in absence but rather oversignifies presence in informative ways that unravel colonial logics that are dependent on binary constructions of settler/native, black/white, and master/slave' (Byrd 2011: xxxvi). Furthermore, Byrd suggests that the interpretations of Caliban as 'black, African, native, Amerindian, Irish, US settler, Latin American, Fidel Castro, and, and, and' constitute 'a process of simultaneous signification that activates the Indian as the field of transit and the field of ontological justification that serves nationalist, anticolonial and imperial projects' (Byrd 2011: 66). That is, Caliban-as-indigenous gets specifically overlooked as Caliban comes to stand in for any and every other type of colonised people/person, a 'translocation' of 'new world indigeneity onto those forced labor diasporas (themselves arising from African indigeneities) that made the colonization of indigenous peoples on both sides of the Atlantic possible in the first place' (Byrd 2011: 67). Byrd continues by arguing that the result of this translocation is that 'descendents of the Black Atlantic become, now, the "real" new world native at the site of exception where indigenous peoples in the American South and Caribbean are rendered fossils, specters, relics, or pushed from their homes to the hinterlands and territories beyond' (Byrd 2011: 67). That is, indigenous peoples are 'cast off, disavowed, and misremembered' (Byrd 2011: 67) when Caliban is not understood as a native but rather as an arrivant who claims Indigeneity, thereby obliterating once again the 'true' native.

When Coco Fusco adopted the character of Miranda as a figure for giving expression to her Cuban femininity, she did so because writers like Rodó, Lamming and Césaire had concentrated 'little attention on Miranda, *The Tempest*'s only significant female character' (Fusco 2015: 201). While the reduction of white women to property for the sake of 'protection' is indeed to be questioned, Fusco has nonetheless been criticised for this perspective, since she would seem to have identified with neither arrivant nor native, but with the 'idealized' (if subjugated?) white woman (who nonetheless fails to find solidarity with Caliban, since Shakespeare has the latter confirmed as threat, while also having Miranda fall in love with Ferdinand, the son of Alonso, thereby meaning that racism is shown to be a more powerful force than sexism in Shakespeare's play, since it is better for Miranda to be the property of a white man than to be touched at all by a black man).[1]

There is a case to be made, though, that Miranda is not the only woman in *The Tempest* with whom Fusco could have identified. This is not a case of Caliban not being male enough to merit mention by Miranda when she numbers the men that she has met in her life, which is two (her father Prospero, and Ferdinand, also shipwrecked on the island; see Act III Scene I, lines 50-52). For while this might make of Caliban a potential trans* figure in keeping with the idea that Blackness falls outside of gender, there is in fact a second woman who has inhabited the island, and who is mentioned, but whom we never see. This is Sycorax, Caliban's now-dead mother, who was banished while pregnant to the island from her native Algiers for being a witch.

In order slightly to nuance Byrd's critique of arrivant writers, therefore, we might argue a) that in addition to being ungendered, Caliban is characterised repeatedly as a monster, and thereby is animalised, with his animalisation making of him a *cimarrón*/wild animal, or a maroon (see Chapter 9, Note 2); and b) that Caliban himself 'arrived' on the island with Sycorax, who is overlooked by Byrd and Fusco alike, even as Byrd does briefly mention her (see Byrd 2011: 59). In other words, Caliban has an African mother who does not appear in Shakespeare's play, instead being relegated to the background. If Sycorax and Caliban, now understood as Algerian, thus come to give expression to contemporary and ongoing Islamophobia, thereby adding another possible layer of 'cacophonous textualisation' and 'simultaneous signification' to *The Tempest* (see also Fuchs 1997: 60), we might nonetheless productively suggest that this allows for the development of a more integrated maroon coalition, whereby rather than trying to find the 'true' identity of Caliban (is he a native or not?), we instead understand that 'these rhetorical strategies [of seeing Caliban as black, native, Irish, etc]...make sense only when viewed from the perspective of multiple contexts' (Fuchs 1997: 62). That is, multiversally, all of these versions of Caliban co-exist at the same time.

More than this, though, we might shift our focus from Caliban to precisely Sycorax, in order to identify how we might achieve what Tiffany Lethabo King, à propos of Charmaine Lurch's 2015 sculpture *Revisiting Sycorax*, would term 'an open state of Black and Indigenous relationality' (King 2019: 204). As King also writes, where in the Americas there are black fungible bodies, they 'index the imagined (surface) and actual sites of colonial expansion and, in turn, the space of Indigenous genocide' (King 2019: 23; see also Day 2021: 5). That is, Sycorax helps us to consider Blackness and Indigeneity as entangled, rather than as competing identities. As M. NourbeSe Philip summarises, then, '[t]o find the true source of authenticity, a more autochthonous lineage and line of descent, it is to Sycorax that we must turn' (Philip 1997: 166).

Abena P.A. Busia points out in her consideration of Sycorax that

> [i]f both African men and European women are of questionable legitimacy, African women demonstrably have none. Like Caliban's mother, they are seldom present as billed players on the stage, and when they are, they do not speak coherently. It is one of their burdens that they are called upon to be fully *embodied* – fleshy beings but unvoiced. Rarely rendered as human beings, they are presented as insubstantial symbols. **(Busia 1989-1990: 94; original emphasis)**

What is more, Busia does not limit her argument to African women, acknowledging that 'the "native woman" remains the most decentered of silent spaces for the purposes of maintaining and sustaining doubtful authorities' (Busia 1989-1990: 100). And so, if '[f]or much of structuralist and postmodernist discourse, "woman" becomes a category without subjectivity and sometimes without historical reference, perpetuating a phallocentric symbolic economy', it is the woman of colour who is even more absent, to the extent, even, that '[o]ur supposed absence of voice becomes, in the end, paradigmatic of the incomplete and incompletable nature of imperial cultural conquest' (Busia 1989-1990: 103).

Irene Lara follows Busia in proposing that it is Sycorax's silence and her failure to appear on stage that function as her most powerful mode of critique. For, in Lara's estimation, '[n]ot only have decolonial and feminist intellectuals, as the heirs to colonialism, learned to speak the master's languages – including English, Spanish, academic, and other forms of legitimised writing – [but] many of us have also inherited the master's fear, loathing, and suppression of the spirit and the body, especially the racialized and feminized spirit and body' (Lara 2007: 86). That is, in the language of recognition used earlier, in trying so hard to be recognised by the hegemonic forces of white patriarchy, women and people of colour betray their bodies and, perhaps especially, their spirit. Conversely, as a figure who never appears on stage, Sycorax functions as precisely a kind of spirit, thereby carrying out something akin to her fellow diasporic Algerian Jacques Derrida's *hantise*, haunting the stage, haunting *The Tempest*, becoming 'a nagging memory' (Lara 2007: 83).[2]

King understands Sycorax to be 'depicted as a subject without language, and therefore without humanity, who passes on her aporetic, or language-less state to her son Caliban', before adding as per Lara, that 'Sycorax functions as a haunt, or a haint, that refuses to be excluded…[and that, for Lurch] Sycorax used other, perhaps poetic, forms of communication that were illegible to Western narrative forms' (King 2019: 181).

In this way, it is the very invisibility of Sycorax, her 'resounding silence', that, in the spirit of Audre Lorde:

creates an alternative counter-hegemonic positionality for social change. In this positionality one will not uncritically take up 'the master's tools' (be it language, the pen, the gun, or other 'tools') in an attempt to 'dismantle the master's house'… The silence of and around Sycorax points to something else. It signals the existence of a powerful epistemology that lives alongside of, yet reaches beyond, the disenchanted secular modern nation. **(Lara 2007: 90; see Lorde 2017)**

In other words, Sycorax presents to us a different way of being, perhaps outside of being, beyond the stage, beyond the purview of surveillance, and, with *The Navigator* in mind, beyond cinema. This perverse 'paraontological' existence/'survivance' is hard to grasp, however, because, as Philip points out, 'we are still dumb in the language of Sycorax' (Philip 1997: 167), to which Lara adds: 'we are also *deaf* in her language' (Lara 2007: 82; original emphasis). For, the language that we use to discuss and to evoke Sycorax, perhaps language in and of itself, is 'too patriarchal', too much a master's tool, which is why Silvia Federici imagines a different outcome to Caliban's failed attempt to overthrow Prospero – if only the instigators had 'been not Caliban but his mother, Sycorax, the powerful Algerian witch that Shakespeare hides in the play's background, and not Trinculo and Stephano but the sisters of the witches who, in the same years of the Conquest, were being burned in Europe at the stake' (Federici 2014: 107). It is by speaking and understanding the language of silence, and by fathoming the meaning of absence, that we can progress from the White Anthropocene to the Black or Maroon (Auto)Chthulucene.

Philip, in her essay 'A Piece of Land Surrounded', recounts how, '[f]ive hundred years ago Cristobal Colon came upon Watling Island: he enc(o)untered another world and that first enc(o)unter with the land of the Natives would be the palimpsest for Europe's subsequent enc(o)unter with the New World. The New World would become both womb (*cunt*) and wound (*cut*)' (Philip 1997: 164). In other words, white Western modernity is born from Sycorax, the woman of colour, the black background, the nothing, the paraontological survivor, whose black hole, whose cunt, generates all that is. More than this, the maroon Sycorax is that which lies between, outside of, or beyond cinema's images, in that Sycorax is cut from the picture, and from this cut emerges cinema (especially as a 'legible', Western narrative form), as well as a legible white cinematic modernity, which relies so much on recognition and visibility, and which is narrativised/made sensible through tropes/myths like Manifest Destiny. Because she is 'female and dark', white Western modernity nonetheless fears Sycorax (Philip 1997: 166), who is what Edward Kamau Brathwaite (1975) would call a 'submerged mother'.

Indeed, Brathwaite, who is not unaware of Sycorax (see Brathwaite 1977: 44), argues that:

> [w]oman – especially the black woman – has always occupied a special place in books because she has always been a submerged/invisible presence and force, becoming therefore in the male chauvinistic mind totemic queen either of good or evil, but basically romantic and almost totally unrelated to the real thing. **(Brathwaite 1975: 48)**

This leads Brathwaite further to say that '[i]n the world of letters, it is bad enough to be Caliban; to be his sister is almost unthinkable' (Brathwaite 1975: 49). And, of course, when Brathwaite elaborates his theory of tidalectics, it is to an old woman of colour that he turns, describing her actions as 'like the movement of the ocean she's walking on, coming from one continent/continuum, touching another, and then receding ("reading") from their island(s) into the perhaps creative chaos of the(ir) future' (Brathwaite 1999: 34). The submerged mother, then, is a combination of land and sea, bringing together past, present and future, working with chaos and against the controlling forces of narrative and surveillance in order to chart wormhole routes to queer new dimensions or continuums (see also Amideo 2021: 6-7).

Elizabeth DeLoughrey and Tatiana Flores analyse Jean-Ulrick Désert's *The Waters of Kiskéya/Quisqueya* (2017), 'a hand-painted map of the Caribbean spread over nine folios of calfskin vellum measuring six feet high by nine feet across'

(DeLoughrey and Flores 2020: 139). Among other things, the map features squids, octopuses and coral, as well as maps of supposed landforms, meaning that the work 'represents a terraqueous view that brings land and sea into tidalectic relation' (DeLoughrey and Flores 2020: 141). Also featured on the map is a legend that reads 'Tabula Nova Insulae e Maria de Caribaeum', which means 'New Map of the Islands and Mary of the Caribbean'. As DeLoughrey and Flores point out, where typically we would see the Latin word *mare*, meaning sea ('New Map of the Islands and the Caribbean Sea'), we instead see *Maria*/Mary (Mary of the Caribbean), a link that also works in French via the homophonous words *mer* (sea) and *mère* (mother; see DeLoughrey and Flores 2020: 143). Complementing this linguistic wordplay is 'a drawing of a woman wearing a long, flowing gown and a crown emerging from the waves with an octopus seeming to swim out of her sleeves' (DeLoughrey and Flores 2020: 144). As DeLoughrey and Flores explain, '[s]he represents the transplanted Yoruba deity of the ocean, the orisha (spirit in human form) Yemayá (also Yemoja) who is worshipped throughout the Caribbean and Brazil…As a caretaking figure, Yemayá is also associated with the Virgin Mary and suggests not just a syncretic culture but a creolized sea' (DeLoughrey and Flores 2020: 144). Finally, DeLoughrey and Flores explain that the image becomes a 'feminized triumvirate of mer, mère and Maria', with 'the fantastic hybrid octopus/Virgin Mary' being what Désert himself describes as 'a "feminine nature spirit force"' (DeLoughrey and Flores 2020: 146).

With this in mind, might we not surmise that the octopus in *The Navigator* is also a 'submerged mother', tidalectically a combination of mother/*mère*/Mary and sea/*mer*. More than this, we can from these associations understand that the octopus/ocean is Mary, and thus the mother of god. Not only does Rollo kill this black/native Yoruba god, then, but he does so in order to instate whiteness as god, a white god born from the black hole/black cunt, confirming the link between the octopus and motherhood identified by Schnier, who nonetheless overlooks the racial components of this mythology: the mother of god is not white, but maroon (she is white Western modernity's night-mare/night-*mère*).

Finally, then, we might recall that the only non-white female presence in *The Navigator* is the newly-wed bride, since the black natives seem exclusively to be a male community (perhaps to exacerbate the appeal of Betsy, or perhaps because they have, in Keaton and Crisp's fevered projections of Blackness, eaten all of the women). Is she Sycorax, silent, easily overlooked, and linked to the octopus-ocean-mother whom Rollo later kills? Is Rollo therefore destroying his desire for the black (m)other, in the process creating and ensuring whiteness as the supreme race, even as it is that desire for the black (m)other that spurs him to seek to marry (and thus to subjugate) Betsy in the first place? As we look tidalectically at *The Navigator* from the maroon shoal, it would appear that this is indeed the case.[3]

## Chapter 19

# The Keaton legacy

In an article on Yasser Arafat, Gilles Deleuze suggests that 'the Palestinians are the new Indians, the Indians of Israel' (Deleuze 1998: 31). Deleuze says this because Israel is emptying Palestinian territory in order to occupy it, much as the United States emptied the land of North America to create its own nation – a point of comparison that for Deleuze explains ongoing American support for Israel. As Kathryn Medien points out in her analysis of Deleuze's article, there is 'a global matrix of settler colonial violence and a shared terrain of native solidarity' (Medien 2019: 56).

Deleuze, meanwhile, has been used to consider the work of renowned Palestinian filmmaker Elia Suleiman by both Laura U. Marks (2015) and Patricia Pisters (2012: 213-240). Significantly, Marks defines some of Suleiman's early works as 'war machines' that 'take advantage of his lack of control over language' (Marks 2015: 67), by which she means that Suleiman tries to create a new language for Palestine by destroying the existing language, both verbal and audiovisual, that is used to define this 'landless nation'. By this token, Suleiman's is a 'terrorist' cinema, since all activities that attempt to represent 'palestine' are considered by the 'majority' power (i.e. the powerful settler/coloniser) to be terroristic.

For Pisters, meanwhile, Suleiman's *Yadon ilaheyya/Divine Intervention* (France/Morocco/Germany/Palestine, 2002) does something similar when it aims to give expression to 'the force of life outside the text' (Pisters 2012: 258), in that Pisters, like Marks, is trying to demonstrate how Palestine exists – but outside of the official codes and language (hence why for Marks, Suleiman tries to invent a new language in order to express

Palestine, since 'palestine' does not in effect exist, especially since it is landless, or in Deleuze/Medien's terms, 'empty'). Notably, Pisters likens Suleiman at one point to Buster Keaton (Pisters 2012: 250), before suggesting that his films involve 'laughter in the midst of the intolerable, in the midst of violence, and hence...laughter that is necessarily and vitally related to the world' (Pisters 2012: 261). In Bergsonian terms, Suleiman in effect demonstrates how the non-existence that is imposed upon Palestine is *du mécanique* that is 'encrusted' over a living space (*du vivant*) – and comedy functions as a tool, here, for engaging critically with that negated reality. Laughter is thus in this instance terroristic, not least in the sense that it plays a role in reclaiming land/*terra* for Palestinians – at least within the virtual realm of the cinema, if not in the actual realm of the Israeli and Palestinian occupied territories.

In her treatment of Abu Ghraib, and especially the controversial photographs depicting abused prisoners that emerged from there in 2004, Jasbir K. Puar charts how the 'Muslim terrorist' has in general been marked as 'sexually conservative, modest and fearful of nudity (and it is interesting how this conceptualisation is rendered both sympathetically and a problem), as well as queer, animalistic, barbarian and unable to control his (or her) urges' (Puar 2007: 86). Especially since 11 September 2001, the terrorist has been invoked in the West, then, 'as a queer, nonnational, perversely racialised other [who] has become part of the normative script of the US war on terror' (Puar 2007: 37) – with Palestinians and Palestine being offered by Puar as examples to illustrate both of these quotations. As Puar does in her work, though, we might also create a 'terrorist assemblage' out of Suleiman's 'terroristic' cinema in order to (illustrate how his films) 'queer' (i.e. subvert) power, and that Suleiman does this in a Keaton-esque fashion. Significantly, however, Suleiman is a non-white and racialised terrorist other who 'punches up' at the occupying Israeli forces, rather than Keaton, who 'punches down' against black folk, indigenous people, women, queerness, trans* being and animals (the octopus) in order to establish his own birth right. Furthermore, while this exercise of power allows Keaton to have a happy ending, the same is not necessarily the case for Suleiman, since even though towards its end *Divine Intervention* sees a female terrorist superhumanly defeat Israeli soldiers in a combat sequence that riffs visually upon *The Matrix* (Lana and Lilly Wachowski, USA, 1999), the film nonetheless ends with the muted image of a man (Suleiman) and his mother staring at a pressure cooker: tensions are always on the rise.

In other words, if Suleiman embodies some sort of neo-Keatonian aesthetic, all the same he does it from the perspective of non-whiteness, and in this sense he turns the antiblack Keatonian logic on its head. It is perhaps telling, therefore, that Pisters segues away from Deleuze in her analysis of *Divine Intervention*, and ends up discussing more the ideas of Frantz Fanon in order to suggest how the 'paradoxical pleasures and pains of violence and laughter...[can] change established visions of the actual world' (Pisters 2012: 264).[1] That is, while Deleuze is certainly useful for helping us to understand Suleiman's cinema, it is in fact by reaching beyond Deleuze and into a foundational text from black studies that Suleiman's work comes fully to make sense. In this vein, when Deleuze explains that 'Palestinian-ness...[is] co-extensive with death' (Medien 2019: 58), he brings to mind the necropolitical thought of Achille Mbembe, who describes the contemporary colonial occupation of Palestine as '[t]he most accomplished form of necropower' (Mbembe 2003: 27).

In terms that recall the simultaneous 'pleasures and pains of violence and laughter', Mbembe charts how under the necropolitical regime in Palestine, *the logic of martyrdom* and *the logic of survival* in effect come down to being the same thing, or there is no difference between them, since 'from the perspective of slavery or of colonial occupation, death and freedom are irrevocably interwoven' (Mbembe 2003: 38). If you will, where Keaton is free to kill the black native and the octopus in order, via a circular logic, to assert his freedom (Keaton is free to kill the (m)other; killing the (m)other, especially the (m)other goddess, reaffirms his freedom, his own divinity), the Palestinian suicide bomber can only kill himself in order to (try to) achieve the same, since their status otherwise is, as per the necropolitical discussion of Blackness earlier, that of the *living dead* (Mbembe 2003: 40).[2] The Palestinian terrorist, and by extension the Palestinian terrorist filmmaker, thus gives expression to an 'outside' (divine intervention) that, notably, never comes, even as we might reckon the work of art/the film itself as an intervention that endeavours to help to change the actual world via its unreal/virtual/cinematic status (see Pisters 2012: 261). Compared to *The Navigator*, where intervention does take place as Rollo and Betsy are rescued by the submarine – an event that would suggest that whiteness is indeed divine, a *deus* that is *ex machina* – in *Divine Intervention*, the filmmaker and his mother (a reminder of the filmmaker's earthly/terrestrial/ human birth) are in the end simply left waiting – looking at a machine that offers nothing in return. If there is a *deus*, it is not coming to help Suleiman, or Palestinians more generally; and if it does anything, this white divinity, it imposes the machinic existence of war on its others (the white man declares war on both nature and non-whiteness in order to create *economy*, which in turn is reaffirmed when, despite economy leading to the destruction of the environment, 'saving' that environment becomes an issue of *ecology*, i.e. saving the white home – not through stopping the killing of nature and the non-white other, but through intensifying the violence towards them).[3]

Deleuze's elision of Palestinians with 'Indians' might seem to contradict Frank B. Wilderson III's claim, discussed earlier, that black humans alone have never effectively been recognised as alive during the lifetime of the USA. It is not that we need choose one or the other, though, and the link between the wider Islamic world and 'Indians' in fact has precedence. Jodi A. Byrd, for example, recalls that arch-terrorist Osama bin Laden was regularly referred to as Geronimo by US military forces, especially during Operation Neptune Spear, which culminated in bin Laden's assassination (see Byrd 2011: 19). Furthermore, in *Habeas Viscus* Alexander G. Weheliye explains how the Jews who had given up on life in the death camps of World War II were referred to as *Muselmanns*, or, literally, Muslims (see Weheliye 2014: 53-73). Not only does this convey how Jews were generally recognised as white, since they had to be given a non-white name when they in effect became the *living dead*, but it also conveys how in the white imagination, the non-white is indeed always already dead (and we might add further resonances between already dead Jews and already dead black folk by reflecting on how they both are captured within ghettos, from which they seek to get 'out').

That said, while the clearing of land in Palestine means that there certainly are resonances between Palestinians and 'Indians' (and between Israel and the USA), black studies can nonetheless help us more fully to get to grips with the plight of Palestinians, for their reality is also preceded by the 'survival' and the necropolitical existence of black people in America.[4] By this token, we might surmise that the necropolitical logic of antiblackness that was initiated in the plantations and perfected during slavery has become globalised coextensively with the globalisation of capital, meaning that when Mbembe suggests the 'Becoming-Black-of-the-World' (Mbembe 2017:7), he is referring to how the 'blackening' of populations – the rendering already dead of vast swathes of people – is indeed intensifying under a globalised neoliberal capitalist regime, a living death that is shared by indigenous peoples, but which is not born out of anti-Indigeneity so much as a kind of generalised antiblackness.[5]

While this detour into the work of Suleiman allows us to think once again about the 'whiteness' of Deleuze's perspective, the comparison between Suleiman and Keaton, especially in their differences (Keaton punches straight down; Suleiman queerly punches up) also helps us to see how even in his legacy, Keaton is demonstrably a white, or more pressingly an antiblack and anti-indigenous, filmmaker, redolent of a system of cinema that might as a whole be antiblack and anti-indigenous.[6] As we shall now see, this antiblack logic of Keaton's work is also made clear by Steve McQueen, who as mentioned turns to Keaton in his short experimental film *Deadpan*, which with his *Caribs' Leap* (UK, 2002) we shall consider presently as the final analytical gesture of this book.

As mentioned earlier, *Deadpan* restages the famous gag in *Steamboat Bill, Jr.* whereby the façade of a house collapses, threatening to crush a figure standing in its path – only for the building to drop in such a way that an open doorway falls over the figure, allowing them to survive. In *Steamboat Bill, Jr.*, this figure is of course Keaton, while in *Deadpan*, the figure is McQueen.

Potentially an example of 'divine intervention' (what a lucky escape!), the stunt is of course carefully planned in both instances – albeit that the calculations made for ensuring the survival of Keaton and McQueen alike could have been wrong, or various atmospheric and other conditions, such as a strong gust of wind, could have changed the outcome of events. That is, there is a still a considerable amount of risk involved in carrying out such a stunt. In this sense, there is perhaps some irony that in *Steamboat Bill, Jr.*, the event is supposed to take place during a cyclone. That is, the logic of controlling the environment is what makes the stunt work – even as the film itself is trying to suggest the uncontrollability of that environment as it brings down the house. As Fay points out, however, even 'natural' disasters are really the result of white humanity's meddling with the environment; they were/are, she says, 'often attributable to industry and war…"nature" was already a product of "culture"' (Fay 2018: 26), such that events like the Great Mississippi Flood of 1927 were a result of white human geo-engineering rather than simply evidence of nature at work independent of humans.

Fay does briefly turn her attention to *Deadpan* in her consideration of Keaton, and her analysis is astute when she notes various distinctions between Keaton's and McQueen's versions of the stunt. As follows:

> [w]hat is fortuitous in the narrative sequencing of Steamboat (the storm just happens to damage the house whose falling façade just happens to not kill [Keaton's character] Will) is arbitrary but inevitable in *Deadpan*. McQueen just stands there waiting for the fall. Using several cameras to capture the singular event, McQueen edits the footage so that we see the stunt several times from different angles over the course of just over four and a half minutes: as an installation, the entire sequence plays on a loop in its exhibition setting. As one critic [Andrew Gellatly] observes, McQueen remakes Keaton's gag into a 'compulsive' and 'compelling study of purgatory.' One wonders if this willing exposure to 'accidental' death – a suicide that is also a survival – distills the risks of living in modernist climates by absenting their sensational features. **(Fay 2018: 57-58)**

While Fay, via Gellatly, notes the 'purgatorial' aspects of the never-ending loop that the setting of the gallery installation creates, and while Fay unwittingly evokes a necropolitical logic when she suggests that suicide and survival amount to the same thing, conspicuously absent from Fay's analysis, and arguably from her analysis of 'cinema in the time of the Anthropocene' more generally, is an engagement with race.

And yet, when McQueen puts his own life on the line, such that for Thomas Mulcaire '[t]he author is alive and dead at the same time' (Mulcaire 1998: 13), there is a sense in which his status as *living dead* cannot but have resonances with his Blackness/his blackened identity. Indeed, as we see McQueen threatened over and over again with death, the suicidal impulse that is at work in the making of *Deadpan* makes of this film a 'terrorist cinema' that recalls the disempowered suicide bomber analysed above in relation to the work of Elia Suleiman, as well as the black 'revolutionary suicide' mentioned in Chapter 9.

Discussing *Caribs' Leap*, meanwhile, it is perhaps unsurprising that T.J. Demos sees the *interval* as being 'a structural condition' of McQueen's work in general (Demos 2005: 71). For on one of the two screens that comprise that installation, we see the sky at the place in Grenada, the ancestral home of McQueen's family, where in 1651 the island's last native Caribs reputedly leapt to their deaths rather than be subjected to European rule.[7] At various points in the looping film, we see bodies falling through the air/the frame, but never do we see them commence their jump or impact the water, meaning that they are quite literally suspended perpetually between life and death, much as McQueen himself is in *Deadpan*. For Demos, this makes of McQueen's films an example of Deleuzian cinema, where the interval is 'an essential condition of film' (Demos 2005: 71).

Demos is not unaware of the role that race plays in McQueen's work, suggesting even that it 'relates the visual signifiers of identity – of race and of gender – to the structural conditions of the projection, which enact a perpetual play between presence and absence, and oscillate about between belief in the filmic illusion and recognition of the space of exhibition' (Demos 2005: 70). Indeed, while Demos does not fully expand upon what he means here, we might interpret this as meaning that McQueen's work helps us to reflect upon how the medium of cinema, via its processes of projection and exhibition, is linked to race; that is, race is projected on to and exhibited by people as part of the 'epidermal schema' identified by Fanon and those critical race theorists who have followed him. However, Demos goes on to say that '[i]t's as if identity falls away from itself, exposed as mere appearance, posed in exteriority to itself, neither grasped by the stereotypical codes of race and gender, nor firmly positioned within historical traditions or cultural matrices' (Demos 2005: 71). That is, Demos seems to be suggesting that McQueen allows us to achieve a 'colour blind' position in which race and gender do not matter, since these have been exposed as matters of 'projection' and 'exhibition', and thus are not 'real' but simply cultural codes – or, if you will, metaphors.

While Demos is not wrong to consider McQueen's work as exposing the way in which race and gender are in effect constructs, with regard to *Deadpan* and *Caribs' Leap* alike, this 'colour blind' reading nonetheless has shortcomings. We might contend, for example, that in recreating the famous scene from *Steamboat Bill, Jr.*, McQueen is with *Deadpan* clearly positioning his work 'within historical traditions or cultural matrices', namely the history of cinema and its (raced and gendered) visual codes. However, while the metaphorical nature of Blackness and, with regard to *Caribs' Leap*, Indigeneity may be exposed in McQueen's work, McQueen also is certain to convey that even if 'only' a metaphor, it is a metaphor that nonetheless structures reality, and which is experienced on a corporeal level, especially by the artist's own black(ened) body – and those indigenous bodies that leapt to their deaths in Grenada in 1651. That is, the metaphoricity of race – it is a construct – is what allows race to be deniable for whites, such that they can claim to be colour blind (race 'falls away', supposedly exposed as 'mere appearance'). However, for the blackened and indigenous body, race is no(t just a) metaphor, since Blackness and Indigeneity are a lived experience. Or, more pertinently, Blackness and Indigeneity are a *dying* experience; they are lived, died, survived and died again – over and over, much like the loops of McQueen's installations.

Perhaps it is unsurprising, then, that David Marriott disagrees with Demos, suggesting that:

> [o]nly by conceiving the interval as a 'crisis' within representational meaning can one begin to see the fall [the fall of the house, the fall of the native bodies] as metaphor, and the chances are that this will be an entirely formal notion of crisis that is again representable, exposable, graspable. But the reference to the interval can also be misleading, for what McQueen is definitely not invoking is any 'vertigo of spacing' (to use the words of Deleuze, again cited by Demos), nor a sense of putting 'truth into crisis' by releasing the image from rational sequence. **(Marriott 2013: 209; see also Demos 2005: 73)**

That is, we do not wonder whether what we are seeing is true or false, a dream or reality, as might happen in a Deleuzian time-image. Unlike with a time-image, where the difficulty of parsing the oneiric from the representational might lead us to a state of wonder, for Marriott there is 'nothing *spiritualised* in *Deadpan*' (Marriott 2013: 216), and the cinema of the time-image is revealed in this way to 'fall into a racism in the full sense of the word' (Marriott 2013: 226). Marriott continues:

> [c]inematic temporality, whether in its early or modern form, has always grounded itself in narratives of race, so what may appear as flight into the virtual can only do so by making the past appear via the represented or articulated meanings of subjects who are less than human, less than shadows, and who, in their abjection, prove their nothingness, or nonexistence. Subjects, in brief, who are dead to the world precisely because they are already dead, and whose aliveness only makes us

aware of their being already dead, from which their petrified existence is indistinguishable. **(Marriott 2013: 226)**

Instead of a Deleuzian frame, then, Marriott, like Pisters, turns to Fanon to explain how the non-being that *Deadpan* and *Caribs' Leap* both depict – suspended between life and death – is inherently tied to Blackness and Indigeneity, such that McQueen's restaging of Keaton's stunt, as well as his restaging of the suicidal leap, functions not just as a regular *mise-en-abîme*, but as a placement in the depths (a *mise en abîme*) of the black and indigenous body that inevitably recalls both the Middle Passage and indigenous genocides – not virtual histories, but real abjections.[8] This gives us not a line of flight away from the world of capital, but a ver-tiginous (i.e. worm-like or tentacular) fall into the blackened world that is the enabling context for capital to emerge.

Edward Bacal and Alessandra Raengo alike note the stillness of McQueen in *Deadpan*, a stillness that gives to the film a palpable physicality. In the descriptive treatment of Bacal, McQueen is 'stoic' and 'oddly moving' (see Bacal 2013: 11), while in her more theoretical consideration Raengo argues that it is the stillness of McQueen's figure that leads critics (perhaps we can include Demos among their number) erroneously to believe that *Deadpan* is not, or has no clear meaning, about race. For her, however, McQueen's 'willed immobility, his performances of stasis and suspension' are precisely part of his racial critique (akin to the silence of Sycorax?), but this is missed because that same immobility resists 'the expectation of black motility as a conduit to legible blackness' (Raengo 2016: 198). Raengo uses the term motility to convey how 'black movement is so structurally mistaken for compulsion, "surplus liveness," or an innate overabundance of performativity and affectability' (Raengo 2016: 192). Stillness, then, demonstrates supreme control on McQueen's part – a stillness that again conveys a sort of living death, in that it is only by not moving (not living?) that the black McQueen demonstrates that he is alive (since as a black man, for him to be mobile/motile would only convey how Blackness is defined in the white imagination by/as a kind of uncontrolled/uncontrollable and 'animal' movement). It is by being *deadpan*, then, that McQueen affects us; but the machinic mask of stillness that he wears over his living face is not the source of laughter, as it might be for Keaton, but rather of a sort of horror, as we watch the building fall again and again.

Where Keaton shows the falling house once, McQueen repeats it *ad infinitum*. In effect, Keaton is rescued by narrative, thereby betraying Trahair's argument that narrative is merely coincidental in Keaton, who would otherwise prefer simply to have a series of gags. The drive towards narrative is, we might say, inscribed into whiteness, and perhaps therefore inscribed into the medium of cinema, even as cinema is and can be non-narrative (but only ever in a minor mode). McQueen, meanwhile, is trapped in the 'gag' forever, with narrative not coming to his rescue, with the plot never progressing past this spectacular stunt moment, and with there being no happy ending, let alone any other sort of resolution for him. The *oikos* may fall apart in *Steamboat Bill, Jr.*, but it will be restored. In *Deadpan*, there is no *oikos*, as the home is always falling; and while one might dream of a room of one's own or have what Robin D.G. Kelley might call a freedom dream (see Kelley 2002), *Deadpan* reveals that there is no such room or freedom except as a dream for the black body, condemned as it is to stillness, or an imposed black motility that in this instance would surely kill them (if McQueen did move, he would be dead).

*Deadpan* might thus be understood as showing how cinema for Blackness is a *deadpanopticon*, as death is rendered pan-present (*dead-pan*) in the era of globalised neoliberal capital. And it is perhaps significant that McQueen's film does not show in theatres but on a loop in a gallery, since cinema, driven as it is by whiteness, narrative, economy and antiblackness, cannot directly convey Blackness, even as it is built upon it. In this way, McQueen's film uses what we might call non-cinema to convey the non-being and the non-existence, or paraontology, of Blackness (for more on non-cinema as a concept, see Brown 2018, especially 113-136).[9]

However, in one last twist, perhaps we can gain something 'positive' from *Deadpan*, much as there might be black survival in the paraontic. In her analysis of Lurch's *Revisiting Sycorax*, Tiffany Lethabo King explains that since the sculpture is a mass of wire, Sycorax is therefore, unlike most statues, 'a figure that is porous and full of holes' (King 2019: 186). If Sycorax is a black hole, then it makes sense that she is full of holes; she is full of Blackness. The house in *Steamboat Bill, Jr.* also has a hole, very specifically the hole that falls over Keaton, thereby allowing him to survive. Not only does the image of the house falling thus stage Keaton being 'birthed' from a black hole, but it also suggests that Keaton-as-white is himself, once again, born from Blackness. McQueen, meanwhile, is not born from Blackness; he remains always suspended in the hole, passing in and out of it; he in this sense is (and is not) Blackness (which itself is not).

When read side by side, the two images remind us that the white house always has within it at least one black hole, if not more. That is, black holes are everywhere, much as Blackness is everywhere, indelible, unsettling (might we suggest that unlike the white Keaton, Chaplin's moustache, as well as, dare I say it, that of Adolf Hitler, is a black hole; Chaplin's is there perhaps because he recognises that he cannot and should not seek to destroy Blackness; Hitler's is there because, try as he might, he cannot destroy Blackness, with this difference clarifying how Hitler was a poor imitation of Chaplin). It is not, then, that the master's tools will or even need to dismantle the master's house. Rather, the master's house will crumble the master's tools, because the master's house is full of (black) holes; it is always already full of an indestructible Blackness. It, too, will die, and white Western modernity might try ceaselessly to build and to rebuild, or to have built and rebuilt, the White House. But as Persian poetess Forough Farrokhzad knows better than anyone through her consideration of a leper colony, *the house is in fact black* (Iran, 1962).

Returning to Keaton, his work functions as a means of demonstrating the whiteness of modernity, the whiteness of cinema (especially in its drive towards narrative as a primary form), the whiteness of economy, and the whiteness of ecology. If for Deleuze there is a 'black' interval between each frame of the cinematic image, and if for Deleuze the time-image shows us this 'structuring interval', or this 'intervallic darkness', then cinema, like the *oikos*/white house, like the economy and like ecology, is always on the verge of collapse. This is in some senses the ongoing exploitation of Blackness for the purposes of perpetuating the white world. Whiteness is built upon the threat of collapse, the weather, time, Blackness and the outside.

If Blackness is negative, then when inverted, there is as Marriott recognises a 'black potentiality of the time-image' (Marriott 2013: 231). This final 'recuperation' of Deleuze, though, runs against his concept of the line of flight (an idea taken from George Jackson) and in some senses against his idea of the virtual, since for Marriott, to 'figure time in its purity' can only be done if time is understood as 'the precarious chance and ruin of the subject in its activities and intentions' (Marriott 2013: 231). That is, there is in Blackness not a certain pessimism *per se* (although the inevitability of ruin might lead us to suspect so), but an acceptance of death, a living with death, a dying with life, a sur-vival that is otherwise alien to whiteness, not least because the latter is overly concerned not just with the eradication of death, the control of the weather and of time, but also with value and hierarchies, a perhaps inevitably 'vertical' form of thought for a genre of human so vertebrate as the white human. Brokeback, invertebrate, queer and black thought, like an octopus, fathoms the world beyond the human and otherwise. Tentacular rather than panoptic, embracing rather than trying to build over black holes and wormholes, this is an oceanic/os-eanic/tidalectic form of existence and thought, one that survives without air, breathing underwater, suspended in the white world between life and death, but certain, as the oceans will rise, to be humanity's future, just as humans emerged from the oceans in the long non-human past. The Anthropocene is (or has been) white, but the (Auto)Chthulucene will be (and already is) black and red, it is maroon. A close consideration of Buster Keaton's *The Navigator* can help us to navigate from the one era to the other, even as the film itself treads a way that aims to sustain whiteness in its supreme position, building that whiteness upon a structural antiblackness in which cinema also plays a key role. Crossing Keaton with strands of posthumanism and, more particularly, critical race studies (especially black and indigenous studies) helps us to draw out the potential for a maroon planetary future, even if the age of man, over-represented historically as white, is coming to an end.

# Chapter 20

# Apostasy or apocalypse

If Zakiyyah Iman Jackson writes that Blackness has been rendered plastic by white supremacy, becoming simultaneously human, superhuman and sub-human (or non-human), then my scholarly considerations of cinema might similarly suggest a plasticity to the medium. For in describing cinema in the digital age as successively a *supercinema* (Brown 2013) and a *non-cinema* (Brown 2018), while also acknowledging both as 'still' cinema, then I perhaps consider cinema equally to be plastic, perhaps even implicitly to be black, in the sense of being an other constructed to bring whiteness into being (see also Brown 2022). There is in my consideration of digital effects cinema ('supercinema') an unthinking whiteness that I hope to pick apart in other future work, while my consideration of low-budget digital filmmaking might have pushed further with its analysis of the role of race in 'non-cinema', seeking to avoid the pitfall of prescribing that filmmakers of colour and other 'minority' filmmakers cannot or should not make 'cinema' (whatever that is). Towards the end of a book on cephalopods and cinema, meanwhile, David H. Fleming and I begin to outline how the posthuman turn, the animal turn and the turn to objects in effect do not make any sense except as a means to preserve white supremacy unless they engage critically with race (see Brown and Fleming 2020: 265-266). *Navigating from the White Anthropocene to the Black Chthulucene* is, then, a step in that direction.

That being said, Herman Melville in *Benito Cereno*, a text that we encountered earlier, asks 'who ever heard of a white so far a renegade as to apostatize from his very species, almost, by leaguing in against it with negroes?' (Melville 2016: 86). Not only does Melville here claim whiteness as a species, thereby demonstrating that black people are not (perceived as) human, but he also demonstrates that whiteness is a religion, such that to go against it is betrayal, or apostasy. This is in keeping with Marquis Bey's argument that John Brown became through his abolitionist work an 'ex-white man', and that since 'man' assumes whiteness, then Brown in effect became an 'ex-man' (Bey 2021: 79).

For whites to apostastise from their white existence is perhaps impossible, although the aim here is not to run through ways in which my own white thinking and being come up constantly against my own unthinking antiblackness and anti-Indigeneity. As Isabelle Stengers points out, to be interesting is to be 'between', from the Latin *inter* and *esse* (see Stengers 2000: 94), meaning that it is not *interesting* for a white person to lament any perceived difficulty in addressing the antiblackness and anti-Indigeneity within themselves. Indeed, it is not interesting to lament one's own whiteness, which would simply and perversely be to lament power (while, conversely, it is precisely *interesting* that Olaudah Equiano should write his *Interesting Narrative*; see Equiano 2018). Fred Moten, in discussing Frantz Fanon, emphasises that 'the fact that there are whites who don't talk down to blacks is irrelevant for the study of the effects produced by whites who do' (Moten 2013: 761). Not only uninteresting, then, but also irrelevant (to celebrate attempts at breaking free from racism is both delusory and racist).

What is relevant, though, and the aim of this final chapter, is to remind the reader that our planet is dying. And what is killing our planet can be summed up as patriarchal capitalism, an endeavour that is overwhelmingly white in terms of its most powerful protagonists, and which certainly is born out of whiteness in terms of its most influential ethea. This whiteness in turn is built upon antiblackness, an antiblackness that after Achille Mbembe is becoming increasingly widespread, as (at least a metaphorical) Blackness (read: economic and other abjections) also grows, such that the disparities between peoples become unfathomable, and such that there is, with a tip of the hat to Steve McQueen, what we might call 'pan-death'. The plastic use of Blackness, as well as the plastic use of cinema, is matched by our everyday use of plastic as it is derived from fossil fuels: it is a weapon to construct whiteness by killing all other life both on land and in our oceans.

Nonetheless, the mutually *viscus* and intelligent forms of Blackness, Indigeneity and the octopus might give us clues regarding how to 'survive' this latest apocalypse. But this is not simply a question of whites stealing (again) from non-whites the techniques that the latter have developed in order to survive the earlier apocalypses that whites visited upon them, which in and of itself would suggest a refusal to acknowledge that it is whiteness that is driving the current planetary apocalypse itself. That is, it is not that whites alone must learn to survive the apocalypse that they otherwise create. Rather, it is that whites, in the face of apostasy or apocalypse, must choose at least the former, if not in some senses both. For, to reject whiteness (apostasy) will involve the death of whiteness and learning how to die (apocalypse); but this apostasy might apocalyptically lead to ecstasy, a movement away from 'standing aside' (apo-stasis) from whiteness, and, like an invertebrate that has no backbone, towards not standing at all (ex-stasis).

Frank B. Wilderson III asks us to admit that:

> the 'Negro' has been inviting Whites, as well as civil society's junior partners (for example, Palestinians, Native Americans, Latinx) to the dance of social death for hundreds of years, but few have wanted to learn the steps. They have been, and remain today (even in the most anti-racist movements, like anti-colonial insurgency) invested elsewhere. Black liberation, as a prospect, makes radicalism more dangerous to the US and the world. **(Wilderson 2020: 249-250)**

Perhaps those 'junior partners' have been dealing with versions of 'social death' of their own, a system of division and conquest that plays into the hands of hegemonic whiteness – meaning that from those many versions, or many peoples, there emerges only one order, one people (*e pluribus unum*). All the same, we must learn this *danse macabre*, even if it is no piece of cake(walk). Indeed, through this dance, or what Lisa Lowe (2015) might term the *intimacies of four continents*, the (white) human will come to an end, falling into the black hole from which it came. And yet hegemonic whiteness is cathected to its hegemony, to its whiteness, to life, because it has convinced itself and tries to convince the rest of the world that (white) life (life as whiteness/whiteness as life) is all that there is. It tries to tell us that there is only one white god ('Man'), in the process killing off other gods like Na Kika and Yemayá (hybrid cephalopods and trans* women of colour). Whiteness, in other words, must kill in order to live (whiteness as psychopathic). But here I say let that white 'god' die. Let the white house (*oikos*) fall down. No more economy, no more ecology. No more (narrative) cinema. Outside of space, outside of time, beyond the cinematic society, and outside of language, perhaps. Out, but happier for it, ecstatic even. Indeed, perhaps it is only after coming out that finally one is able (queerly) to love. Knowing love, black (w) holes offer only generation, love and 'sur-life'; there is nothing to fear, not even nothing itself.

# Endnotes

## Chapter 3

1. My thanks to Mila Zuo for suggesting this latter point. It is worth mentioning, too, that Native Americans were granted full US citizenship in 1924 (see Byrd 2011: 166), meaning that *The Navigator* potentially gives expression to anxieties not just about black migration, but also to the further 'dilution' of white supremacy that such an integration of indigenous peoples might provoke.

2. Cedric J. Robinson (2007: 336), drawing on Rhona J. Berenstein (1994), argues that the trope of black natives in the jungle and other locations, and who typically pursue the white heroine, begins in the early 1930s with films like *Ingagi* (William Campbell, USA, 1930) and *Trader Horn* (W.S. Van Dyke, USA, 1931) – even as *King Kong* is its most famous exemplar. Even taking into account how the book upon which *Trader Horn* is based was published in 1927 (Robinson 2007: 323-324), Keaton would seem with *The Navigator* to have been ahead of the curve in his backward depiction of black natives.

3. Such an animalisation of the black natives would not be anything new, and indeed it might already be perversely at work in the image of the newly-weds. For, in their discussion of J.L. Austin's consideration of marriage between a human and a monkey, Mel Y. Chen suggests that the union also contains a trace of racism in its 'intimations of sexual oddity with racial nonwhiteness and figural blackness' (Chen 2012: 14). Even as it is Rollo who 'apes' the newly-weds, there might well be a sense in which Keaton suggests that marriage between black humans is as absurd as marriage between animals. Notably, shortly after their discussion of 'congruences between animals and slaves' and 'colonial

animalisation' (Chen 2012: 98), Chen goes on to discuss the 'frighteningly indefinable and disallowable sexual practices' of 'multilimbed octopus sex' (Chen 2012: 99). It would seem that the octopus and Blackness are never far from each other.

## Chapter 4

1. Spillers notably proposes that '"gendering" takes place within the confines of the domestic, an essential metaphor that then spreads its tentacles for male and female subject[s] over a wider ground of human and social purposes' (Spillers 1987: 72). Spillers' invocation of tentacles seems opportune, even though she is suggesting that domesticity is (negatively) a tentacular monster, rather than seeing the tentacular as a release from, or an alternative to, such straight and straitened existence.

2. Although without reference to Agamben, Toni Morrison describes in an interview with Paul Gilroy how:

> [s]lavery broke the world in half, it broke it in every way. It broke Europe. It made them into something else, it made them slave masters, it made them crazy. You can't do that for hundreds of years and it not take a toll. They had to dehumanize, not just the slaves but themselves. They have had to reconstruct everything in order to make that system appear true. It made everything in World War II possible. It made World War I necessary. Racism is the word that we use to encompass all this. **(Morrison, quoted in Gilroy 1993: 178; see also Gilroy 1996: 221)**

Mapped back on to the philosophy of Agamben, it is not that World War II and the Holocaust led to the (normalisation of the) state of exception and the *homo sacer*; it is the prior *state of normality* whereby the black human is always already the exception that leads to World War II and the Holocaust. In this way, Agamben reproduces the 'normal exceptionalisation' of the black human in order to put forward his theory of a white state of exception.

## Chapter 5

1. While flesh rots before bone in the earth, this is not necessarily the case in the brine. Indeed, large blob-like creatures, known as globsters, occasionally wash up on terrestrial shores, and while historically numerous were reckoned to be the mythical *Octopus giganteus*, or giant octopus, it turns out that many (all?) such carcasses are in fact the flesh of other marine creatures, such as sperm whales, but now without any shape or form as a result of the decomposition (or perhaps just the filleting) of their bones (see Pierce et al 1995). That such otherwise unidentified or unidentifiable blobs were thought to be octopuses is of course telling, in that it demonstrates the way in which the octopus is linked with the unknown (if you don't know what it is, and it is weird and a bit scary, then let's assume it is an octopus!). Furthermore, as per Saidiya Hartman's invocation of slave corpses washed up from the ocean in the form of human-molluscs towards the end of this chapter, this link between unknown flesh and the octopus (which is indeed a mollusc) is also raced: black humans are in the white Western imagination themselves mere flesh, alien, boneless and soft. For a hypothetical consideration of how humans actually decompose at sea, the reader might consult Anderson and Bell (2016).

2. In *2001: A Space Odyssey* (Stanley Kubrick, UK/USA, 1968), a black monolith leads an ape to become intelligent. What marks the intelligent ape out from the others is not just tool usage, as it picks up a bone and attacks a conspecific, but the logic of the white bone itself. Indeed, as per Kubrick's famous match-cut of the bone with a space ship, the exploitation and then abandonment of this planet for the purpose of

conquering space suggests that all so-called 'intelligence' is part of a 'white boner' logic taken from an otherwise black intelligence that is then suppressed. Indeed, *2001* points to how the bone, even when inside the human body, is a tool, and that the logic of white Western modernity (or capitalism) is to turn bony human bodies into tools, in the process often reducing those humans to mere flesh and bone. In the case of the black human, they are considered not to have bones, since they are just flesh; that is, bones are imposed upon otherwise invertebrate black humans, especially via images from the white racist imaginary of the black native with a bone through their nose, only for those bones to be broken. Perhaps we can see an example of how this paradoxical ossuary logic works in Toni Cade Bambara's posthumous novel, *Those Bones Are Not My Child*, which reworks in a heart-rending fashion the way in which bones do not and cannot be considered a part of Blackness. Uttered twice in the novel, the words of the title are first spoken in the Prologue in the second person as Cade Bambara puts herself and the reader in the place of a mother being shown the remains of a child – as per the Atlanta child murders of the 1970s and 1980s upon which the novel is based (Cade Bambara 1999: 12). And then, after her eldest child Sonny has been found, albeit beaten, Marzala/Zala Spence recalls saying the same words about the remains of two boys found months earlier in a Quonset hut in Atlanta. Of particular note is that just before Zala has this flashback, she notices the 'Darth Vader laser sword' of her younger son Kofi in a mirror (see Cade Bambara 1991: 517). It is a complex image that is created, then, not least because *Star Wars* in itself is a text about filial recognition and which casts darkness (and the 'dark father' that is Darth Vader, voiced of course by James Earl Jones) in a stereotypical position of evil. But this interruption of a licensed product from a science-fiction film into the world of antiblack violence otherwise depicted in *Those Bones Are Not My Child*, especially at a moment when Sonny is in fact present, albeit heavily beaten, would seem to reinforce the associations between flesh and alienness – that Blackness is not of this (antiblack) world, even as Blackness is produced by this antiblack world. In other words, Blackness is invented by an antiblack world only to be destroyed by this antiblack world, just as Blackness is perceived as boneless, only for slavery to be used as a tool to give to black humans some sort of form, or a backbone, which in turn is then destroyed, or broken, rendering the black human once again invertebrate. It is a twisted logic, indeed.

To return to *2001*, I might add that white humanity's exploitative journey into the cosmos leads to the well-known Starchild image, whereby a human infant comes face to face with Planet Earth. This new cosmic consciousness involves the white human seeing the planet as if it were equally a child (the film's famous image sees the child and planet before each other as if face to face, equivalent). That is, having abandoned Earth, the white human only comes to realise that he should have looked after Earth as he did himself, and/ or as he might a child. Black and indigenous consciousness, however, knew this all along, and it might be noted that the Starchild is not drifting in space detached, but rather is inside a uterine sac. The image reminds us, then, that the future human will, like the human about to be born, need to be able to breathe in a liquid environment, a notion that only accrues in power as the oceans rise and we all face collectively a submarine existence (see also Brown 2021). Unsurprisingly, it is precisely the ability to breathe underwater that Detroit-based electronic-music pioneers Drexciya attribute to their afrofuturist creations, the Drexciyans, who are 'a marine species descended from "pregnant America-bound African slaves" thrown overboard "by the thousands during labour for being sick and disruptive cargo"' (Eshun 1998: 83; see also Weheliye 2014: 153; for some other Drexciya-inspired literature, see Rivers Solomon and colleagues' 2019 novella, *The Deep*). That is, a submarine Blackness does constitute the future of the world – but notably not the future of humanity, since the Drexciyans are not human. That is, humanity as white can only survive by becoming black (and/or indigenous), in the process giving up their whiteness and their humanity. Is this possible for the white human psyche, or will it only seek to steal from Blackness the very ability to survive that it cruelly forced Blackness to develop in the first place, thereby 'justifying', and in its psychotic mind necessitating, the perpetuation of the cruelty that it instantiated (for more on whiteness as psychosis, see Andrews 2016)?

While I suspect not, we can nonetheless surmise that white consciousness is simply an endeavour to force into existence and then to claim as its own/to steal a black consciousness, the very Blackness of which it will then immediately seek, unsuccessfully, to destroy. Indeed, as per Glissant and the other theorists evoked here, Blackness is indestructible – whereas whiteness reveals nothing more than its own fragility in its very quest to create an equally indestructible whiteness that is separate from Blackness. As well as wasting a planet and numerous black lives, then, we might conclude that whiteness – and the quest for an indestructible, pure white consciousness – is, quite literally, a waste of time (if, as we shall see, Blackness is outside of time, then whiteness involves the invention of time in order then to seek to get outside of time, a process that is, effectively, pure waste).

## Chapter 6

1. As Lovecraft's first Cthulhu story was published in *Weird Tales*, so has the term weird been used to define a Lovecraftian outlook, as per the work of China Miéville (2008), Graham

Harman (2012) and Mark Fisher (2016).

2.  Jackson elaborates further on this matter in her book-length study *Becoming Human: Matter and Meaning in an Antiblack World* (Jackson 2020). Meanwhile, similar arguments have been made using other terms by J. Kameron Carter and Sarah Jane Cervenak, who posit a 'black ether' as a 'fence-breaking, boundary-crossing, paratheological, paraontological, insovereign, paralegal, and parapossessive ambulation' (Carter and Cervenak 2016: 211), and by Marquis Bey, who similarly uses the term 'paraontological' to define 'a sort of originary impurity, which is no origin at all if origin is definitionally a pure, unperturbed beginning state. We [black folk] are and must be impure from the start' (see Bey 2021: 47; see also Chandler 2013). Paraontology is itself a concept discussed by Fred Moten, who indeed asks whether black people might 'choose – while also choosing not to assume the barrenness of – the paraontic field'; that is, perhaps outside of what is (in the para-ontic), we might yet find new dimensions of existence (see Moten 2013: 765).

3.  Notably, C.L.R. James reckons only Captain Ahab from *Moby Dick* as 'a new type of human being' in the literature of Herman Melville. 'Bartleby is not,' he succinctly adds. 'Still less is Babo,' the leader of the slave revolt in *Benito Cereno* (1855), whom we shall encounter in Chapter 13. 'The Negro slaves and their leaders are shown to be human', writes James of the latter, a line of thought that might contradict the argument that black people are excluded from humanity. However, James' critique is not of Babo as a creation so much as of Melville as a creator; for, Melville was in James' opinion slipping into a kind of conservatism post-*Moby Dick*, having 'lost his vision of the future'. That is, Melville could tell not new stories but stories we have heard 'ten thousand' times before, being unable to penetrate and thus accurately to describe 'existing reality', but instead repeating the

clichés used to cloak it. In relation to *Benito Cereno*, then, Melville could not see through antiblackness to critique it, but instead only repeated it. And in relation to *Bartleby, the Scrivener* (1853), perhaps it is James who fails to see how his formlessness does make of him an original creation/a new type of human being (see James 1985: 119).

4. If Roderick A. Ferguson notes the migration of black folk in the 1920s, Kadji Amin notes a trend during the same decade of skin grafts from chimpanzee testicular matter into human testicles in a bid to enhance virility. Amin importantly notes the racialised aspects of these practices, in that apes and Blackness were often conflated in the white popular imagination, while also suggesting that there is a 'plasticity' at work in these transhuman operations, which also embody a plastic and trans* logic. In particular, Amin writes at one point that there was 'a veritable hunger for the plasticity housed in the sex glands of the other, a cannibalistic and erotic hunger that sought to consume, incorporate, and metabolize that other in order to restore the (sexual) vitality of the white self' (Amin 2020: 57). Perhaps it goes without saying that Amin could be describing Rollo's typically white relationship with Blackness, whereby he consumes the black other in order to assert his (sexual) vitality, even as he projects cannibalism on to the black islanders.

## Chapter 7

1. A further link between blackness and California can be found, perhaps surprisingly, in the medieval French text *La chanson de Roland/The Song of Roland*, where Charlemagne mourns his nephew, the titular Roland, who supposedly conquered many lands for his uncle, including *cil d'Affrike e cil de Califerne* ('those of Africa and those of Califerne/ California'; see Anonymous 2016: 97). Unlikely, of course, to be the California where Keaton made the majority of *The*

*Navigator*, the resonance nonetheless bears a mention – not least because *The Navigator*, through its hero's conquest of 'Africans' off the coast of California, might thus be thought of as *La chanson de Rollo*.

2. 'Asleep in the Deep' has further possible links with Blackness when we consider that it is a song sung by Goofy in Disney's *Clock Cleaners* (Ben Sharpsteeen, USA, 1937). Art Babbitt, who created Goofy, said in a memo in 1934 that the character is:

> a composite of an everlasting optimist, a gullible Good Samaritan, a half-wit, a shiftless, good-natured colored boy and a hick...His brain is rather vapoury. He laughs at his own jokes, because he can't understand any others. He is very courteous and apologetic and his faux pas embarrass him, but he tries to laugh off his errors. He talks to himself because it is easier for him to know what he is thinking if he hears it first. **(quoted in Hasted 1996)**

In other words, if Goofy is a 'dumb colored boy', and if *A Goofy Movie* (Kevin Lima, USA/Australia/France/Canada, 1995) is 'the Blackest Disney movie of all time' (see Calhoun 2015; Jones 2019), then his singing of 'Asleep in the Deep' in *Clock Cleaners* would suggest that Goofy also is haunted by the Middle Passage. Significantly enough, not only is *Clock Cleaners* about the violent labour that goes into keeping time, as Mickey Mouse, Donald Duck and Goofy all three suffer various knocks and scrapes as they endeavour to clean a clock, but Goofy in particular gets deafened when first a figure of a man with a scythe and then a replica of the Statue of Liberty knock loudly against a bell, the inside of which Goofy is cleaning, as the clock strikes 4pm. That a 'black' Goofy in effect gets hit by the Statue of Liberty is suggestive of the outsider status of black people in American society, even as black labour is what allows that society to 'run like clockwork'. That Keaton's *Steamboat Bill, Jr.* (Chas F. Reisner, USA, 1928) inspired Disney's *Steamboat Willie* (Ub Iwerks, USA, 1928) perhaps only further cements the shared (white supremacist) worldview of the two.

## Chapter 8

1. There is some uncertainty as to whether Equiano actually lived through the Middle Passage. As Brycchan Carey notes, 'at one point in his life, Equiano told people he was born in Carolina', meaning that he might not have gone to America from Africa, as he reports in *The Interesting Narrative*. Nonetheless, as Carey goes on to suggest, 'Equiano's outstanding contribution to the cause of freedom should never be doubted' (Carey 2018: xxii). Hortense J. Spillers, who herself adopts Equiano's narrative as a key text in helping her to make the distinction between body and flesh, does not explicitly engage with doubts surrounding the veracity of *The Interesting Narrative*. However, when Spillers discusses how one might deny the 'inveterate obscene blindness' of slave traders, in that they were not even 'curious about this "cargo" that bled, packed like so many live sardines among the immovable objects', she does go on to assert that 'we know it happened' (Spillers 1987: 70). Likewise, even if Equiano never made the Middle Passage (making of his work an example of *the powers of the false*?), it happened, and the graphs of how its human 'cargo' was packed, as per the cargo ship *Brooks* that both Spillers (1987: 73) and Simone Browne (2015: 46ff) discuss, are real.

2. If Betsy is not Rollo's 'ball and chain', then she is at least his mate – with 'mate' of course being a nautical term that suggests a sexualised link between those who travel together at sea, which is not to mention clichés of homosexuality among sailors, as made most famous by the fashion designs of Jean Paul Gaultier and the Village People's camp classic

'In the Navy' (1979), which features the great line 'what am I gonna do in a submarine?', and which, perhaps uncoincidentally, appears on their *Go West* album, itself a wry celebration of the myth of American Manifest Destiny. *Go West* (Buster Keaton, USA, 1925) is itself the title of one of Keaton's subsequent films to *The Navigator*, telling as it does the story of a cowboy, Friendless (Keaton), who ends up in a queer relationship with a cow (Brown Eyes). Making kin with non-human species is perhaps always queer.

Meanwhile, Omise'eke Natasha Tinsley points out that in Suriname, the Creole term *mati*, which is derived from mate/shipmate, came to mean 'she who survived the Middle Passage with me' (Tinsley 2008: 192). That is, in its nautical tale of white (ship)mating, *The Navigator* cannot but queerly evoke the founding tragedy of white, Western modernity, something that *Go West* perhaps also attempts to do.

For her part, L.H. Stallings draws upon the germinal work of Gloria Wekker (2006) to point out that '*mati* work', whereby (typically) working-class women undertake sexual relationships with both male and female partners, 'rebuffs capitalist understandings of sexual orientation, labor, and expression' (Stallings 2015: 16), not least because *mati* work is often a life choice taken in contradistinction to heterosexual marriage. As Tiffany Lethabo King clarifies, *mati* work, 'which can take the form of same-sex, opposite-sex erotics and transactional sex...happen[s] in the context of how survival is intimately tethered to the erotic in postcolonial conditions of poverty' (King 2019: 168). Where the white, bourgeois Rollo finds a heteronormative and white (ship) mate, there is in the post-Middle Passage reality of the Americas scope for non-normative, queer and anti-capitalist relations/relationships/matings – black matings that are unrecognisable to white Western modernity (which often mistakes *mati* work for 'straight' prostitution, rather than, as per Stallings, something empowering and *funky*; many thanks to Jamie Ann Rogers for helping me to clarify this point).

3. Rex Ingram, the Irish-American director of *Mare Nostrum*, is not to be confused with Rex Ingram, the African-American actor who appeared in such films as *The Thief of Bagdad* (Michael Powell, Ludwig Berger and Tim Whelan, UK/USA, 1940) and *Sahara* (Zoltán Korda, USA, 1943).

4. Given that an octopus has eight arms, and thus is exceptional at holding, dare we suggest that to find paraontological survival 'in the hold' à la Harney and Moten is in some senses also to find a paraontological survival in the embrace of the cephalopod?

5. Even sticking just to submarines (i.e. without reverting to ships and boats), we might note that when Frantz Fanon critiques the treatment of black folk in cinema, one of the prime examples that he draws upon is *Crash Dive* (Archie Mayo, USA, 1943), the French title of which, *Requins d'acier* (literally 'steel sharks'), is left untranslated in various versions of *Black Skin, White Masks*. Fanon fumes at how the 'Negro crewman' in that film (unnamed by Fanon, but called Oliver Cromwell Jones, a telling name in that it recalls not just the English republican Oliver Cromwell, but also the Trinidadian radical black ideologue Oliver Cromwell Cox, with Jones being played in the film by Ben Carter) is dubbed in such a way as to be:

> all *n[*****]*, walking backward, shaking at the slightest irritation on the part of a petty officer; ultimately he was killed in the course of the voyage. Yet I am convinced that the original dialogue did not resort to the same means of expression. And, even if it did, I can see no reason why, in a democratic France that includes sixty million citizens of color, dubbing must repeat every stupidity that crosses

the ocean. It is because the Negro has to be shown in a certain way...the black man is supposed to be a good n[*****]. **(Fanon 2008: 22; original emphasis)**

While Fanon makes room for the English-language version of the film being less overtly racist, John Nickel (2004) names *Crash Dive* (as well as *Sahara*, mentioned in Note 3 above) as among a slew of films from the 1940s through to the 1960s that aimed to 'promote racial tolerance', and yet various of which saw the black characters disabled over the course of the film. However, what both Nickel and Fanon fail to mention, together with David Marriott, who in his extended essay, 'Waiting to Fall', also engages with this passage from *Black Skin, White Masks*, is the role that the submarine, as a surveillance technology that helps to 'grammatize' human behaviour, plays in producing the controlled black character that irritates Fanon so much. Here, the submarine literally places Jones in 'the abyss', or what Marriott also refers to as 'being stranded *en abŷme*' [sic.] (Marriott 2013: 224). If, finally, Deane fails to make the connection between surveillance, race and the war on terror, Marriott draws out precisely these connections in his excellent *Haunted Life: Visual Culture and Black Modernity* (Marriott 2007), as does Jasbir K. Puar in her *Terrorist Assemblages: Homonationalism in Queer Times* (2007), a text that we shall encounter in due course.

6. For a description of *By Right of Birth*, see Cedric J. Robinson (2007: 236).

## Chapter 9

1. Looking further beyond the USA, we might note that in regions like Putumayo, which straddles modern-day Brazil, Colombia and Peru, indigenous peoples were very much forced into slavery, especially by the Anglo-Peruvian Amazon Rubber Co., meaning that slavery is not just limited

to black people in the Americas, even as it was nonetheless racialised, and racialised specifically via antiblackness in the USA. Rollo's adventures in the Pacific bear little resemblance to those of British-Irishman Roger Casement in Putumayo; where the latter was moved to anti-colonial action by the cruelty that he saw, the former merely enacts the white colonialist mindset through his elimination of the native.

2. Sylvia Wynter reminds us that 'maroon' is a term 'derived originally from the Spanish word *cimarrón*: that is, the non-tamed, nondomesticated animal' (Wynter 1989: 638). Albeit that here I am claiming maroon as a colour, we might also contend that in reclaiming animality in a positive sense, a case could be made for the red, black and maroon also to be at work in that most nondomesticated and nondomesticable animal, the alien, colour-changing octopus.

   Meanwhile, Frank B. Wilderson III takes to task an interracial group with whom he does some work in Copenhagen called Marronage precisely for not being 'exclusively Black' (Wilderson 2020: 166). In the spirit of Lisa Lowe, cited above, the aim here is not to elide difference and thus to perpetuate antiblackness; antiblackness is not the same as anti-Indigeneity, but the two are tools for creating and perpetuating a white world. As Wilderson is not against solidarity (Wilderson 2020: 170), so do I hope that the conceptual maroonage being proposed here is not misguided. I will be honoured to have my own conceptual shortcomings corrected in due course.

3. As Rollo would in principle be bound for his honeymoon in Honolulu, so does the island that he reaches in *The Navigator* come in some senses to stand in for Hawai'i, which had been an annexed territory of the USA since 1898, but which would only become a recognised state in 1959. At the time of the making of *The Navigator*, Hawai'i was becoming an increasingly popular tourist destination, thanks in particular

to the Matson Navigation Company, which in the mid-1920s sought to make of 'Waikīkī an upper-class resort and residential community' (Skwiot 2010: 103). Furthermore, in the year that *The Navigator* was made (1924), 'the first English-standard school system opened in Honolulu' (Skwiot 2010: 119). In this way, tourism, including honeymoon tourism, to places like Oahu works alongside (re-)education to play a key role in settler colonialism (see also Wilderson 2010: 207). Indeed, as Christine Skwiot reports:

> [t]he Waik īk ī *Beach reclamation project opened fourteen hundred acres for development, a broad swath of it for an exclusive recreational and residential enclave. The three-mile Ala Wai Canal built to drain Waik īk ī and keep it dry reached completion in 1924. Building it destroyed Hawaiian fish ponds, temples, and dwellings, archaeological remains of which date to 1100 c.e., and erased from memory the centuries when Waik īk ī was shared by ordinary and chiefly Hawaiians, long before ali'i became royals.* **(Skwiot 2010: 95)**

The creation of Waik īk ī as a tourist destination thus leads to '[m]ultistory hotels disgorg[ing] over six million tourists a year onto stunningly beautiful (and easily polluted) beaches, closing off access to locals' (Trask 1999: 2-3). Creating another link between tourism and clearing, but this time of arrivants conflated with indigenes, M. NourbeSe Philip similarly describes the offensively named and offensively priced *Plantation Beach Villas* in Tobago as follows: 'the owners... are planting bushes around the swimming pool because they "don't want the *natives*" – read Black people – "looking at the people swimming." Read white people swimming' (Philip 1997: 170). Rollo and Betsy are just the advance party that will see the island in *The Navigator*, like their would-be destination Oahu, cleared for white tourists to enjoy.

Furthermore, Keaton/Rollo might in some senses be understood as inspired by Mark Twain, who in his *Letters from Hawai'i* (1866) imagines himself as Captain James Cook, who first sighted Oahu in 1778, before being slain there by a native the next year. Jodi A. Byrd sees Twain's text as the inauguration of 'the touristic fascinations and nationalistic narrative that link the Pacific sea of islands to Atlantic imperial sites across an intervening continent that is itself rhizome, oceanic. Cook's surname, then, gives rise to the cannibalistic fetish the Western mind evokes when it thinks of Pacific indigenous worlds' (Byrd 2011: 22), a cannibalistic fetish that is clearly expressed in *The Navigator*.

Given that Hawai'i would become 'home to the largest portage of nuclear-fuelled ships and submarines in the world' (Trask 2004: 12), we might go further and propose that it seems only apt that a submarine is already there in Keaton and Crisp's film. Furthermore, nuclear testing in and around the Pacific islands has not just involved historically the development of white Western (and destructive) science, but it has also functioned as a continuation of the clearing process, and the extermination of natives via other means – above and beyond the destruction of the natural world that Jennifer Fay attributes to such nuclear testing (see Fay 2018: 59-96). With this in mind, Haunani-Kay Trask notes not just that cancer is widespread among inhabitants of the Marshall Islands, a key historical nuclear testing site, but also that '[t]hey have one of the highest rates of severely deformed children, including "jellyfish babies" who have no heads, arms, legs, or human shape. Native women from these islands have given birth to babies they describe as "octopuses"' (Trask 2004: 12). Without wishing unduly to conflate native Hawai'ians (Kanaka Maoli) with Marshall Islanders with continental Native Americans (which themselves span 574 legally recognised, but distinct tribes; for more on this issue, see Byrd 2011: 158-165), might we nonetheless query that mutant indigenous children are in fact related to the black human-molluscs who can breathe underwater and whom we identified earlier, suggesting that the inhabitants of the maroon shoal are indeed a combination of the red and the black? For more on the links between radiation as an Anthropocene technology at work in and against Pacific islands, see DeLoughrey 2019: 63-97).

4. In relation to the concept of land, we might make mention of *terra nullius*, which Glen Sean Coulthard describes as 'the racist legal fiction that declared Indigenous peoples too "primitive" to bear rights to land and sovereignty when they first encountered European powers in the continent, thus rendering their territories legally "empty" and therefore open for colonial settlement and development' (Coulthard 2014: 175). As Byrd clarifies, 'colonialism...enters lands already inhabited by peoples with their own laws, customs, languages, and orderings of the world; declares said lands "uninhabited"; and then proceeds to establish another alien world as the dominant order' (Byrd 2011: 64). By rendering the indigenous population nobody/*nullius*, it would seem that there is always an annihilation of the body in (settler) colonialism, while one need look no further than the infamous exhortation to 'exterminate all the brutes' from Joseph Conrad's *Heart of Darkness* (1899) to understand that elimination was key to colonialism in Africa, and that this logic extended into the Middle Passage. *Exterminate All the Brutes* and *Terra Nullius* are notably both titles of books by Sven Lindqvist (2007a; 2007b), with the former being the basis for Raoul Peck's mini-series of the same name (USA, 2021). Settler colonialism and racialisation would appear to be intimately linked, even as we must acknowledge their subtle distinctions.

5. Dare we say, as we move towards critiques of Henri Bergson, Gilles Deleuze and others in the chapters to follow, that if

the island and, by extension, the maroon shoal, allows us to think beyond the continent, then maroon philosophy offers a way to open up new dimensions beyond 'continental philosophy'? That is, do Black and Indigenous studies, or critical race theory more broadly defined, provide us with the next wormhole through which thought can and will travel?

## Chapter 10

1. While these uses of the term black hole might seem metaphorical, they do reflect a physical reality, in that 'real' black holes generate new stars. That is, across the multiverse, light/whiteness is generated from blackness. For a brief introduction to this, see Urdaneta (2019).

2. Another proponent of the black (w)hole concept is Samantha N. Sheppard, who applies it to discuss the 'absent-present history of Black female athletic practices, leagues, and teams, including the places and communities where her abilities were taught, learned and honed' (Sheppard 2020: 109). Interestingly, Sheppard develops this as part of her consideration of *Sporting Blackness*, which title to her monograph suggests that Blackness is a kind of epidermal clothing (one 'sports' Blackness as one might sport a jacket) – thereby suggesting that one is not black so much as *blackened*, as Zakiyyah Iman Jackson might put it (see Jackson 2020). Furthermore, in his consideration of manhunts, philosopher Grégoire Chamayou discusses how certain humans, known as helots, were dressed up in (or sported) a dog-skin cap in order to be marked as prey, while hunters wore wolf skins (see Chamayou 2012: 9) – before going on to discuss how modernity is built upon the hunting by white humans of non-white humans in various different ways, including hunting those with black skins (see Chamayou 2012: 43-56). If this is the case, then we might understand that sport as

a whole is the sporting of skins in order for some (white) humans to hunt (non-white) others, a practice that continues to this day in the sense that, as Orlando Patterson points out, sports remain a realm where human bodies are bought and sold to the highest bidder (see Patterson 1982: 25-26). As a result, sport also plays a role in the construction of a white, Western modernity, especially when considered as a history of blood sports involving manhunts. That is, as hunting for Chamayou involves in some respects the invention of the animal for the purposes of being able to hunt fellow humans *as if they were animals* (i.e. as if they were not human), then so are sports historically a means to cast certain human beings into a 'blackened' and non-human realm.

By this token, the history of manhunt films, from *The Most Dangerous Game* (Irving Pichel and Ernest B. Schoedsack, USA, 1932) through to *The Hunt* (Craig Zobel, USA, 2020) might be read through the lens of race. The former film might especially be noteworthy because it was of course made by the same team (Schoedsack and Cooper), as well as at the same time and on the same sets, as *King Kong*, a film so incisively deconstructed along racial lines by James Snead, as mentioned. What is more, the film also features Noble Johnson in a key role as 'savage' mute Cossack servant Ivan, one of several non-white actors playing henchmen in the film (others include Steve Clemente, credited as Steven Clemento, and an unnamed black actor in the role of Ahmed). While there is much to say about the film, this will have to await for another occasion, although in its depiction of a Russian dressed in black (Leslie Banks) hunting a white American dressed in white (Joel McCrea), with a white woman as the stake of the hunt, it seems clear that *The Most Dangerous Game* projects a white logic of manhunting on to a non-white/ blackened/foreign set of characters. In being set on a Pacific island seemingly emptied of natives, one could even read the film as talking to *The Navigator* some years later, after the natives have been slaughtered.

Meanwhile, Ernest R. Dickerson's *Surviving the Game* (USA, 1994) perhaps makes the racial logic of cinematic manhunts most clear, since Ice T's Jack Mason is the target of the hunters, led by Thomas Burns, played by Rutger Hauer. What is of particular note about Dickerson's film is that T is made at times in his dreadlock hairstyle to resemble the titular monster in John McTiernan's 'classic' vehicle for Arnold Schwarzenegger, *Predator* (USA, 1987). As that film is also about hunting, in that aliens come to Earth to hunt humans as prey, then so, too, does Dickerson's riff on McTiernan reveal the implied racialised logic at work in the Schwarzenegger movie – except that *Predator*, like *The Most Dangerous Game*, simply reverses roles and has the white man hunted, a projection of what Chamayou charts as the white man's own propensity to hunt black humans for sport. Intriguingly, Schwarzenegger (whose name means 'black ridge') only manages to defeat the Predator in McTiernan's film when he 'blacks up' by covering his face in mud, such that he cannot be seen by the alien's thermal surveillance cameras. A clear irony emerges here when we compare der Arnold mudding up with Keaton doing the same in *Neighbors*. For while *Neighbors* sees Keaton immediately arrested for being black, thereby highlighting the state/ police surveillance of black people, in *Predator* Arnie evades surveillance by a 'black' Predator by himself blacking up. The stuff of pure fantasy – for the ultimate hard-bodied white man, who expresses *e pluribus unum* in his title as Mr Universe (as opposed to multiverse), gets to become black in order to defeat a black enemy. Or perhaps, more accurately, this story is the stuff of pure reality...

3. The killing by cannon of the black native of course anticipates a similar firing of a cannon in *The General* (Clyde Bruckman

and Buster Keaton, USA, 1926). Notably, the cannonball in *The General* hits another train (see Trahair 2002: 584). In *The Navigator*, meanwhile, the cannonball hits a black native, suggesting an odd (queer?) equivalence between train and native. For the purposes of the present argument, the resonance would suggest Keaton's view of Blackness as a technology, or perhaps even a tool of death. Maybe Keaton seeks even to 'can(n)onise' himself and/or whiteness by destroying Blackness.

## Chapter 11

1. Jack Halberstam suggests that the asterisk in trans* 'modifies the meaning of transitivity by refusing to situate transition in relation to a destination, a final form, a specific shape, or an established configuration of desire and identity' (see Halberstam 2018: 4). In other words, trans* also takes on the plasticity or paraontological status that has been used to describe Blackness, with Claire Colebrook defining trans through transitivity, or 'a not-yet differentiated singularity from *which* distinct genders, race[s], species, sexes, and sexualities are generated in a form of relative stability' (Colebrook 2015: 228; also quoted in Snorton 2017: 5). Talia Mae Bettcher, however, queries the effectiveness of the asterisked trans* as an 'umbrella term for *transgender*', even though it seeks to get away from 'binary-identified trans people' and more fully to include 'gender-nonbinary, genderqueer, gender fluid, and agender people'. As Bettcher says, the term may be short-lived since 'it doesn't do the work needed to really have nonbinary people included (that is, the problem that afflicted *transgender* similarly afflicts *trans**). Another concern is that it is not accessible to and understandable by people who are not already deeply familiar with the intricacies of trans/trans* politics' (Bettcher 2019: 664). Acknowledging that this may be the case, I

nonetheless follow Hayward in using the term.

2. Harriet Jacobs famously hid in a 'loophole of retreat' for 7 years in her journey towards escaping slavery (see Jacobs 2015). As Katherine McKittrick points out, the 'loophole' is also a 'dark hole', perhaps even a black hole as well as a wormhole, in the sense that upon emerging from it, Jacobs entered into a new reality, freedom (see McKittrick 2006: 41). Notably, Jonathan Beller describes Jacobs' experience inside the loophole/wormhole as akin to being inside a camera obscura, since Jacobs observed from there life on the plantation of James Norcom (referred to in *Incidents in the Life of a Slave Girl* as Dr Flint). More than this, he says that '[s]he lives the life of the negative' (Beller 2018: 101), thereby highlighting the associations between negativity and Blackness.

3. In *Disclosure: Trans Lives on Screen* (Sam Feder, USA, 2020), Laverne Cox describes how on the New York subway she was laughed at for her appearance as a trans woman. The moment recalls Frantz Fanon's famous "Look, a Negro!" scene, which we shall discuss in more detail in Chapter 14. The moment thus serves to elide Blackness and trans-ness, with both emerging as threatening to white heteronormativity. Furthermore, while in Fanon the interpellation is driven by fear, the role of laughter in Cox's experience suggests added layers of complexity. If, as we shall see, Henri Bergson finds the black face funny because it looks like it is dirty (?!), then the black trans face – if it is recognised as such – is in the white imagination also 'fake'. That is, if Bergson's theory of laughter relies on the machinic (which here I am characterising as 'fake') being encrusted on to the 'living', then the racism that Bergson expresses in finding the black face funny would suggest the inadmissibility of the black and the trans to white heteronormativity. Small wonder, then, that lethal violence is visited upon both populations,

especially as they intersect; or, as Bettcher argues, the vital philosophical engagement with trans-ness should not rest upon how trans existence complicates or elucidates our understanding of what is a man or what is a woman, but rather trans philosophy should answer the question: '[w]hy do people want to kill us?' (Bettcher 2019: 657). The answer, it would seem, is because hegemonic whiteness and those who embody it (regardless of their skin colour) structurally have to.

What is more, the white heteronormative reaction of laughter towards the black trans woman reveals the constructed nature of all genders and races, perhaps especially the normative/white ones, since the trans person demonstrates that these are not fixed in their being, with the black trans woman specifically demonstrating that whiteness reaffirms heteronormative and binaristic sexes, while Blackness inherently challenges them all. This can be seen in the much-studied history of figures like Saartjie Baartman/the Hottentot Venus, whose body was understood to defy the binaristic white categories of gender, meaning that to be non-white meant also to fall outside of the male/female dichotomy. Should we believe that this is all ancient history, then we might look at the continuing controversy surrounding an athlete like Caster Semenya and realise that history continues to repeat itself, even if Tavia Nyongo'o is also wary of direct comparisons between Semenya and Baartman (see Nyongo'o 2010). What we might productively glean from this, though, is that all faces are fake; and deriding certain faces/fakes for their colour and/or non-binaristic gender is thus not a question of the disturbance of a 'natural' order that does not in reality exist, but rather a matter of *power*, which is established precisely through the making-natural of a particular conception of reality, such that said conception of reality is accepted as the only one possible. This ethos of making-exclusively-real we might summarise in shorthand as *e pluribus unum*, which of course is the founding ethos of the USA. For more specifically on Baartman, see, for example, Ferguson (2004: 9-10) and Jackson (2019).

## Chapter 12

1. The most clear expression of cinema as a wormhole in Keaton's work is the celebrated sequence in *Sherlock, Jr.* (Buster Keaton, USA, 1924), where Keaton's protagonist, who works as a movie projectionist, dreams while asleep on the job that his love interest is in the movie that he is projecting. Keaton's character enters into the screen and tries to intervene in the story, only for the film on the screen to keep cutting, meaning that Keaton also experiences various pratfalls, like falling from a bench, nearly falling from a cliff, finding himself with a group of tigers and so on. The moment surely is ingenious and one of the finest commentaries on the way in which cinema is akin to a dream (the famous 'dream screen' analogy). That said, for Keaton to signal these transitions as clearly a dream arguably undermines their radically subversive potential. Furthermore, it is a shame that the film projected by the protagonist likely does not really feature the succession of almost random images that allow for Keaton's character to progress into ever-more-dangerous situations, not least because these images do not feature narrative elements such as characters. Were this succession of often empty landscapes the film being projected, then truly a subversion of cinema's confinement within narrative might take place, and truly would a wormhole cinema be suggested. However, that in *Sherlock, Jr.* the entangled nature of the multiverse is a dream does suggest not that cinema haunts our dreams, but rather that the universal (rather than multiversal) logic of cinema shapes our (perception of) reality. Had Keaton more explicitly exposed this, rather

than merely implied it, then *Sherlock, Jr.*, already a 'classic' of some grandeur, might yet have become literally *timeless*.

2. Beyond the scope of this study, I should like all the same to point out how the links between Irish and African-American identities might also be linked through the concept of the wake, as expressed in James Joyce's monumental *Finnegans Wake* (1939) and Christina Sharpe's *In the Wake* (2016). Something also to explore elsewhere would be the links between Fred Moten's conception of *mu* (as in mu-sic), which involves 'a circling or spiralling or ringing, this roundness or rondo linking beginning and end' (Moten 2013: 746), just as Finnegan will also always begin again. I wonder that Keaton might yet also play a role in such considerations of race, Irishness, cinema, surveillance and other themes that are raised here thanks to his star turn in Samuel Beckett's *Film* (Samuel Beckett and Alan Schneider, USA, 1965).

## Chapter 13

1. In *The Paleface*, Keaton plays a butterfly collector who wanders on to the territory of a Native American tribe whose lands have been fraudulently signed over to an oil company. Angry at the loss of their land, they imprison him, but somewhat incompetently, in that Keaton simply escapes from them at will. That is, the Native Americans are characterised as naïve and stupid, especially when they make Keaton their chief after he uses asbestos in order not to burn in a fire – which they take as a miracle. Even though the film would see Keaton's character demonstrate sympathy for the indigenous people (in keeping with the afore-mentioned claim by Keaton's sister that he was descended from Native Americans), he is of course shown to be far smarter than they are, while also having a seemingly limitless libido for their women. Indeed, at the film's climax, when Keaton's character has by chance

returned to the 'Indians' the deed to their land, they allow him to take a bride (played in brownface by Virginia Fox). Keaton leans in to kiss her and the film cuts to a title card: two years later. However, instead of seeing little brown children running about, Keaton is still kissing the woman. On one level a funny gag, in that our expectations for a reproductive coupling are subverted, the cut simultaneously suggests Keaton's desire for the Indian woman to be much more libidinal than procreative, which in turn pushes the attraction for her outside of heteronormativity. Maybe some interracial queerness is no bad thing; but *The Paleface* might also suggest that Keaton treats the Native woman as a fuck object rather than as a human partner.

2. If cinema is about the construction of whiteness, or the pale face, then does this mean that cinema constructs a pale-ontology? Can this pale-ontology be linked to the study of the fossils (paleontology) that the white world consumes in order to dominate, and ultimately to destroy, the planetary environment?

   We might also note that the Pale was a term applied to portions of Ireland occupied by the English as early as the twelfth century. To be 'beyond the Pale', then, meant to be 'beyond the Pale of English authority' (Fuchs 1997: 48) – or beyond 'pale'/white English authority, especially if the Irish were not at this point in time considered exactly white, as discussed earlier. Such a racialised understanding of the term 'pale' also finds support in the slave narrative of Harriet Jacobs, who asserts that her freedom 'can be fully understood only by those who have been accustomed to be treated as if they were not included within the pale of human beings' (Jacobs 2015: 151).

3. The story of *Benito Cereno* is told from the perspective of Delano, captain of the *Bachelor's Delight*, which comes to the aid of Cereno's *San Dominick*, where the mutiny led by slave

leader Babo has taken place – albeit that this fact is hidden for much of the duration of the story. In a fashion that recalls Fanon and, as we shall see, Henri Bergson, Delano laughs when he first encounters 'the odd-looking blacks, particularly those old scissor-grinders, the Ashantees; and those bed-ridden old knitting-women, the oakum-pickers; and almost at the dark Spaniard himself, the central hobgoblin of all' (Melville 2016: 81), before also taking an erotic interest in a 'slumbering negress... like a doe in the shade of a woodland rock...Like most uncivilized women, they seemed at once tender of heart and tough of constitution; equally ready to die for their infants or fight for them. Unsophisticated as leopardesses; loving as doves' (Melville 2016: 86). Finally, Babo's intelligence as the mutiny's ringleader is what makes him most sinister in Delano's eyes, since it was his 'brain, not body, [that] had schemed and led the revolt, with the plot – his slight frame, inadequate to that which it held' (Melville 2016: 137). As suggested in the second chapter, it is black intelligence that is most fearsome to whites/whiteness.

## Chapter 14

1. For a sense of how 'out of place' has 'subversive potential', see Browne (2015: 72).

## Chapter 15

1. A further resonance between trans-ness and blackness might be elaborated here around the concept of the nation as white and heteronormative. As Susan Stryker, Paisley Currah and Lisa Jean Moore explain, trans- as a term 'becomes the capillary space of connection and circulation between macro- and micro-political registers through which the lives of bodies become enmeshed in the lives of nations, states, and capital-formations' (Stryker et al 2008: 14; see also Stryker and Sullivan 2009: 52). In other words, as the nation is born

with capital, whiteness, heternomativity, binaristic gender formations and so on, so does the trans body, like the black body, fall outside of the nation. In this sense, the trans body is always 'transnational'. (Perhaps it is worth saying, after Jasbir K. Puar, that heteronormativity can be accompanied by what she terms 'homonormativity', in that the queer does not *de facto* subvert the nation, but often enough is, at least in the US context, co-opted, especially through specifically *white* homonormativity, to reinforce the whiteness of the nation; see Puar 2007. If only white and not intersected with critical race theory, then trans* also runs the risk of being/becoming trans*normative.)

## Chapter 16

1. To reinforce this hypothesis, let us recall that the octopus, along with the cuttlefish and the squid, abandoned the shell that the slower and less intelligent nautilus retained. That is, the octopus has evolved to be homeless, but that homelessness enables its others to create a home. The *oikos* emerges from the homeless octopus: *oiktopus* (for more on cephalopods losing their shells, see Godfrey-Smith 2016: 49).

## Chapter 18

1. The perceived shortcoming in Fusco's argument might also be reflected in her 1992 performance with Guillermo Gómez-Peña, *The Couple in the Cage: Two Undiscovered Amerindians Visit the West*. This show saw Fusco and Gómez-Peña impersonate captured indigenous peoples being exposed to Westerners for the first time, a performance that famously had various audience members believe the pair genuinely to be 'natives'. As Byrd says of the performance, it 'relies on racial tropes to express otherness and presents us with an elision between colonization and racialization' (Byrd 2011: 52).
2. As Sycorax haunts *The Tempest*, so might it be that Jacques

Derrida's concept of the *arrivant*, as elaborated in his consideration of 'hostipality' (Derrida 2000), is haunted by the unacknowledged and earlier use of the same term by Edward Kamau Brathwaite (1973).

3. A further Shakespeare-influenced engagement with indigeneity comes in the form of the dictum from Oswald de Andrade's famous 1928 'Cannibalist Manifesto': 'Tupi or not tupi, that is the question' (de Andrade 1991: 38). The phrase makes reference to the Tupi, or Tupinamba, 'the popular, generic name for the Native Americans of Brazil' (de Andrade 1991: 44n2), and it effectively suggests that if Brazil is to achieve social, economic and philosophical autonomy, then it must embrace indigeneity. Once again, then, it is worth looking beyond North America in order to find philosophical and other histories that can help us to maroon. (For more on Oswald de Andrade, and the wider *Tropicalismo* movement of which he formed a key part, in relation to film, see Stam 1997: 70-78; and Martin-Jones 2018: 124-134.)

## Chapter 19

1. Pisters' shift away from Deleuze is even more pronounced in a separate version of her Suleiman essay, where in a book entitled *Deleuze and the Postcolonial*, the shift into Fanonian as opposed to Deleuzian theory suggests even more the possible blind spots in the latter's work (see Pisters 2010).xx

2. Curiously enough, in the earlier version of Pisters' essay on Suleiman, she at one point describes 'terrorist fundamentalism' as 'a serious challenge to society' (Pisters 2010: 216). It is unsure whether she means that this challenge is conceptual (it is hard for Westerners to get their head around terrorist fundamentalism) or what we might call genuine (terrorist fundamentalists might overthrow Western society). If the latter, then lacking from Pisters' analysis is Mbembe's conception of necropolitics, which would help

to convey relatively clearly that terrorist fundamentalism is at base an expression of powerlessness, with little ability seriously to challenge hegemonic power, even as terrorism produces deadly and catastrophic results for all involved. Acknowledging, after Ghassan Hage, that one cannot speak of terrorists without having to condemn them (quoted in Puar 2007: 216), one wonders all the same that the reason for Pisters' (over-)estimation of terrorist fundamentalism is a result of her own Dutch nationality, in that the Netherlands, like the UK, considers 'Muslim populations as an especial threat to LGBTIQ persons, organisations, communities, and spaces of congregation' (Puar 2007: xxiv), which for Puar is redolent of the sway held by conservatism in these countries, where 'homonormativity', or the harnessing of the white homosexual population for the purposes of preserving white national identity, would seem to be especially strong, as exemplified in the controversial if tragic figure of Pim Fortuyn (I use the term 'tragic' here in the journalistic sense that Fortuyn was murdered in 2002 by white environmentalist Volkert van der Graaf; his demise being unfortunate and untimely, I do not mean to suggest a more 'classical' reading whereby Fortuyn was, is, or should be considered a 'tragic hero'; see also Puar 2007: 48-49). All the same, Pisters removes the sentence from *The Neuro-Image*, suggesting a slight change in her thinking on the matter between 2010 and 2012.

3. Perhaps Suleiman's mother is another Sycorax. Indeed, if we learn to hear and/or to speak the language of Sycorax, then we know that her silence is telling us that the white world will collapse under the weight of its own unsustainability. It is, in effect, riddled with wormholes.

4. Thinking about Muslims in a necropolitical fashion as 'already dead' potentially helps us to rethink Albert Camus' 1942 novel, *L'étranger*, which notably is translated often

as *The Outsider* (also the name of one of Richard Wright's novels, from 1953). The outsider in Camus, however, is not necessarily Meursault, the story's anti-hero, but the Arab whom he kills. The murder, which takes place on a beach (i.e. where the ocean/os-ean laps the shore), almost happens automatically (*la gachette a cédé*/the trigger gave way), not here in any comic sense (*du mécanique plaqué sur du vivant*), but rather as if 'killing an Arab' (to namecheck the 1978 Cure song inspired by the novel) were the 'natural' thing to do with one. Meursault, like a typical white, then claims 'outsider' status for himself, having in effect taken it from the Arab whom he has slaughtered.

In other words, the novel tells the story of white supremacist business as usual, not unlike Keaton, and in an anti-Islamic tradition that dates back at least until our old 'friend' Roland, who helped kill Muslims under Charlemagne in 778 (Cedric J. Robinson reminds us that the term 'blackamoor' conflates Islam with Blackness, noting the presence of Islam in Europe from the seventh century, while also suggesting that by the eleventh century, Muslims had become 'the enemy whose very being mocked the beliefs of Europe and materially diminished its daily life'; see Robinson 1983: 89). With Roland in mind, we might note that he sometimes also is known as Orlando, as in Ludovico Ariosto's *Orlando furioso* (1516). Not only does Ariosto's epic poem feature the eponymous paladin slaughtering Muslim Saracens, but another literary Orlando, namely the titular character of Virginia Woolf's 1928 'biography', significantly transitions from a man to a woman after a discussion of 'negresses' with Shelmerdine, as Rachel Carroll has pointed out (the novel even opens with Orlando 'slicing at the head of a Moor'; see Carroll 2020: 15). In other words, Roland and Rollo, as well as the trans*sexual Orlando, all take their being from Blackness, especially as it is conflated with Islam. (By this token, might we not also understand Frantz Fanon as 'becoming black' thanks to his time in Algeria, the homeland of Sycorax, and itself an Islamic country afflicted by settler colonialism?)

Thinking psychogeographically, it is perhaps not quite a coincidence, even if disturbing, that Orlando would also be the venue for the mass murder of many queers of colour (i.e. people doubly outside of the white normative realm) at the Pulse nightclub on 12 June 2016, an event the racist undertones of which have been noted by various trans* scholars (for example, Steinbock 2019: 150).

5. We might note, as do Noura Erakat and Mark Lamont Hill, that there is a 'longstanding history of Palestinian solidarity from Black communities outside of North America, specifically on the African continent, as well as in Latin America and the Caribbean' (Erakat and Hill 2019: 12). What is more, the kinship between the black American struggle and Palestine (as well as the Islamic world more broadly) is not linear, in that black leaders like Marcus Garvey initially saw not in Palestine but in Israel the model for a homeland, as Robin D.G. Kelley reports (see Kelley 2002: 24). Indeed, it was, as Kelley writes elsewhere, Stokely Carmichael (Kwame Ture) who in 1967 changed the narrative when with Ethel Minor he wrote a report for the newsletter of the Student Nonviolent Coordinating Committee (SNCC) about how the Six-Day Arab-Israeli War of June that year was 'a war of dispossession, Israel as a colonial state backed by US imperialism, and Palestinians as victims of racial subjugation' (Kelley 2014: 36).

While Black and Palestinian solidarity has been relatively constant since then, this seems all the same to have intensified in the contemporary moment, as highlighted by various writers, including Kelley, Michelle Alexander (2019) and Angela Y. Davis (2016). The latter in particular notes how Palestinian protestors offered advice to Black Lives Matters protestors after spotting that the same tear gas cannisters, made by the American company Combined Systems, Incorporated, were being deployed in Ferguson, Missouri, in 2014 and 2015 as in occupied Palestine (see Davis 2016: 139-140).

Perhaps characteristically, Frank B. Wilderson III contends that, when a Palestinian friend professes to grave humiliation at being stopped and searched by an Ethiopian (black) Jew working for the Israeli army,

> Palestinian insurgents have more in common with the Israeli state and civil society than they do with Black people. What they share is a largely unconscious consensus that Blackness is a locus of abjection to be instrumentalized on a whim. At one moment Blackness is a disfigured and disfiguring phobic phenomenon; at another moment Blackness is a sentient implement to be joyously deployed for reasons and agendas that have little to do with Black liberation. **(Wilderson 2020: 12)**

Wilderson goes on to argue, somewhat hyperbolically, and in spite of the solidarity evidenced by Davis, that, as a result of Palestinian antiblackness, 'Ferguson is a threat to Palestine, a threat far greater than that of Israel's occupying army' (Wilderson 2020: 244).

While there is no doubt truth in Wilderson's claims, in that certain Palestinians are surely capable of and do express antiblack racism, and while Palestine might indeed *need* structurally to be antiblack in order to be recognised (or reborn/rebirthed) as a nation, then we might again suggest, after Glen Sean Coulthard, that the politics of recognition, like the framework of the nation, is always already too 'white' (and thus antiblack). That is, Black-Palestinian solidarity exists (and must exist) beyond the politics of recognition and beyond the nation – something that hopefully is well understood by those facing Zionist settler colonialists who seek to establish/birth, as well as to maintain, their own nation. Many thanks to Laurence Kent for helping me to elaborate this point.

6. For Tiffany Lethabo King, Deleuze and Guattari's 'non-representational theory of lines of flight is only possible as a form of White self-actualizing posthumanism due to the death of Indigenous peoples and their excision from the Earth/land. White posthumanism and its flows and lines of flight are made possible through Native death' (King 2019: 100).

7. Jamie Ann Rogers notes that various Carib people did survive colonial genocide (Rogers 2018: 170). Many thanks to Rogers for helping to bring the analysis of *Caribs' Leap* into fuller consideration.

8. Although there is little room to analyse it in detail, it might be worth noting McQueen's consistent engagement with Irishness in his feature filmmaking work. This is most notable in *Hunger* (Ireland/UK, 2008), which is a recounting of the hunger strike undertaken in 1981 by imprisoned Irish republican Bobby Sands (Michael Fassbender). However, traces remain in his use of Irish actors such as Fassbender, Colin Farrell and Liam Neeson in *Shame* (UK/Canada/USA, 2011), *12 Years a Slave* (USA/UK, 2013) and *Widows* (UK/USA, 2018). It would seem that the relationship between Blackness and Irishness (and quareness) continues to be explored, even if obliquely.

9. I should note that while the gallery might well function as a non-cinematic institution, it nonetheless is an institution bound up in its own power struggles. Kobena Mercer, for example, sees the museum as 'the key site upon which the last will and testament of liberal humanist Man has been so bitterly contested' (Mercer 2016: 40). Or, put differently, the white cube of the gallery is as much a white space as

the black box of the cinema. Nonetheless, as Mercer writes that '[t]he aim [of black diaspora art practices] is to subvert the codes of museological authority precisely by perverting our aesthetic contract with the artefact as a signifier of power, knowledge, and truth' (Mercer 2016: 43), so might we suggest that the use of the museum/gallery as a site of 'cinema' potentially subverts both the museum/gallery and cinema alike as spaces of hegemony. That is, the (non-) cinematic museum/gallery installation potentially functions as a kind of unsettling shoal, putting the museum/gallery and cinema tidalectically in relation with each other. It is a shame, then, that, more even than in theatres, museum and gallery staff regularly police visitors and enforce a would-be reverential and non-interactive relationship between the visitor/viewer and the installation (do not touch anything, do not cross this line and approach the screen, sit here, be silent, etc) – leading to visitors feeling discouraged from, say, staying in the installation for an extended period of time; that is, the installation might seek to undermine the authority of the institution, but the institution is regularly seeking to reassert its position of power. Many thanks to James Harvey in helping to discuss this point.

# References

Agamben, Giorgio (1998) *Homo Sacer: Sovereign Power and Bare Life* (trans. Daniel Heller-Roazen, Stanford: Stanford University Press.

Alexander, Michelle (2019) 'Time to Break the Silence on Palestine,' *The New York Times*, 19 January, https://www.nytimes.com/2019/01/19/opinion/sunday/martin-luther-king-palestine-israel.html. Accessed 22 October 2021.

Amadahy, Zainab, and Bonita Lawrence (2009) 'Indigenous Peoples and Black People in Canada: Settlers or Allies?' in Arlo Kempf (ed.) *Breaching the Colonial Contract: Anti-Colonialism in the US and Canada*, New York: Springer, pp. 105-136.

Amideo, Emilio (2021) *Queer Tidalectics: Linguistic and Sexual Fluidity in Contemporary Black Diasporic Literature*, Evanston: Northwestern University Press.

Amin, Kadji (2020) 'Trans* Plasticity and the Ontology of Race and Species,' *Social Text*, 38:2/143 (June), pp. 49-71.

Anderson, Gail S., and Lynne S. Bell (2016) 'Impact of Marine Submergence and Season on Faunal Colonization and Decomposition of Pig Carcasses in the Salish Sea,' *PLoS ONE*, 11:3, e0149107. doi:10.1371/journal.pone.0149107.

Andrews, Kehinde (2016) 'The Psychosis of Whiteness: The Celluloid Hallucinations of *Amazing Grace* and *Belle*,' *Journal of Black Studies*, 47:5, pp. 435-453.

Anonymous (2016) *The Song of Roland and Other Poems of Charlemagne* (trans. Simon Gaunt and Karen Pratt), Oxford: Oxford University Press.

Bacal, Edward (2013) 'Sharon Lockhart and Steve McQueen: inside the frame of structural film,' *CineAction*, 91 (Spring), pp. 4-13.

Baker Jr., Houston A. (1984) *Blues, Ideology and Afro-American*

*Literature: A Vernacular Theory*, Chicago: University of Chicago Press.

Barad, Karen (2007) *Meeting the Universe Halfway: Quantum Physics and the Entanglement of Matter and Meaning*, Durham, N.C.: Duke University Press.

Barker, Jennifer M. (2018) 'A Horse Is a Horse, of Course, of Course: Animality, Transitivity, and the Double Take,' *Somatechnics*, 8:1, pp. 27-47.

Bataille, Georges (1986) *Visions of Excess: Selected Writings, 1927-1939* (trans. Allan Stoekl, with Carl R. Lovitt and Donald M. Leslie Jr), Minneapolis: University of Minnesota Press.

Baucom, Ian (2001) 'Specters of the Atlantic,' *The South Atlantic Quarterly*, 100:1 (Winter), pp. 61-82.

Beller, Jonathan (2006) *The Cinematic Mode of Production: Attention Economy and the Society of the Spectacle*, Lebanon, N.H.: University Press of New England.

Beller, Jonathan (2018) *The Message is Murder: Substrates of Computational Capital*, London: Pluto Press.

Berenstein, Rhona J. (1994) 'White Heroines and Hearts of Darkness: Race, Gender and Disguise in 1930s Jungle Films,' *Film History*, 6:3 (Autumn), pp. 314-339.

Bergson, Henri (2004) *Matter and Memory* (trans. Nancy Margaret Paul and W. Scott Palmer), Mineola: Dover Publications.

Bergson, Henri (2005) *Laughter: An Essay on the Meaning of the Comic* (trans. Cloudesley Brereton and Fred Rothwell), Mineola: Dover Publications.

Berkman, Alexander (1976) *The Russian Tragedy*, Montreal: Black Rose Books.

Bettcher, Talia Mae (2019) 'What is Trans Philosophy?' *Hypatia*, 34:4 (Fall), pp. 644-667.

Bey, Marquis (2017) 'The Trans*-ness of Blackness, the Blackness of Trans*-ness,' *TSQ: Transgender Studies Quarterly*, 4:2 (May), pp. 275-295.

Bey, Marquis (2021) *The Problem of the Negro as a Problem for*

*Gender*, Minneapolis: University of Minnesota Press.

Bilton, Alan (2006) 'Buster Keaton and the South: The First Things and the Last,' *Journal of American Studies*, 40:3 (December), pp. 487-502.

Bogle, Donald (1973) *Toms, coons, mulattoes, mammies, and bucks: an interpretive history of Blacks in American films*, New York: Viking Press.

Bordwell, David (1982) 'Happily Ever After, Part Two,' *The Velvet Light Trap*, 19, pp. 2-7.

Bradley, Rizvana (2016) 'Living in the Absence of a Body: The (Sus)Stain of Black Female (W)holeness,' *Rhizomes: Culture Studies in Emerging Knowledge*, 29, https://doi.org/10.20415/rhiz/029.e13. Accessed 10 November 2020.

Brand, Dionne (2010) *Ossuaries*, Toronto: McCelland & Stewart.

Brand, Dionne (2011) *A Map to the Door of No Return*, Toronto: Vintage.

Brathwaite, Edward (Kamau) (1973) *The Arrivants: A New World Trilogy*, Oxford: Oxford University Press.

Brathwaite, Kamau (1975) 'Submerged Mothers,' *Jamaica Journal*, 9:2/3, pp. 48-49

Brathwaite, Edward Kamau (1977) 'Caliban, Ariel, and Unprospero in the Conflict of Creolization: A Study of the Slave Revolt in Jamaica in 1831-32,' *Annals of the New York Academy of Sciences*, 292:1 (June), pp. 41-62.

Brathwaite, (Edward) Kamau (1999) *ConVERSations with Nathanial Mackey*, Staten Island: We Press.

Brown, William (2013) *Supercinema: Film-Philosophy for the Digital Age*, Oxford: Berghahn.

Brown, William (2018) *Non-Cinema: Global Digital Filmmaking and the Multitude*, London: Bloomsbury.

Brown, William (2021) 'Making Kin, Making Children, and Making *Coyote* Under Lockdown,' *The Projector: A Journal of Film, Media, and Culture*, 21:2 (Summer), https://www.theprojectorjournal.com/making-coyote-under-lockdown.

Accessed 18 October 2021.

Brown, William, and David H. Fleming (2020) *The Squid Cinema from Hell:* Kinoteuthis Infernalis *and the Emergence of Chthulumedia*, Edinburgh: Edinburgh University Press.

Brown, William, and David Martin-Jones (2012) 'Introduction: Deleuze's World Tour of Cinema,' in David Martin-Jones and William Brown (eds.), *Deleuze and Film*, Edinburgh: Edinburgh University Press, pp. 1-17.

Browne, Simone (2015) *Dark Matters: On the Surveillance of Blackness*, Durham, N.C.: Duke University Press.

Busia, Abena P.A. (1989-1990) 'Silencing Sycorax: On African Colonial Discourse and the Unvoiced Female,' *Cultural Critique*, 14 (Winter), pp. 81-104.

Byrd, Jodi A. (2011) *The Transit of Empire: Indigenous Critiques of Colonialism*, Minneapolis: University of Minnesota Press.

Byrd, Jodi A. (2014) 'Arriving on a Different Shore: US Empire at Its Horizons,' *College Literature*, 41:1 (Winter), pp. 174-181.

Cade Bambara, Toni (1999) *Those Bones Are Not My Child*, New York: Pantheon Books.

Calhoun, Jordan (2015) '20 Years Ago, 'A Goofy Movie' Became the Blackest, Most Underrated Nerd Classic of All Time,' *Huffington Post*, 27 October, https://www.huffpost.com/entry/20-years-ago-a-goofy-movi_b_8402650?guccounter=1. Accessed 5 November 2020.

cárdenas, micha (2015) 'Shifting Futures: Digital Trans of Color Praxis,' *ada: A Journal of Gender, New Media & Technology*, 6, https://adanewmedia.org/2015/01/issue6-cardenas/. Accessed 14 January 2021.

Carey, Bryechan (2018) 'Introduction,' in Olaudah Equiano, *The Interesting Narrative*, Oxford: Oxford University Press, pp. vii-xxiv.

Carroll, Noël (2009) *Comedy Incarnate: Buster Keaton, Physical Humor, and Bodily Coping*, Chichester: Wiley-Blackwell.

Carroll, Rachel (2020) 'Making whiteness visible: transgender, race and the paradoxes of in/visibility in *Orlando* (1928), *The Passion of New Eve* (1977) and *Sacred Country* (1992),' *European Journal of English Studies*, 24:1, pp. 13-24.

Carter, J. Kameron, and Sarah Jane Cervenak (2016) 'Black Ether,' *CR: The New Centennial Review*, 16:2 (Fall), pp. 203-224.

Césaire, Aimé (2002) *A Tempest* (trans. Richard Miller), New York: TCG Translations.

Chamayou, Grégoire (2012) *Manhunts: A Philosophical History* (trans. Steven Rendall), Princeton: Princeton University Press.

Chandler, Nahum D. (2008) 'Of Exorbitance: The Problem of the Negro as a Problem for Thought,' *Criticism*, 50:3 (Summer), pp. 345-410.

Chandler, Nahum D. (2013) *X: : The Problem of the Negro as a Problem for Thought*, New York: Fordham University Press.

Chen, Mel Y. (2012) *Animacies: Biopolitics, Racial Mattering, and Queer Affect*, Durham, N.C.: Duke University Press.

Chun, Wendy Hui Kyong (2009) 'Introduction: Race and/as Technology; or, How to Do Things to Race,' *Camera Obscura: Feminism, Culture, and Media Studies*, 70/24:1, pp. 6-35.

Colebrook, Claire (2015) 'What Is It Like to Be a Human?' *TSQ: Transgender Studies Quarterly*, 2:2, pp. 227-243.

Coleman, Beth (2009) 'Race as Technology,' *Camera Obscura: Feminism, Culture, and Media Studies*, 70/24:1, pp. 176-207.

Coulthard, Glen Sean (2014) *Red Skin, White Masks: Rejecting the Colonial Politics of Recognition*, Minneapolis: University of Minnesota Press.

Courage, Katherine Harmon (2013) *Octopus!: The Most Mysterious Creature in the Sea*, New York: Penguin.

Cripps, Thomas (1993) *Slow Fade to Black: The Negro in American Film, 1900-1942*, Oxford: Oxford University Press.

Davis, Angela Y. (2016) *Freedom is a Constant Struggle: Ferguson, Palestine, and the Foundations of a Movement*, Chicago:

Haymarket Books.

Day, Iyko (2015) 'Being or Nothingness: Indigeneity, Antiblackness, and Settler Colonial Critique,' *Critical Ethnic Studies*, 1:2 (Fall), pp. 102-121.

Day, Iyko (2021) 'On Immanence and Indeterminacy: Black Feminism and Settler Colonialism,' *EPD: Society and Space*, 39:1, pp. 1-8.

de Andrade, Oswald (1991) 'Cannibalist Manifesto' (trans. Leslie Bary), *Latin American Literary Review*, 19:38 (July-December), pp. 38-47.

Deamer, David (2016) *Deleuze's* Cinema *Books: Three Introductions to the Taxonomy of Images*, Edinburgh: Edinburgh University Press.

Deane, Cormac (2015) 'The Control Room: A Media Archaeology,' *Culture Machine*, 16, pp. 1-34.

Deleuze, Gilles (1997) *Cinema 1: The Movement-Image* (trans. Hugh Tomlinson and Barbara Habberjam), Minneapolis: University of Minnesota Press.

Deleuze, Gilles (1998) 'The grandeur of Yasser Arafat' (trans. Timothy S. Murphy), *Discourse*, 20:3 (Fall), pp. 30-33.

Deleuze, Gilles (2005) *Cinema 2: The Time-Image* (trans. Hugh Tomlinson and Robert Galeta), London: Continuum.

DeLoughrey, Elizabeth (2010) 'Heavy Waters: Waste and Atlantic Modernity,' *PMLA*, 125:3 (May), pp. 703-712.

DeLoughrey, Elizabeth (2019) *Allegories of the Anthropocene*, Durham, N.C.: Duke University Press.

DeLoughrey, Elizabeth, and Tatiana Flores (2020) 'Submerged Bodies: The Tidalectics of Representability and the Sea in Caribbean Art,' *Environmental Humanities*, 12:1 (May), pp. 132-166.

Demos, T.J. (2005) 'The Art of Darkness: On Steve McQueen,' *October*, 114 (Autumn), pp. 61-89.

Derrida, Jacques (2000) 'Hostipitality' (trans. Barry Stocker and Forbes Matlock), *Angelaki: Journal of Theoretical Humanities*,

5:3, pp. 3-18.

Diaz, Vicente M. (2015) 'No Island is an Island,' in Stephanie Nohelani Teves, Andrea Smith and Michelle H. Raheja (eds.), *Native Studies Keywords*, Tucson: University of Arizona Press, pp. 90-108.

Douglas, Mary (2001) *Purity and Danger: An Analysis of the Concepts of Pollution and Taboo*, London: Routledge.

Du Bois, W.E.B. (2008) *The Souls of Black Folk*, Oxford: Oxford University Press.

Dyer, Richard (1979) *Stars*, London: British Film Institute.

Dyer, Richard (1997) *White*, London: Routledge.

Eastwood, Steven (2015) 'A Budding Cinema,' paper presented at Film-Philosophy 2015 Conference 'The Evaluation of Form,' St Anne's College, University of Oxford, 22 July.

Epstein, Jean (2014) *The Intelligence of a Machine* (trans. Christophe Wall-Romana), Minneapolis: Univocal.

Equiano, Olaudah (2018) *The Interesting Narrative*, Oxford: Oxford University Press.

Erakat, Noura, and Marc Lamont Hill (2019) 'Black-Palestinian Transnational Solidarity: Renewals, Returns, and Practice,' *Journal of Palestinian Studies*, 48:4 (Summer), pp. 7.16.

Eshun, Kodwo (1998) *More Brilliant Than the Sun*, London: Quartet Books.

Fanon, Frantz (2008) *Black Skin, White Masks* (trans.Charles Lam Markmann), London: Pluto Press.

Fay, Jennifer (2018) *Inhospitable World: Cinema in the Time of the Anthropocene*, Oxford: Oxford University Press.

Federici, Silvia (2014) *Caliban and The Witch: Women, the Body and Primitive Accumulation*, Brooklyn: Autonomedia.

Ferguson, Roderick A. (2004) *Aberrations in Black: Toward a Queer of Color Critique*, Minneapolis: University of Minnesota Press.

Ferreira da Silva, Denise (2007) *Toward a Global Idea of Race*, Minneapolis: University of Minnesota Press.

Fisher, Mark (2016) *The Weird and the Eerie*, London: Repeater

Books.

Flaig, Paul (2021) 'Bergson's Boffo Laughter,' *JCMS: Journal of Cinema and Media Studies*, 60:2 (Winter), pp. 4-31.

Forbes, Jack D. (2011) *The American Discovery of Europe*, Urbana: University of Illinois Press.

Fuchs, Barbara (1997) 'Conquering Islands: Contextualizing *The Tempest*,' *Shakespeare Quarterly*, 48:1 (Spring), pp. 45-62.

Fusco, Coco (2015) 'El Diario de Miranda/Miranda's Diary,' in Ruth Behar (ed.), *Bridges to Cuba/Puentes a Cuba*, Ann Arbor: University of Michigan Press, pp. 198-216.

Gaines, Jane (2005) 'In-and-out-of-race: The Story of Noble Johnson,' *Women & Performance: A Journal of Feminist Theory*, 15:1, pp. 33-52.

Gates, Racquel J. (2018) *Double Negative: The Black Image and Popular Culture*, Durham, N.C.: Duke University Press.

Gillespie, Michael Boyce (2016) *Film Blackness: American Cinema and the Idea of Black Film*, Durham, N.C.: Duke University Press.

Gilroy, Paul (1993) *Small Acts: Thoughts on the Politics of Black Cultures*, London: Serpent's Tail.

Gilroy, Paul (1996) *The Black Atlantic: Modernity and Double Consciousness*, London: Verso.

Gleick, James (1998) *Chaos: Making a New Science*, London: Vintage.

Glissant, Édouard (1996) *Caribbean Discourse: Selected Essays* (trans. J. Michael Dash), Charlottesville: University Press of Virginia.

Glissant, Édouard (2010) *Poetics of Relation* (trans. Betsy Wing), Ann Arbor: University of Michigan Press.

Godfrey-Smith, Peter (2016) *Other Minds: The Octopus and the Evolution of Intelligent Life*, New York: Farrar, Straus and Giroux.

Goeman, Mishuana (2015) 'Land as Life: Unsettling the Logics of Containment,' in Stephanie Nohelani Teves, Andrea

Smith and Michelle H. Raheja (eds.), *Native Studies Keywords*, Tucson: University of Arizona Press, pp. 71-89.

Goldman, Emma (2003) *My Disillusionment in Russia*, Mineola: Dover Publications.

Gumbs, Alexis Pauline (2018) *M Archive: After the End of the World*, Durham, NC: Duke University Press.

Gumbs, Alexis Pauline (2019) 'Being Ocean as Praxis: Depth Humanisms and Dark Sciences,' *Qui Parle*, 28:2 (December), pp. 335-352.

Gunning, Tom (1986) 'The Cinema of Attraction, Early Film, Its Spectators and the Avant-Garde,' *Wide Angle*, 8:3-4, pp. 63-70.

Gunning, Tom (1995) 'Crazy Machines in the Garden of Forking Paths: Mischief Gags and the Origins of American Film Comedy,' in Kristine Brunovska Karnick and Henry Jenkins (eds.), *Classical Hollywood Comedy*, New York: Routledge, pp. 87-105.

Halberstam, Jack (2018) *Trans*: A Quick and Quirky Account of Gender Variability*, Berkeley: University of California Press.

Hallward, Peter (2006) *Out of this World: Deleuze and the Philosophy of Creation*, London: Verso.

Hammonds, Evelynn (1994) 'Black (W)holes and the Geometry of Black female sexuality,' in Jacqueline Bobo, Cynthia Hudley and Claudine Michel (eds.), *The Black Studies Reader*, London: Routledge, pp. 301-314.

Haraway, Donna (2015) 'Anthropocene, Capitalocene, Plantationocene, Chthulucene: Making Kin,' *Environmental Humanities*, 6, pp. 159-165.

Haraway, Donna J. (2016) *Staying with the Trouble: Making Kin in the Chthulucene*, Durham, N.C.: Duke University Press.

Harman, Graham (2012) *Weird Realism: Lovecraft and Philosophy*, Winchester: Zero Books.

Harney, Stefano, and Fred Moten (2013) *The Undercommons: Fugitive Planning & Black Study*, Wivenhoe: Minor

Compositions.

Harney, Stefano, and Fred Moten (2015) 'Michael Brown,' *boundary 2*, 42:4, pp. 81-87.

Harris, Cheryl I. (1993) 'Whiteness as Property,' *Harvard Law Review*, 106:8 (June), pp. 1707-1791.

Hartman, Saidiya (2007) *Lose Your Mother: A Journey Along the Atlantic Slave Route*, New York: Farrar, Straus and Giroux.

Hasted, Nick (1996) 'So what is Goofy?' *The Independent*, 17 October, https://www.independent.co.uk/arts-entertainment/so-what-is-goofy-1358726.html. Accessed 5 November 2020.

Hayward, Eva (2008a) 'Lessons from a Starfish,' in Noreen Giffney and Myra J. Hird (eds.), *Queering the Non/Human*, Burlington: Ashgate, pp. 249-263.

Hayward, Eva (2008b) 'More Lessons from a Starfish: Prefixial Flesh and Transspeciated Selves,' *WSQ: Women's Studies Quarterly*, 36:3-4 (Fall/Winter), pp. 64-85.

Hayward, Eva (2010) 'Fingeryeyes: Impressions of Cup Corals,' *Cultural Anthropology*, 25:4 (November), pp. 577-599.

Hayward, Eva (2012) 'Sensational Jellyfish: Aquarium Affects and the Matter of Immersion,' *differences: A Journal of Feminist Cultural Studies*, 23:3, pp. 162-196.

Hayward, Eva, and Jami Weinstein (2015) 'Introduction: Tranimalities in the Age of Trans* Life,' *TSQ: Transgender Studies Quarterly*, 2:2 (May), pp. 195-208.

Hechter, Michael (1975) *Internal Colonialism: The Celtic Fringe in British National Development*, Berkeley: University of California Press.

Holtmeier, Matthew (2019) *Contemporary Political Cinema*, Edinburgh: Edinburgh University Press.

Houellebecq, Michel (2005) *H.P. Lovecraft: Against the World, Against Life* (trans. Dorna Khazeni), London: Orion.

Ignatiev, Noel (1995) *How the Irish Became White*, London: Routledge.

Jacobs, Harriet (2015) *Incidents in the Life of a Slave Girl*, Oxford:

Oxford University Press.

Jackson, Zakiyyah Iman (2016) 'Losing Manhood: Animality and Plasticity in the (Neo)Slave Narrative,' *Qui Parle: Critical Humanities and Social Sciences*, 25:1/2 (Fall/Winter), pp. 95-136.

Jackson, Zakiyyah Iman (2018) '"Theorizing in a Void": Sublimity, Matter, and Physics in Black Feminist Poetics,' *The South Atlantic Quarterly*, 117:3 (July), pp. 617-648.

Jackson, Zakiyyah Iman (2019) 'Suspended Munition: Mereology, Morphology, and the Mammary Biopolitics of Transmission in Simone Leigh's *Trophallaxis*,' *e-flux*, 105 (December), https://www.e-flux.com/journal/105/305272/suspended-munition-mereology-morphology-and-the-mammary-biopolitics-of-transmission-in-simone-leigh-s-trophallaxis/. Accessed 31 January 2021.

Jackson, Zakiyyah Iman (2020) *Becoming Human: Matter and Meaning in an Antiblack World*, New York: New York University Press.

James, C.L.R. (1985) *Mariners, Renegades and Castaways: The story of Herman Melville and the world we live in*, London: Allison & Busby.

James, Joy (2013) 'Afrarealism and the Black Matrix: Maroon Philosophy at Democracy's Border,' *The Black Scholar*, 43:4 (Winter), pp. 124-131.

Johnson, E. Patrick (2005) '"Quare" Studies, or (Almost) Everything I Know about Queer Studies I Learned from My Grandmother,' in E. Patrick Johnson (ed.), *Black Queer Studies: A Critical Anthology*, Durham, N.C.: Duke University Press, pp. 124-160.

Jones, Dillon Thomas (2019) 'Is Goofy Black, Too?' *The Outline*, 11 June, https://theoutline.com/post/7549/a-goofy-movie-black-classic. Accessed 5 November 2020.

Judy, Ronald (1993) *(Dis)Forming the American Canon: African-Arabic Slave Narratives and the Vernacular*, Minneapolis: University of Minnesota Press.

Keeling, Kara (2007) *The Witch's Flight: The Cinematic, the Black Femme, and the Image of Common Sense*, Durham, N.C.: Duke University Press.

Keeling, Kara (2019) *Queer Times, Black Futures*, New York: New York University Press.

Kelley, Robin D.G. (2002) *Freedom Dreams: The Black Radical Imagination*, Boston: Beacon Press.

Kelley, Robin D.G. (2014) 'Another Freedom Summer,' *Journal of Palestine Studies*, 44:1, pp. 29-41.

Kelley, Robin D.G. (2017) 'The Rest of Us: Rethinking Settler and Native,' *American Quarterly*, 69:2 (November), pp. 267-276.

Kelley, Robin D.G. (2019) 'From the River to the Sea to Every Mountain Top: Solidarity as Worldmaking,' *Journal of Palestine Studies*, 48:4, pp. 69-91.

Kerr, Walter (1980) *The Silent Clowns*, New York: Alfred A. Knopf.

King, Tiffany Lethabo (2019) *The Black Shoals: Off-Shore Formations of Black and Native Studies*, Durham, N.C.: Duke University Press.

King, Tiffany Lethabo (2021) 'Some Black feminist notes on Native feminisms and the flesh,' *EPD: Society and Space*, 39:1, pp. 9-15.

Koerner, Michelle (2011) 'Line of Escape: Gilles Deleuze's Encounter with George Jackson,' *Genre*, 44:2 (Summer), pp. 157-180.

Kravanja, Peter (2005) *Buster Keaton: portrait d'un corps comique*, Rome: Portaparole.

Krell, Elías Cosenza (2017) 'Is Transmisogyny Killing Trans Women of Color? Black Trans Feminisms and the Exigencies of White Femininity,' *TSQ: Transgender Studies Quarterly*, 4:2 (May), pp. 226-242.

Lakoff, George, and Mark Johnson (2003) *Metaphors We Live By*, Chicago: University of Chicago Press.

Lamming, George (2016) *Water with Berries*, Leeds: Peepal Tree Press.

Lara, Irene (2007) 'Beyond Caliban's Curses: The Decolonial Feminist Literacy of Sycorax,' *Journal of International Women's Studies*, 9:1, pp. 80-98.

Lindqvist, Sven (2007a) *'Exterminate All the Brutes': One Man's Odyssey into the Heart of Darkness and the Origins of European Genocide* (trans. Joan Tate), New York: The New Press.

Lindqvist, Sven (2007b) *Terra Nullius: A Journey Through No One's Land* (trans. Sarah Death), New York: The New Press.

Linville, Susan E. (2007) 'Black Face/White Face,' *New Review of Film and Television Studies*, 5:3, pp. 269-284.

Lippit, Akira Mizuta (2000) *Electric Animal: Toward a Rhetoric of Wildlife*, Minneapolis: University of Minnesota Press.

Lippit, Akira Mizuta (2005) 'Oectopus,' *Octopus*, 1 (Fall), pp. 9-13.

Lorde, Audre (1984) 'Grenada Revisited: An Interim Report,' *The Black Scholar*, 15:1 (January-February), pp. 21-29.

Lorde, Audre (2017) *The Master's Tools Will Never Dismantle the Master's House*, Milton Keynes: Penguin.

Lowe, Lisa (2015) *The Intimacies of Four Continents*, Durham, N.C.: Duke University Press.

Mannoni, O. (1990) *Prospero and Caliban: The Psychology of Colonization* (trans. Pamela Powesland), Ann Arbor: University of Michigan Press.

Marks, Laura U. (2000) *The Skin of the Film: Intercultural Cinema, Embodiment, and the Senses*, Durham, N.C.: Duke University Press.

Marks, Laura U. (2015) *Hanan Al-Cinema: Affections for the Moving Image*, Cambridge, Mass.: MIT Press.

Marriott, David (2007) *Haunted Life: Visual Culture and Black Modernity*, New Brunswick: Rutgers University Press.

Marriott, David (2013) 'Waiting to Fall,' *CR: The New Centennial Review*, 13:3 (Winter), pp. 163-240.

Martin-Jones, David (2011) *Deleuze and World Cinemas*, London: Bloomsbury.

Martin-Jones, David (2018) *Cinema Against Doublethink : Ethical Encounters with the Lost Pasts of World History*, London: Routledge.

Mast, Gerald (1979) *The Comic Mind: Comedy and the Movies*, Chicago: University of Chicago Press.

Mather, Jennifer A., Roland C. Anderson, and James B. Wood (2010) *Octopus: The Ocean's Intelligent Invertebrate*, Portland, OR: Timber Press.

Mbembe, Achille (2003) 'Necropolitics' (trans. Libby Meintjes), *Public Culture*, 15:1, pp. 11-40.

Mbembe, Achille (2017) *Critique of Black Reason* (trans. Laurent Dubois), Durham, N.C.: Duke University Press

McGowan, Todd (2016) 'The Location of Silent Comedy: Charlie Chaplin's Outsider and Buster Keaton's Insider,' *Quarterly Review of Film and Video*, 33:7, pp. 602-619.

McKittrick, Katherine (2006) *Demonic Grounds: Black Women and Cartographies of Struggle*, Minneapolis: University of Minnesota Press.

Meade, Marion (1997) *Buster Keaton: Cut to the Chase*, New York: Da Capo Press.

Medien, Kathryn (2019) 'Palestine in Deleuze,' *Theory, Culture & Society*, 36:5, pp. 49-70.

Mercer, Kobena (2016) *Travel & See: Black Diaspora Art Practices Since the 1980s*, Durham, N.C.: Duke University Press.

Miéville, China (2008) 'M.R. James and the Quantum Vampire: Weird; Hauntological: Versus and/or and and/or or?,' in Robin Mackay (ed.), *Collapse IV*, Falmouth: Urbanomic, pp. 105-128.

Morrison, Toni (2004) *Beloved*, New York: Vintage.

Morton, Timothy (2007) *Ecology without Nature: Rethinking Environmental Aesthetics*, Cambridge, Mass.: Harvard University Press.

Moten, Fred (2003) *In the Break: The Aesthetics of the Black Radical Tradition*, Minneapolis: University of Minnesota Press.

Moten, Fred (2013) 'Blackness and Nothingness (Mysticism in the Flesh),' *The South Atlantic Quarterly*, 112:4 (Fall), pp. 737-780.

Mulcaire, Thomas (1998) 'Deadpan: The Film Installations of Steve McQueen,' *Nka: Journal of Contemporary African Art*, 8 (Spring/Summer), pp. 10-13.

Muñoz, José Esteban (2009) *Cruising Utopia: The Then and There of Queer Futurity*, New York: New York University Press.

Musser, Amber Jamilla (2012) 'Anti-Oedipus, Kinship and the Subject of Affect: Reading Fanon with Deleuze and Guattari,' *Social Text*, 112/30:3 (Fall), pp. 77-95.

Neale, Steve, and Frank Krutnik (1990) *Popular Film and Television Comedy*, London: Routledge.

Newton, Huey P. (1973) *Revolutionary Suicide*, London: Penguin.

Nickel, John (2004) 'Disabling African American Men: Liberalism and Race Message Films,' *Cinema Journal*, 44:1 (Fall), pp. 25-48.

Nyongo'o, Tavia (2010) 'The unforgiveable transgression of being Caster Semenya,' *Women & Performance: a journal of feminist theory*, 20:1, pp. 95-100.

Patterson, Orlando (1982) *Slavery and Social Death: A Comparative Study*, Cambridge, Mass.: Harvard University Press.

Philip, M. NourbeSe (1997) *A Genealogy of Resistance and Other Essays*, Toronto: The Mercury Press.

Philip, M. NourbeSe (2008) *Zong! As told to the author by Setaey Adamu Boateng*, Toronto: The Mercury Press.

Pierce, Sidney K., Gerald N. Smith Jr, Timothy K. Maugel, and Eugenie Clark (1995) 'On the Giant Octopus (*Octopus gigmteus*) and the Bermuda Blob: Homage to A. E. Verrill,' *The Biological Bulletin*, 188:2, pp. 219-230.

Pisters, Patricia (2010) 'Violence and Laughter: Paradoxes of Nomadic Thought in Postcolonial Cinema,' in Simon

Bignall and Paul Patton (eds.), *Deleuze and the Postcolonial*, Edinburgh: Edinburgh University Press, pp. 201-219.

Pisters, Patricia (2012) *The Neuro-Image: A Deleuzian Film-Philosophy of Digital Screen Culture*, Stanford: Stanford University Press.

Puar, Jasbir K. (2007) *Terrorist Assemblages: Homonationalism in Queer Times*, Durham, N.C.: Duke University Press.

Puar, Jasbir K. (2015) 'Bodies with New Organs: Becoming Trans, Becoming Disabled,' *Social Text*, 124/33:3 (September), pp. 45-73.

Raengo, Alessandra (2016) 'Blackness and the Image of Motility: A Suspenseful Critique,' *Black Camera*, 8:1 (Fall), pp. 191-206.

Reeh-Peters, Christine (2018) 'Machine Thinking, Thinking Machine: Considerations on Film as Artificial Intelligence,' in José Miranda Justo, Paulo Alexandre Lima and Fernando M.F. Silva (eds.), *Questioning the Oneness of Philosophy: I. Philosophy and the Arts II. Philosophy, Gender and Sexual Difference*, Lisbon: Centre for Philosophy at the University of Lisbon, pp. 113-126.

Retamar, Roberto Fernández (1989) *Caliban and Other Essays* (trans. Edward Baker), Minneapolis: University of Minnesota Press.

Robinson, Cedric J. (1983) *Black Marxism: The Making of the Black Radical Tradition*, Chapel Hill: University of North Carolina Press.

Robinson, Cedric J. (2007) *Forgeries of Memory and Meaning: Blacks and the Regimes of Race in merican Theater and Film before World War II*, Chapel Hill: University of North Carolina Press.

Rodó, José Enrique (1988) *Ariel* (trans. Margaret Sayers Peden), Austin: University of Texas Press.

Rogers, Jamie Ann (2018) *After the Revolution: Memory, Absence, and Carrying On in Black Literature and Film of the Americas*, PhD thesis, submitted to the University of California, Irvine.

Rogers, Jamie Ann (2021) Margin note on a draft of this book, received 28 June.

Schnier, Jacques (1956) 'Morphology of a Symbol: The Octopus,' *American Imago*, 13:1, pp. 3–31.

Sexton, Jared (2011) 'The Social Life of Social Death: On Afro-Pessimism and Black Optimism,' In *Tensions Journal*, 5 (Fall/Winter), https://www.yorku.ca/intent/issue5/articles/pdfs/jaredsextonarticle.pdf. Accessed 27 January 2021.

Sexton, Jared (2016) 'The *Vel* of Slavery: Tracking the Figure of the Unsovereign,' *Critical Sociology*, 42:4-5, pp. 583-597.

Shakespeare, William (1993) *The Tempest* Act 2 Scene 2, http://shakespeare.mit.edu/tempest/tempest.2.2.html. Accessed 21 October 2021.

Sharpe, Christina (2016) *In the Wake: On Blackness and Being*, Durham, N.C.: Duke University Press.

Sheppard, Samantha N. (2020) *Sporting Blackness: Race, Embodiment, and Critical Muscle Memory on Screen*, Berkeley: University of California Press.

Shoatz, Russell Maroon (2013) 'Maroon Interviewed by Lisa Guenther, Associate Professor of Philosophy at Vanderbilt University,' 23 May, *Free Russell Maroon Shoatz! US Held Political Prisoner*, https://russellmaroonshoats.wordpress.com/2013/05/23/maroon-interviewed-by-lisa-guenther-associate-proffesor-of-philosophy-at-vanderbilt-university/. Accessed 19 October 2021.

Skidmore, Emily (2011) 'Constructing the "Good Transsexual": Christine Jorgensen, Whiteness, and Heternormativity in the Mid-Twentieth-Century Press,' *Feminist Studies*, 37:2 (Summer), pp. 270-300.

Skwiot, Christine (2010) The Purposes of Paradise: US Tourism and Empire in Cuba and Hawai'i, Philadelphia: University of Pennsylvania Press.

Smith, Imogen Sara (2008) *Buster Keaton: The Persistence of Comedy*, Chicago: Gambit.

Snead, James (1994) *White Screens, Black Images: Hollywood and the Dark Side*, London: Routledge.

Snorton, C. Riley (2017) *Black on Both Sides: A Racial History of Trans Identity*, Minneapolis: University of Minnesota Press.

Solomon, Rivers, Daveed Diggs, William Hutson, and Jonathan Snipes (2019) *The Deep*, New York: Saga Press.

Spillers, Hortense J. (1987) 'Mama's Baby, Papa's Maybe: An American Grammar Book,' *diacritics*, 17:2 (Summer), pp. 64-81.

Spivak, Gayatri Chakravorty (1994) 'Can the Subaltern Speak?' in Patrick Williams and Laura Chrisman (eds.), *Colonial Discourse and Post-Colonial Theory: A Reader*, New York" Columbia University Press, pp. 66-111.

Stallings, L.H. (2015) *Funk the Erotic: Transaesthetics and Black Sexual Cultures,*' Urbana: University of Illinois Press.

Stam, Robert (1997) *Tropical Multiculturalism*, Durham, N.C.: Duke University Press.

Steele, Edward J., Shirwan Al-Mufti, Kenneth A. Augustyn, Rohana Chandrajith, John P. Coghlan, S. G. Coulson, Sudipto Ghosh, Mark Gillman, Reginald M. Gorczynski, Brig Klyce, Godfrey Louis, Kithsiri Mahanama, Keith R. Oliver, Julio Padron, Jiangwen Qu, John A. Schuster, W. E. Smith, Duane P. Snyder, Julian A. Steele, Brent J. Stewart, Robert Temple, Gensuke Tokoro, Christopher A. Tout, Alexander Unzicker, Milton Wainwright, Jamie Wallis, Daryl H. Wallis, Max K. Wallis, John Wetherall, D. T. Wickramasinghe, J. T. Wickramasinghe, N. Chandra Wickramasinghe, and Yongsheng Liu (2018) 'Cause of Cambrian Explosion: Terrestrial or Cosmic?,' *Progress in Biophysics and Molecular Biology*, 136, pp. 1–21.

Steinbock, Eliza (2012) 'The violence of the cut: transsexual homeopathy and cinematic aesthetics,' in Gender Initiativkolleg Wien (eds.), *Gewalt und Handlungsmacht: Queer_Feministische Perspektiven*, London: Campus Publications, pp. 154-171.

Steinbock, Eliza (2019) *Shimmering Images: Trans Cinema, Embodiment, and the Aesthetics of Change*, Durham, N.C.: Duke University Press.

Stengers, Isabelle (2000) *The Invention of Modern Science* (trans. Daniel W. Smith), Minneapolis: University of Minnesota Press.

Stryker, Susan (1994) 'My Words to Victor Frankenstein Above the Village of Chamounix: Performing Transgender Rage,' *GLQ*, 1, pp. 237-254.

Stryker, Susan, Paisley Currah and Lisa Jean Moore (2008) 'Introduction: Trans-, Trans, or Transgender?' *Women's Studies Quarterly*, 36:3/4 (Fall/Winter), pp. 11-22.

Stryker, Susan, and Nikki Sullivan (2009) 'King's Member, Queen's Body: Transsexual Surgery, Self-Demand Amputation and the Somatechnics of Sovereign Power,' in Nikki Sullivan and Samantha Murray (eds.), *Somatechnics: Queering the Technologisation of Bodies*, Farnham: Ashgate, pp. 49-64.

Tinsley, Omise'eke Natasha (2008) 'Black Atlantic, Queer Atlantic: Queer Imaginings of the Middle Passage,' *GLQ: A Journal of Lesbian and Gay Studies*, 14:2-3, pp. 191-215.

Tompkins, Kyla Wazana (2017) '"You Make Me Feel Right Quare": Promiscuous Reading, Minoritarian Critique, and White Sovereign Entrepreneurial Terror,' *Social Text*, 133/35:4 (December), pp. 53-86.

Trahair, Lisa (2002) 'The Ghost in the Machine: The Comedy of Technology in the Cinema of Buster Keaton,' *The South Atlantic Quarterly*, 101:3 (Summer), pp. 573-588.

Trahair, Lisa (2004) 'The Narrative-Machine: Buster Keaton's Cinematic Comedy, Deleuze's Recursion Function and the Operational Aesthetic,' *Senses of Cinema*, 33 (October), https://www.sensesofcinema.com/2004/comedy-and-perception/keaton_deleuze/. Accessed 15 January 2021.

Trahair, Lisa (2007) *The Comedy of Philosophy: Sense and Nonsense in Early Cinematic Slapstick*, Albany: State University of New York Press.

Trask, Haunani-Kay (1999) *From a Native Daughter: Colonialism and Sovereignty in Hawai'i*, Honolulu: University of Hawai'i Press.

Trask, Haunani-Kay (2004) 'The Color of Violence,' *Social Justice*, 31:4, pp. 8-16.

Urdaneta, Inés (2019) 'Supermassive Black Holes Birthing Stars at "Furious Rate"!' *Resonance Science Foundation*, 22 November, https://www.resonancescience.org/blog/Supermassive-Black-Holes-Birthing-Stars-at-Furious-Rate?fbclid=IwAR1c0dBQLLBSQcGw0bo_u2Ckc4dNv7fCY0In2x5gHXtKKArkpQyD0H8BEAk. Accessed 31 January 2021.

Vizenor, Gerald (1998) *Fugitive Poses: Native American Indian Scenes of Absence and Presence*, Lincoln: University of Nebraska Press.

Walcott, Derek (1992) *Collected Poems 1948-1984*, London: Faber and Faber.

Walcott, Rinaldo (2021) 'The Black Aquatic,' *liquid blackness*, 5:1 (April), pp. 63-73.

Wallace, Michele (2016) *Invisibility Blues: From Pop to Theory*, London: Verso (eBook).

Warren, Calvin L. (2018) *Ontological Terror: Blackness, Nihilism, and Emancipation*, Durham, N.C.: Duke University Press.

Weheliye, Alexander G. (2014) *Habeas Viscus: Racializing Assemblages, Biopolitics, and Black Feminist Theories of the Human*, Durham, N.C.: Duke University Press.

Wekker, Gloria (2006) *The Politics of Passion: Women's Sexual Culture in the Afro-Surinamese Diaspora*, New York: Columbia University Press.

Wilderson III, Frank B. (2010) *Red, White and Black: Cinema and the Structure of U.S. Antagonisms*, Durham, N.C.: Duke University Press.

Wilderson III, Frank B. (2020) *Afropessimism*, New York: Liveright.

Wolfe, Patrick (2001) 'Land, Labor, and Difference: Elementary Structures of Race,' *The American Historical Review*, 106:3, pp. 866-905.

Wolfe, Patrick (2006) 'Settler colonialism and the elimination of the native,' *Journal of Genocide Research*, 8:4, pp. 387-409.

Wolfe, Patrick (2016) *Traces of History: Elementary Structures of Race*, London: Verso.

Wynter, Sylvia (1984) 'The Ceremony Must be Found: After Humanism,' *boundary 2*, 12:3/13:1 (Spring/Autumn), pp. 19-70.

Wynter, Sylvia (1989) 'Beyond the Word of Man: Glissant and the New Discourse of the Antilles,' *World Literature Today*, 63:4 (Autumn), pp. 637-648.

Wynter, Sylvia (1990) 'Afterword: "Beyond Miranda's Meanings: Un/silencing the "Demonic Ground" of Caliban's "Woman,"' in Carol Boyce Davies and Elaine Savory Fido (eds.), *Out of the Kumbla: Caribbean Womena and Literature*, Trenton: Africa World Press, pp. 355-370.

Wynter, Sylvia (2001) 'Towards the sociogenic principle: Fanon, identity, the puzzle of conscious experience, and what it is like to be "Black,"' in Mercedes F. Durán-Cogan and Antonio Gómez-Moriana (eds.), *National Identities and Sociopolitical Changes in Latin America*, New York: Routledge, pp. 30-66.

Wynter, Sylvia (2003) 'Unsettling the Coloniality of Being/Power/Truth/Freedom: Towards the Human, After Man, Its Overrepresentation—An Argument,' *CR: The New Centennial Review*, 3:3 (Fall), pp. 257-337.

Wynter, Sylvia (2006) 'On How We Mistook the Map for the Territory, and Re-Imprisoned Ourselves in Our Unbearable Wrongness of Being, of *Désêtre*: Black Studies Toward the Human Project,' in Lewis R. Gordon and Jane Anna Gordon (eds.), *Not Only the Master's Tools: African-American Studies in*

*Theory and Practice,* Boulder: Paradigm, pp. 107-169.

Yusoff, Kathryn (2018) *A Billion Black Anthropocenes or None,* Minneapolis: University of Minnesota Press.

Žižek, Slavoj (2004) *Organs without Bodies: On Deleuze and Consequences,* London: Routledge.

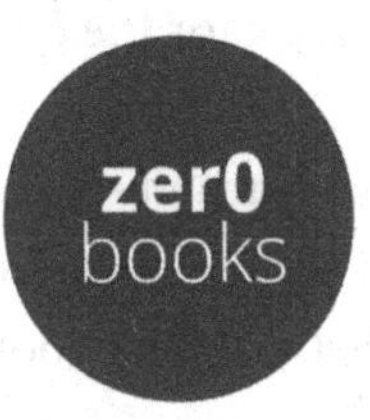

# CULTURE, SOCIETY & POLITICS

Contemporary culture has eliminated the concept and public figure of the intellectual. A cretinous anti-intellectualism presides, cheer-led by hacks in the pay of multinational corporations who reassure their bored readers that there is no need to rouse themselves from their stupor. Zer0 Books knows that another kind of discourse - intellectual without being academic, popular without being populist - is not only possible: it is already flourishing. Zer0 is convinced that in the unthinking, blandly consensual culture in which we live, critical and engaged theoretical reflection is more important than ever before.

If you have enjoyed this book, why not tell other readers by posting a review on your preferred book site.

You may also wish to
subscribe to our Zer0 Books YouTube Channel.

**Capitalist Realism**

Is There No Alternative?

Mark Fisher

An analysis of the ways in which capitalism has presented itself
as the only realistic political-economic system.
Paperback: 978-1-84694-317-1 ebook: 978-1-78099-734-6

**Rebel Rebel**

Chris O'Leary

David Bowie: every single song. Everything you want to know,
everything you didn't know.
Paperback: 978-1-78099-244-0 ebook: 978-1-78099-713-1

**Kill All Normies**

Angela Nagle

Online culture wars from 4chan and Tumblr to Trump.
Paperback: 978-1-78535-543-1 ebook: 978-1-78535-544-8

**Cartographies of the Absolute**

Alberto Toscano, Jeff Kinkle

An aesthetics of the economy for the twenty-first century.
Paperback: 978-1-78099-275-4 ebook: 978-1-78279-973-3

**Malign Velocities**

Accelerationism and Capitalism

Benjamin Noys

Long listed for the Bread and Roses Prize 2015, *Malign Velocities*
argues against the need for speed, tracking acceleration
as the symptom of the ongoing crises of capitalism.
Paperback: 978-1-78279-300-7 ebook: 978-1-78279-299-4

**Meat Market**
Female Flesh under Capitalism
Laurie Penny
A feminist dissection of women's bodies as the fleshy fulcrum of
capitalist cannibalism, whereby women are both consumers and
consumed.
Paperback: 978-1-84694-521-2 ebook: 978-1-84694-782-7

**Babbling Corpse**
Vaporwave and the Commodification of Ghosts
Grafton Tanner
Paperback: 978-1-78279-759-3 ebook: 978-1-78279-760-9

**New Work New Culture**
Work we want and a culture that strengthens us
Frithjof Bergmann
A serious alternative for mankind and the planet.
Paperback: 978-1-78904-064-7 ebook: 978-1-78904-065-4

**Romeo and Juliet in Palestine**
Teaching Under Occupation
Tom Sperlinger
Life in the West Bank, the nature of pedagogy and the role of a
university under occupation.
Paperback: 978-1-78279-637-4 ebook: 978-1-78279-636-7

**Color, Facture, Art and Design**
Iona Singh
This materialist definition of fine-art develops guidelines for
architecture, design, cultural-studies and ultimately social
change.
Paperback: 978-1-78099-629-5 ebook: 978-1-78099-630-1

**Sweetening the Pill**
or How We Got Hooked on Hormonal Birth Control
Holly Grigg-Spall
Has contraception liberated or oppressed women?
*Sweetening the Pill* breaks the silence on the dark side of hormonal
contraception.
Paperback: 978-1-78099-607-3 ebook: 978-1-78099-608-0

**Why Are We The Good Guys?**
Reclaiming Your Mind from the Delusions of Propaganda
David Cromwell
A provocative challenge to the standard ideology that Western
power is a benevolent force in the world.
Paperback: 978-1-78099-365-2 ebook: 978-1-78099-366-9

**The Writing on the Wall**
On the Decomposition of Capitalism and its Critics
Anselm Jappe, Alastair Hemmens
A new approach to the meaning of social emancipation.
Paperback: 978-1-78535-581-3 ebook: 978-1-78535-582-0

**Enjoying It**
Candy Crush and Capitalism
Alfie Bown
A study of enjoyment and of the enjoyment of studying. Bown
asks what enjoyment says about us and what we say about
enjoyment, and why.
Paperback: 978-1-78535-155-6 ebook: 978-1-78535-156-3

**Ghosts of My Life**
Writings on Depression, Hauntology and Lost Futures
Mark Fisher
Paperback: 978-1-78099-226-6 ebook: 978-1-78279-624-4